RAILWAYS FOR THE PEO

The Nationalisation of Britain's railways in 1948

A. J. Mullay

"...will provide an efficient, adequate, economical and properly integrated system of public inland transport and port facilities within Great Britain."

Transport Act 1947

"We 'own' British Railways, but we are allowed no say in them."

John Betjeman, 1953

CONTENTS

Farewell to the old order – painters obliterate the initials of the LMS on a locomotive tender early in 1948.

Introduction

Ten minutes before midnight, on the very cusp of 1948, the last Great Western train to leave Paddington pulled out for Penzance, headed by No. 5037 *Monmouth Castle*. Fifteen minutes later it was followed by the first Western Region departure, a Birkenhead service, with its locomotive, No. 5032 *Usk Castle,* clearing the platforms to a crescendo of detonators. Surprisingly, this was one of the few signs of celebration that Britain's previously privately-owned railways were being taken over by the People. At least *some* railwaymen were determined that British Railways should be brought into the world with a bang and not a whimper.

But a very difficult 45 years lay ahead for the People's Railways.

Just as World War One had ended with a 'khaki election' in the United Kingdom, so did the second conflict, in 1945. This time, the electorate made it clear that it wanted a change from the Conservative Party which had been in power in the years before the war, and which had dominated, through the strength of Prime Minister Winston Churchill, the coalition which had governed through the war from 1940. But a belief in the need for 'reconstruction' was rife in 1945 and the Labour Party was the beneficiary, satisfying the aspirations of a new generation of voters drawing on improved educational standards and increased responsibility in wartime conditions.

The new Labour Government took power with (for those days) a massive majority of 146 seats and was led by the cerebral but less-than-impassioned Clement Attlee. Nevertheless, Attlee's was to be the greatest reforming administration since Asquith's Liberal government in the six years before World War One and was arguably the last Socialist administration the United Kingdom has ever seen. Its work can best be summed up in a chronology and this gives special emphasis to transport matters, while not forgetting climatological conditions – something which took on considerable significance in the late 1940s.

CHRONOLOGY OF POLITICAL, METEOROLOGICAL AND TRANSPORT EVENTS 1944-53

1944	October	Labour Party announces full Nationalisation policy
1945	8th May	End of World War Two in Europe
		Wartime coalition dissolved
	4th June	Churchill's "Gestapo" gibe at former Labour colleagues
	5th July	General Election held, but result announcement delayed
	26th July	Labour wins General Election with majority of 146 seats
1946	March	Bank of England nationalised
	November	Announcement that **transport** is to be nationalised
1947	1st January	Coal industry nationalised
	23rd January	Cold spell begins
	16th March	Cold spell followed by gales and floods
	6th August	**Transport Act** becomes law
	13th August	**British Transport Commission (BTC)** meets for first time
1948	1st January	**Railways** nationalised
		Railway Executive reports to BTC
		London Transport Executive established
	April	Electricity industry nationalised
	July	National Health Service established
		Docks and Internal Waterways Executive established
		Hotels Executive established
		Road Transport Executive established
	August	**East Coast Main Line cut by floods**
	November	**East Coast Main Line reopened**
	December	**Central Transport Users Consultative Committee** begins work
1949	May	Gas industry nationalised
	June	**Road Transport Executive** renamed **Road Haulage Executive**
		Road Passenger Executive established
	July	**TUCCs** established for Scotland and Wales
1950	February	Labour wins General Election narrowly
1951	February	Steel industry nationalised
	May	**First preserved railway (Talyllyn) begins operations**
	October	Conservatives win General Election
1953	May	**Transport Act** passed
		Road freight transport privatised
		Steel privatised
	October	**Railway Executive** abolished

1947 and the Transport Act

When Michael Bonavia's popular history of railway nationalisation was published back in 1979, he was writing from a contemporary background of state ownership which few in the United Kingdom questioned. He suggested that the process of nationalisation was nothing more than an academic axiom, happened "long ago" (in fact some 32 years earlier) and reflected the fact that nearly all major nations in the world, excepting the United States of America, had state-owned railway systems.

One fellow-Briton who did not accept the concept of state ownership was a certain Margaret Thatcher and she happened to become Prime Minister in 1979, the year when Dr. Bonavia's book *The Birth of British Rail* was published. Now, we are almost as distant from that period of n a t i o n a l i s e d industries as Michael Bonavia was from the Transport Act of 1947 and – although it was Mrs. Thatcher's successor John Major who privatised railways – she was to make British transport history turn a half-circle. Nowadays, privatisation is the norm, while state ownership is a historical curiosity and in many thoughts, including those of Labour politicians, is a taboo subject.

But who is to say that this half-circle will not turn again? This is an aspect of transport history which cannot and should not be ignored, if only so future generations can grasp what should, and should not, be done to bring a vital national utility under Government, or other non-profit-making, control.

After all, as a famous Swedish group sang at the time in a song called *Waterloo:*

"The history book on the shelf
is always repeating itself".

Sir Eric Gore-Brown, chairman of the Southern Railway, complained at that company's last Annual General Meeting, on 4th March 1948, that railway nationalisation would cause his company's stockholders "to have their income cut down by, on average, 28%".

It was about to be reduced even more by the Southern's directors accepting £60,000 (approximately £1.26 million nowadays) among them, approved by the meeting to compensate them for their loss of office. This was in addition to a grant from the British Transport Commission of £5,000 to each director, the modern equivalent of £100,000 each – plus expenses – for assisting in the transition to public ownership.

The "redundant" directors could then look forward to the sale of their overrated stock; neither of these points seemed to be mentioned by the Southern chairman.

However, not every SR shareholder was enamoured by this generous award to the directors, with the Chairman being asked why this offer was being made when their Great Western counterparts were expected to decline one. Gore-Brown replied: "I have not the slightest idea, not being in the counsels of the GWR board." In a strained atmosphere a vote was forced, which confirmed the gratuity, by 86 votes to 24. The newly-knighted, and even more newly-enriched, Sir Eric Gore-Brown brought the tension to an end with the reported words "Thank you very much indeed – and goodbye."

At the Great Western AGM held on the following day, that former company's directors declined a similar gratuity from the shareholders as, in the words of chairman Viscount Portal, to have accepted it "would have been to reduce the final payment to stockholders, many of them persons of limited means". In contrast, the LMS directors accepted a total payment of no less than £75,000 (£1.5 million), overcoming an amendment that this should be reduced to £45,000 with "the State" paying the rest.

However, there was even more animation at the LNER AGM, when a resolution was called for the directors to receive £63,000 (£1.28 million) among them. A hostile atmosphere seems to have developed, with a Mr. Thompson, a former driver from the Southern Area, claiming that after his 46 years of company service (the LNER was actually only 25 years old) working for "a pittance ... [he] never had the price of a packet of Woodbine [cheap cigarettes]". A vote was taken there and then, with the resolution being defeated by 55 to 38. Even although a wider, postal vote could have been put in train, the directors retired with good grace, but without this particular bonanza.

Nevertheless, the directors of all the 'Big Four' railways received one-off payments from the BTC "as remuneration for the services rendered by them", former LNER Board members receiving £5,250 (£115,000) each, with £6,250 (£137,500) going to those on the LMS Board and £5,975 (£120,000) to Portal's colleagues at Paddington. "Reasonable expenses" incurred during the transition to nationalisation were additional to this, as well as any payments their shareholders

The last LMS train to leave London St. Pancras before nationalisation – 'Jubilee' 4-6-0 No.5614 **Leeward Islands** *departs with the 11.50pm to the north on 31st December 1947.*

may have voted to them for "loss of office", plus the sale of their company stock, which up-and-coming politician Harold Wilson had already described as overvalued. The 'feeding frenzy' noted among share-buyers at the time of railway privatization in the 1990s may come to the reader's mind.

In an editorial in 1947, the *Glasgow Herald* had deplored "the disappearance of a huge block of stock which had for generations provided an acceptable form of investment for a large number of people in all walks of life."

However, Harold Wilson was to point out that British Transport Stock – offered to existing shareholders in various transport undertakings including railways – was issued at around 20% above its real value and totalled £1.065 milliards. The Government had gone to some lengths to ensure fairness in assessing the worth of stock, the basis of exchange being the average market price of railway shares over the six months immediately prior to the recent General Election, effectively the first half of 1945, or the price obtained in the half-year before the publishing of the Transport Bill, whichever was the greater. If the value of the shares was less than £2,000, it would be paid in cash – although this is around £40,000 in modern values! Wilson's point was proved by the lack of an overwhelming chorus of complaint emanating from smaller shareholders; indeed, as we have seen, more anger appeared to be aimed at company directors as the 1947-48 financial year ended than at the democratically-elected Government so regularly castigated by the right-wing press.

Away from the Stock Exchange, the practical realities of what was happening was the public takeover of the railway companies, comprising 25,000 route-miles of track, 20,000 locomotives and 1.23 million goods wagons – and this would also bring into the Government's arms 70 hotels and inns, 50,000 tons of shipping, such major harbours as Hull, Southampton and Barrow-in-Furness, 1,640 miles of canals and no fewer than 52,000 houses. All this from the railway companies alone, not counting the docks, canals, trucks, and buses which would be inherited from other arms of the transport industry. How all this happened is the subject of this book.

Firstly, however, a glance at the railway companies as they were in 1947.

The largest of these was the **London Midland & Scottish Railway.** When founded in 1923, the LMS was 50 times bigger than the largest steel company at the time. It had a share value of £2,850 million (at today's values) and its annual receipts grossed at £2,400 million in 1923. By 1946 its net revenue for that year was £15.9 million. It employed 268,835 people in 1923 – comparable with the peacetime British Army – and its 6,243 horses could have supplied many a cavalry regiment.

The LMS owned 8,000 route-miles of railway in all four nations of the United Kingdom, 8,000 locomotives, twenty miles of docks, 550 miles of canals, and ran 21,000 road vehicles. It owned major shareholdings in Pickford's Removals and bus companies from Bristol to the Western Isles. To reach the latter, you could have voyaged in one of its 74 steamers. The company partly owned a number of airlines and held powers allowing it to operate services as far east as Yugoslavia. You could have holidayed in Egypt and travelled on a Nile steamer part-owned by the LMS. Its President was paid more than the Prime Minister or even the head of the Post Office. Owning 28 hotels, it was also the biggest operator of railway hotels in the world.

The **London & North Eastern Railway** was the second largest railway company – and that means company of any kind – in the UK in the 1920s and '30s, operating 6,615 steam locomotives on 6,333 route-miles of track. Its issued capital was not far short of that of the LMS and it was 45 times larger than the greatest steel company. Pre-war, its General Manager was paid three times the salary of the head of the Post Office.

Although it was noted for its three streamlined express services – the 'Silver Jubilee', 'Coronation', and 'West Riding' – its staple traffic was freight, particularly mineral traffic. But the war years took their toll and by 1946 the company's net revenue was down to £11 million, making it the poorest-performing of the "Big Four".

The **Southern Railway** was the most modernised of the four companies, stretching from its three major London termini into south and south east England. It also extended a rail tentacle as far as Padstow on the coast of north Cornwall, but was otherwise characterized as almost a suburban, or at least London-orientated, system.

Approximately two-thirds of the Southern's timetabled passenger services had been electrified by 1948, delivering proportionately the best revenue performance of any British railway. Many of its 1,800 steam locomotives were by far the most exciting in terms of modernity, with Chief Mechanical Engineer Oliver Bulleid experimenting with such technical innovations as thermal siphons and chain gearing, as in his Pacific classes, and culminating in the ultimate in innovation, if not efficiency – the 'Leader' class.

Great Western Railway. Needing no introduction to railway enthusiasts, the GWR had remained almost unchanged as a commercial operation for over a century, with neither its conversion to standard gauge by 1892 nor the 1923 Grouping preventing it from claiming to be the nation's premier line. Although centred in the south of England and most of Wales, its 3,741 route-miles penetrated as far north as Warrington. Interestingly, just before World War One, the GWR was claimed to be the nation's greatest rate-payer – an aspect of rail administration not often glimpsed.

COMPARATIVE PERFORMANCE OF 'BIG FOUR' RAIL COMPANIES IN 1946

Company	Route miles	Net revenue	Per route-mile
1 SR	2,156	£7,184,536	£3,332
2 LMS	6,785*	£15,923,680	£2,347
3 GWR	3,741	£7,467,390	£1,996
4 LNER	6,333	£11,078,471	£1,749

* Excludes mileage in Northern Ireland.

Source for mileage and revenue returns: *Railway Yearbook* 1947-48.

"You have just lost us the next General Election." Those words were reportedly spoken by Herbert Morrison to Ian Mikardo after the 1944 Labour Party conference had just approved the latter's motion to enforce Clause IV of the party constitution and take the "means of production, distribution and exchange" into public ownership. Morrison was aghast at this assumption that the public was ready for this almost revolutionary approach to domestic politics, convinced that Mikardo, a thorn in the flesh of Labour leaders over five decades, was pushing a war-weary electorate too far. Ironically, Morrison was to become personally identified with his party's Nationalisation programme to a major degree; indeed he could be described as its architect, following his attempt in 1931 when Minister of Transport to establish a passenger transport board for London, one which was taken up and promulgated by his ministerial successor. Yet his caution in 1944 proved to be unnecessary when, in the following year, the voters showed that they were perfectly comfortable with Nationalisation, electing Labour with a thumping 146-seat majority .

The Prime Minister who oversaw this radical administration was Clement Attlee, a quiet and undemonstrative leader whose donnish appearance belied a steely determination. But, like Morrison, he had felt it necessary to reassure any nervous voters about the way that Labour would go about nationalising

The 10.00am 'Flying Scotsman' from King's Cross to Edinburgh passes Red Hall signal box, near Hatfield, behind LNER A3 Pacific No.60039 Sandwich *on 16th April 1949. Over a year after nationalisation the locomotive has gained British Railways number and lettering but remains in LNER livery, as does the train, with LNER headboard and roofboards.* (Eric Bruton)

the railways, not to mention coal, steel, etc. In 1937 Attlee had confirmed his party's policy to introduce an unprecedented programme of public ownership when next in power. Displaying his lawyer's caution, Attlee emphasised that "proper compensation" would be paid to the existing shareholders. His party's sincerity was not to be tested for a further eight years, but was not found wanting when an election was called as World War Two ended.

A raft of legislation was launched by this new government, exactly in keeping with its 1944 party conference resolutions. The Bank of England was first on the list, then coal mining was nationalised in 1947 and the National Health Service announced. In the following year, transport came under public auspices on 1st January, although the railways were already running under Government control through the existing Executive and hotels, docks and canals only followed later in the year. London Transport was soon brought under the British Transport Commission umbrella, but road transport maintained a considerable semblance of freedom – indeed, more than just a semblance – well into 1949 and even afterwards. Electricity was nationalised in April 1948 and gas in May 1949. Steel followed in 1951, but was soon returned to private hands. (All this is summarised in the Chronology.) Not only was this the proof of an energetically reforming administration, it was a highly creditable achievement for politicians who had given years of public service even before 1945. No wonder so many of the Labour front bench were exhausted by 1951.

Nowadays a retrospective view of nationalised industries is coloured by a tabloid perspective which attributed to them a demonic status and made them favourite whipping-boys for such cartoonists as Low and Vicky at the time and, in later years, Giles in the *Daily Express.*

Yet, while the idea of nationalisation nowadays seems unthinkable even to Labour politicians, it was demonstrably popular with voters. The number of Labour votes counted at the 1945 General Election weighed in at over 12 million. In 1950, after the most intensive nationalisation programme in Britain's history, there were 13 million voting Labour, and in the election in the following year (which Labour narrowly lost, despite polling more votes than did the new Conservative government), nearly 14 million votes were cast for the party which had brought the nation's railways under public control.

Modern journalist Joan Bakewell looks back on that Labour administration's achievements with affection. Writing in the *Guardian* in 2004, she asked:

"How can one possibly convey the euphoria of those postwar years? ... How we loved the Welfare State. How we rejoiced in the National Health Service!"

Yet in some ways, the Nationalisation programme of 1945-50 was a lost opportunity. Driven by ideology which is now discredited by many, the Labour government forcibly converted Britain's main industries, the "means of production, distribution and exchange", into corporations which were theoretically publically-owned, but their operations were soon taken over by members of the existing ruling class who were almost certainly conservative in politics and social outlook. The most obvious example was the appointment, or what one might almost describe as a transfer, of Lord Hyndley from ownership of a coal-mining company to the chairmanship of the new National Coal Board. In a sense, the nationalisation of the railways in 1948 paralleled the 1921 Transport Act, which was passed by politicians who then left it to the existing railway elites to put into effect.

In most cases the top managerial and supervisory posts were not advertised in 1947 as they would be – or should be – today and, if there had been an opportunity to give rein to those from a wider social base who might have had the benefit of a university education and man-management skills in a wartime environment, this opportunity was not taken.

The appointments policy which was put into effect was pragmatic rather than dogmatic. Morrison believed that the new captains of industry would be "men chosen for their ability and technical competence" – in other words, *existing* captains of industry. Harold Wilson supported this 'Morrisonian' theory, opposing the idea of workers' control in favour of seeking administrative talent and experience, if necessary paying £15,000 (£325,000) a year for the right kind of chairman. Wilson was writing about the coal industry, but he had also prepared two pamphlets on railway nationalisation and, although not yet even an MP, his views were obviously influential.

Although economic historian T.R. Gourvish believes that the Government was 'stingy' in its salary allocation for posts on both Commission and Executive, thus discouraging the recruitment of younger management approaching the peak of their careers, this would seem to disregard the politician's tendency to reward friends and colleagues. In any event, even appointments to the Executives were made by the Minister

himself. But Labour's generosity in dispensing offices among its traditional opponents was probably influenced by Attlee and his fellow ministers having experienced office during the previous five years of coalition government. Attlee had held the post of Deputy Prime Minister, with a number of his Labour colleagues brought into the process of government. But this concept of brotherhood was hardly universal. Churchill had adopted a party-political stance even before the end of the war, on 4th June 1945, suggesting that support for the Labour Party, with whose senior members he had been perfectly happy to work for the previous five years, would introduce some kind of Gestapo into the UK. Labour, on the other hand, appointed senior Conservatives – in attitude if not party membership – to some of the highest offices in the land.

Historian Robert Pearce has pointed out that nationalised bodies were often "run by people of generally capitalist outlook and conviction", citing Hyndley's appointment to head the National Coal Board. No doubt in reaction to this kind of appointing from among the existing ruling class, one transport periodical, the NUR's *Railway Review,* called for new rail executives to demonstrate "democratic socialist convictions", but this was a lone voice in the media, immediately savaged by more conventional transport magazines. Pearce also suggests that trade union leaders "wished to preserve traditional, adversarial wage-bargaining", rather than take seats in the boardrooms.

Interestingly, this was certainly the case in 1921, when the Transport Minister at that time, Sir Eric Geddes, a man not usually noted for his sympathy for the working classes, suggested that the workers be represented on the boards of the new 'grouped' companies. Both the railway directors *and* the unions opposed this idea unanimously. In the case of the latter, they feared token representation which could be used by the existing establishment to push through unpopular decisions, such as wage cuts – incidentally, the immediate cause of the 1926 General Strike.

Even Attlee conceded that "in socialised [the then-fashionable term for 'nationalised'] industries, the board is a very long way from the rank and file" and for a time it appeared that a roving group of efficiency experts might examine each industry, but nothing came of this idea. To be

fair to Attlee, it has been said of him that he sought to introduce reforms which would be acceptable to succeeding governments of a different political hue. Pearce remarks sagely of him that Attlee "aimed realistically to bring about a better society, not a perfect one".

In creating the Welfare State which Joan Bakewell described so affectionately, the Labour Party developed a paper on Social Insurance and Allied Services, called colloquially the 'Beveridge Report'. Written by William Beveridge in 1943, this was a non-political document proposing a system for looking after the citizen "from the cradle to the grave". Beveridge was later to stand as a Liberal candidate; one of his principal assistants at both Oxford and at Whitehall was a certain Harold Wilson (although not involved with the report itself), while the cradle-to-grave remark was Churchill's. A better illustration of political consensus at a time when Britain's population was enduring bombs and strict rationing, could scarcely be imagined. However, there was less certainty in the world of transport; in particular, no immediately obvious debate concerning the future method of running Britain's railways as the war ended.

There was no what we call nowadays 'blue sky' thinking. The fact that railways were already overseen by the Ministry of Transport (actually War Transport in the years 1941-6, and incorporating shipping) obviously suggested that this style of Government supervision would be appropriate for other facets of transport, which could then be brought under an umbrella grouping. Why this should take the form of the BTC rather than the existing Ministry is not entirely clear, although 'Morrisonian' thinking – of establishing a public corporation along the lines of that which co-ordinated London's transport – was undoubtedly influential.

The 1923 Grouping had been seen as a means of renewing Britain's railway system after a war of attrition which had left the companies exhausted – just as World War Two would do by 1945 – but there was a determination among legislators at that time to take the opportunity of maintaining competition while removing duplication of services. On this latter point, the Grouping had failed dismally, although permitting two or more routes between cities was by no means the worst of its faults. However, no effort was made to redraw the rail map methodically or sensibly, so geographical anomalies continued – the Southern operated in North Cornwall, while the GWR did so in both north and south. The Great North of Scotland Railway system was some 40 miles separate from the rest of the LNER network.

The lack of new investment for the railways would prove crucial, however. Economist Denys Munby summed up this omission in bloodless academic terms, by describing it as "net disinvestment on the railways for many years on a massive scale". Historians and statisticians have produced a confusing array of different totals for this, although all seem agreed that 'disinvestment' there certainly was. Philip.S. Bagwell gave a figure for itemized inter-war rail investment as being £125 million short of what it should have been – £6.07 milliards adjusted up to 2004 from 1938 figures. A figure curiously similar to Bagwell's was produced by statistician Philip Redfern for the following 15-year period up to 1953 – £126 'net disinvestment', although Gourvish points out that the latter figure would be improved if railway ships – a noticeable 'growth area' – were included. Yet a London School of Economics statistician quotes Redfern as calculating disinvestment between 1937 and 1953 as no less than £440 million at 1948 prices.

In 1946 Chancellor of the Exchequer Hugh Dalton had stated that "the railways are in very poor physical shape" and, possibly on a different occasion, "a very mixed bag of assets". Nobody argued with that, although distinguished railway historian C. Hamilton Ellis, in his book *British Railway History 1877-1947,* described the latter remark as tasteless when coming from the MP for the railway community of Swindon. (Curious, as Hugh Dalton represented Bishop Auckland at the time and was never the representative of the Wiltshire railway stronghold.)

Even a Conservative historian like Richard Lamb conceded that the railways were not properly rewarded – or at the very least, compensated – for their contribution to the war effort. However, Lamb squarely placed the blame for this on the incoming Labour government:

"Between the armistice in 1945 and the date they passed into state ownership in 1947, they [the 'Big Four'] lacked both the necessary finance, and with expropriation around the corner, the motivation to repair the war damage; LNER in fact were [sic] on the verge of bankruptcy".

At least Lamb admits that "neither the Churchill [after 1951] nor Eden governments showed enthusiasm for putting state capital on a large scale into railways". (In fact, it was a Conservative government which recapitalised Britain's railways with the Modernisation Plan announced in 1955, but that was hardly before time.)

In all this discussion about shares and corporate organisation, there was one element of the railway companies' histories that was of vital everyday concern to members of the British public – and not just the travelling British public. As mentioned earlier, the 'Big Four' owned 52,000 houses – more than could be found in such cities as Carlisle or Durham.

There is little mention of this important commodity in the technical press and hardly much more in the archives of the BTC. No instructions on housing were passed to the Regions in their remit documents drafted by the Commission and issued by the Executive on 1st January 1948. On the latter body, W.P. Allen, with his allocation of staff matters, covered 'welfare' within his overview, but there seemed no question of this important subject receiving departmental status on a par with mechanical or civil engineering.

However, the future of staff accommodation excited Parliamentary attention in the summer of 1950, when Alf Barnes was asked to confirm the number of housing units involved, and whether their tenants had rental protection. Mr. Barnes – a Minister of Transport answering questions on housing matters, and unconsciously showing how far Britain's railway networks had permeated the tapestry of everyday life – announced that 21,000 houses were "occupied by protected tenants under the Rent Restriction Acts". This suggests that the majority of railway housing tenants had less than water-tight rental agreements and consequently less security than dedicated workers deserved.

As discussed in the chapter on the 'other' Executives, the BTC had a somewhat muddled attitude to housing, if it displayed any policy at all. One historian believes that the Commission discouraged BR from extending a loan system designed to permit tenant purchase, but if the Commission had wanted to rid itself of responsibility in this area of transport administration, a more obviously logical policy could have been introduced and this is discussed later.

At the beginning of the 1930s Minister of Transport Herbert Morrison introduced a Bill in Parliament to bring London's transport under the aegis of one unitary authority. His Bill failed with the collapse of the first Labour government, but his successor recognised the value of Morrison's proposals and the London Passenger Transport Board came into being in 1933. By then Morrison was applauding from the political sidelines (although he became leader of the London County Council in the following year) and he published an interesting commentary on the capital's – and the nation's – transport called *Socialisation and Transport*. Morrison's volume was dedicated "to the travelling public and the workers by hand and by brain in the transport industry".

Morrison began by analysing the work of the two principal public, non-profit-making, corporations set up in the 1920s, the Central Electricity Board and the BBC – and envisaged this kind of model as ideal for the transport industry (although he noted the conflict between the strong-willed Reith and his Board of Governors at the BBC!). Perhaps this is a clue to the appointment of the (predictably) less dynamic Hurcomb at the later BTC? Suffice to say that Morrison's entry in the new edition of the *Dictionary of National Biography* comments that the years of the Labour government of 1945-51 "witnessed the triumph of the public corporation".

One area where the Minister had to reach a decision which he could not delegate completely to either BTC or RE was in equipment procurement. In the Spring of 1947, the Railway Carriage and Wagon Builders' Association boldly asked for an assurance that at least 50% of all British orders for railway vehicles would be placed with its members, and that a 12-month notice period would be observed for such orders. The latter proviso was not as bare-faced as it might appear nowadays – steel supply was so unreliable at that time as to make tendering a difficult process, as will be related in more detail in the chapter on 1948 operations. Hurcomb answered the Association on Barnes's behalf, ruling out a statutory requirement on BR's procurement of equipment, but assuring the manufacturers of his goodwill in the matter.

We know that the Railway Research Service, an independent 'think tank' originally set up by the LSE, but now financed by the 'Big Four', was asked to examine how things were done overseas – although there is no reference to this in BTC Minutes before the end of 1947. It was the Canadian National Railway service which had caught the attention of the Service's Secretary, C.E.R. Sherrington, early in 1946. Charles Sherrington had held his post for twenty years by this time and in January 1948 was the subject of an encomium in a *Railway Gazette* editorial. The praise lavished on him might suggest an underlying unease that the Service's role in providing information, to allow for the creation of the best possible transport reorganisation, was going to waste. At least Sherrington enjoyed the compensation of a 33% salary increase at the end of 1948, at a time when the BTC decided there would be a moratorium on new staff appointments at the Service.

Sherrington's report of his transatlantic trip consisted of barely two pages of paper, its brevity suggesting that he may have been tipped off that the CNR example would not be followed, whatever it was. Indeed, when the RRS report was considered by the BTC in September 1947, it was taken to indicate the importance of any national model for rail management to incorporate a devolved level of management.

As a matter of interest, Sherrington discovered that the CNR, an amalgam of five railways brought together in 1923 (the year of the Grouping in the UK), was the largest railway concern under a single management in the world, outside the UK or USSR. The railway was run by a non profit-making company which applied to the Canadian House of Commons for capital when required. The salary of its president was fixed by an Order in Council and its board members appointed by the Minister of Transport. The CNR's existence did not prevent the Ottawa government from subsidising some of the activities, particularly ferry operations, run by the Canadian

Southern electric, Pullman-style: the up 'Brighton Belle' near Patcham Tunnel on 30th June 1935. (LCGB/Ken Nunn Collection 6438)

Pacific Railway. None of this seemed to interest Whitehall and the 'British National Railway' was to have a different – and more complicated – structure.

Historians have expressed surprise at how little determined opposition there was to the concept of nationalising the nation's vital arteries. Ernest Barry wrote in his book *Nationalisation in British politics:*

"It was noticeable at the time, and has since been emphasised by historians, that no serious objections were raised, and no anti-nationalisation campaigns organised, before 1949."

The Economist magazine had commented in 1945 on the mildness of the Government's proposals (which would hardly have pleased the Labour faithful), while even *The Times* hanselled the first day of the new British Railways, 1st January 1948, with what Berry calls "a faint cheer", commiserating with the new organization on having to inherit "existing physical equipment badly run down by its intensive war-time usage. The possibility of renewing it at all rapidly are remote".

The *Railway Magazine* had predicted that "there is no reasonable prospect that the dull uniformity of standardisation will be offset by greater efficiency in operation".

This was a fair point although, as the subsequent confusion of numbering and livery policy proved, "dull uniformity" was not to be glimpsed for some time! More positively, the magazine commissioned a painting by Reginald Myers of what a contemporary locomotive would look like in Post Office red – possibly to mobilise public opinion against such an outrage, even taking advice from the Postmaster General (a Labour appointee) to ensure a faithful rendering. It showed an LNER B1 numbered 1948 (by that company's numbering, it should have been a K3) and named *The New Era* – a more apt title might have been *The end of civilization as we know it,* which would have fitted the magazine's editorial leaning. To this author's eyes, the B1 looked far more attractive than in the begrimed, if lined, black which became the norm. Soon, the magazine was complaining about the Bill becoming law, on 6th August 1947, "with practically no newspaper publicity".

This is an interesting echo of a comment made by the editor of the North Eastern Railway (later LNER) magazine in 1923, complaining that the press was allocating to the Grouping "perhaps 0001% of the space they sometimes devote to a really interesting murder". The media never changes, it seems, in its treatment of railway matters!

After what a future Home Secretary called the "trials of its gestation", this complex legislation of the Transport Act reached the Statute Book on 6th August 1947. Of particular interest to the rail historian are Sections 1 to 6, and 13. The first section of the Act dealt with the establishment of a British

Transport Commission, specifying those who could be represented on it; this somewhat threadbare section is examined in the next chapter. Section 2 specified the powers of the Commission and Section 3 its General Duties. Section 4 denoted the powers of the Minister in relation to the Commission and Section 5 outlined the Executives governing various aspects of domestic transport and, again, these are detailed subsequently in this book.

Section 6 covered the establishment of Transport Users' Consultative Committees – perhaps the most highly flawed area of the entire Act (and dealt with in more detail later in this book). The final section of interest to rail enthusiasts was No.13, specifying those transport concerns being taken into public ownership, but this was very much a case of Conan Doyle's dog which didn't bark. It was the not inconsiderable list of those railways which were *not* nationalised which triggered interest among transport enthusiasts at the time and among historians subsequently. An appendix to this book is devoted to this, quoting an official assessment of the reasons why such apparently doomed railways as the Festiniog and Talyllyn, should not be taken into public ownership. Unfortunately, Section 13 of the Transport Act 1947 is so obtusely worded that it defies analysis, certainly by those unqualified in law, while the number of Whitehall reviews in the first two years of Nationalisation of railways not 'vesting' suggests that civil servants were uncomfortably aware that they couldn't understand Clause 13 either!

Not until September 1948 did it seem to occur to the specialized transport press that the Act did not confer a monopoly of railway operation on the BTC or its agents. Indeed, the *Railway Gazette* pointed out that there was nothing in the legislation to prevent anyone promoting an entirely new railway. Thus, poor drafting nullified the spirit and intent of the legislation, certainly as far as railways were concerned.

The Act, with so many faults, nevertheless addressed the temporary problem of the four largest companies in the UK having to negotiate the period between the arrival of the Act on the Statute Book and 'Vesting Day' – in other words, from 6th August 1947 to the following New Year's Day. During this period the railways were expected to "carry on in an efficient manner in the ordinary course of business" but could not enter transactions involving sales of land, sign contracts of more than 12 months' duration or undertake works costing more than £50,000, or £5,000 in the case of the smaller concerns, such as Joint railways. In return the companies were guaranteed payments of £799,000 to the LMS, £574,000 (GWR), £227,000 (Southern), £150,000 (LNER) and £63,000 (LPTB). If compared with the 1946 net revenue, these terms would appear to be over-favourable to the Great Western, possibly at the expense of the Southern.

Another detail of interest to railway historians concerned privately-owned wagons. Until the return of privatisation in the 1990s, private-owner wagons were known only to model railway owners as a means of brightening up an otherwise utilitarian goods train! However, until 1948, they were part and parcel of the transport scene, with more than half a million of them on Britain's railways, most of them pre-war, mainly grease-lubricated (instead of by oil) and all braked by hand. The vast majority of them were owned by coal companies, but the complexities of local government rating had already reduced the value of freight investment by the rail companies themselves after 1931 (as discussed later).

The new Act specified the compensation to be paid to wagon owners for their vehicles, the example given being £159 for a twenty-year old 15-ton steel-framed vehicle rebuilt within the last five years. Payment would be made in British Transport Stock but, if less than £2,000, would be paid in cash. This was for the benefit of smaller firms, such as coal retail merchants owning fewer than thirteen wagons of the type specified above, and guaranteeing someone a trip to the bank with the modern equivalent of some £44,000 in cash! These fiscal arrangements were to generate serious repercussions – and within a year.

Dr. Bonavia recounts a meeting between the BTC and the Railway Executive at which representatives of the latter predicted 1950 traffic demands which could be met *without* requiring nearly 85,000 coal wagons recently acquired from private owners. Apparently, BTC Chairman Sir Cyril Hurcomb registered "pained surprise" at this revelation and well he might. Although RE officials explained that these were largely redundant vehicles, particularly in the manner of their lubrication, that hardly addressed the question as to why they were purchased in the first place. Dr. Bonavia does not put a price on this dubious transaction in his *British Rail: the first 25 years* but this author estimates the cost to the taxpayer of £12,750,000 (£280 million) in purchasing vehicles which could have been foreseen – indeed, were foreseen – as unnecessary to the operation of the newly nationalised railways. By the time of the next Transport Act, in 1953, it was estimated that just over 50% of the low-capacity wagons acquired from private owners were obsolete. No wonder that nationalisation, a good idea in principle, seemed to attract so much criticism!

The confusion inherent in the new Act was scarcely surprising, given the equally confused nature of its inception. As late as spring 1946 the Minister himself, Alf Barnes, had been considering placing all forms of inland transport – road, docks and canals – under four major railway concerns not dissimilar to the 'Big Four'. This was an extraordinary alternative to the Commission structure which former minister

Working conditions at locomotive depots changed little until the end of steam. This is York shed in the 1950s. (Eric Treacy)

Lord Reith had publicly suggested and which was clearly uppermost in the minds of post-war planners such as Morrison and Wilson. Barnes could be forgiven for anticipating the potential conflict between a Transport Minister and transport commissioners who were not democratically accountable and who were quite likely to be unsympathetic to his party's philosophies. This problem undoubtedly began to develop after 1948, although it must be said that many of Barnes's own appointments to the BTC were responsible for such conflicts. These are examined in more detail in the chapter on the Commission and later in the chronological account of the year 1948.

The drafters of the Transport Bill could never be accused of 'feather bedding' their proposed creation, the BTC. Not only would it be responsible for all the local authority rates payable by the railways and canals (a matter discussed in more detail in the next chapter), but the Commission was also not allowed any exemption from Profits Tax "granted to certain trades and businesses carried on by statutory undertakings". To ease its burden, the BTC was however allowed to sell off or lease "any part of their undertaking or property which they do not consider necessary for the discharge of their duties". This

clause was to lead to a wide-ranging interpretation, to say the least.

It was left to a member of the former GWR management, David Blee, to pinpoint the fact that the 1947 legislation, while introducing what he called "compulsion" into transport matters, did not apply this to the transport user. Writing in 1949, he might have gone farther and pointed out that the new Transport Act was equally liberal towards the road lobby. Lorry or van owners carrying their own products were exempt from the Act, while some of the bus companies appear to have virtually dictated their own terms. The Communist Party was quick to seize on this, pointing out in 1948 that the taking over of bus companies "... from the way the shares are rocketing at the Stock Exchange, is proceeding at a ruinous price".

Nowadays, the whole concept of institutionalising transport appears bizarre in an age when the average citizen thinks nothing of motoring to the end of the street to buy a pint of milk at the all-night convenience store. Problems resulting from road congestion and exhaust gases were not foreseen in 1948 and, while known to modern politicians today, do not appear to concern them overmuch. Presumably, this is because no politician worries about anything more than four years in the future – a charge, to be fair, which cannot be levelled at Attlee and his fellow ministers.

While David Blee was correct to emphasise that the transport *users* of 1948 did not come under any degree of compulsion in their choice of journey or means of getting to their destination, it could be argued nevertheless that control existed to a considerable extent. The bus company or railway Region offering transport options was governed by two Government-appointed boards, imposed over the local stratum of management. To those politically right-of-centre in 1948, it might seem suspiciously like a perfect platform to use as a means of *controlling* passenger journeys, as was now happening in half of the world under Communist repression.

It could be said that the 1947 legislation, with its highly-flawed TUCC clause, combined the worst of all possible worlds – it regulated the choices of passengers, without guaranteeing their rights.

Interestingly, the official Communist pamphlet on the 1947 Transport Act was not slow to condemn the legislation for its shortcomings and made a number of points about working conditions. While it was predictable that the appointments to the Commission and Executives would be criticised – "the old gangs are back" – the lack of an obligation on the nationalised railways towards their employees' welfare was highlighted. Pointing out that the new NCB was required by the Mines Act to improve "the safety, health and welfare of persons in their employment", the Party commented that the Transport legislation "has no such clause".

This was not just a propaganda exercise; it appears that even Cabinet Ministers such as Ernest Bevin were appalled at working conditions on Britain's railways in the 1940s. In July 1944 Bevin, who happened to be Minister of Labour and National Service, complained to his colleague, the Minister of War Transport, about the "unsatisfactory conditions under which many railwaymen work". The companies were not even statutorily required to provide First Aid facilities. And not just railway*men*. In the following year the transport ministry was asked to investigate a number of specific complaints and some of the most serious involved the conditions for women rail staff.

Women were found to be working at Stafford Goods Depot on the LMS in a room described as unheated and rat infested, while at Heaton Norris station no woman could have even a cup of tea unless a male member of staff was present. At Exeter and Newton Abbot on the Western and at Plymouth Friary on the Southern, the men's lavatories were so primitive that most employees made other arrangements. Also at Friary, a loco crewman complained that the lack of locker provision meant that foodstuff had to be stored on the floor, resulting in his finding a mouse in the middle of his sandwiches. The Ministry observed that all the 'Big Four' companies had

Welfare Officers for female staff, and all but the LNER for men also, but these did not appear to have "sufficient standing" in the management hierarchy to improve conditions and "the railway companies do not appear to have kept up with industry generally in terms of personnel management".

As for the specific allegations made about horrendous working conditions – the Railway Executive reported that the Friary crews had the use of a "chuck wagon" in the form of a redundant Pullman carriage, no less, but "it is little used by the loco men". (The files fail to record if this curious omission was pursued.) An allegation about conditions at LNER Stratford was too vague to be investigated properly, while the ladies of Heaton Norris were promised tea-making facilites and these were fitted within three months; the problem had been that the only gas ring was located in the men's toilet. Meanwhile, the Stafford case was answered with an assurance that vermin was to be "expected" on railway premises and exterminators visited regularly. An LMS Welfare Officer, a woman, had already distinguished herself in this particular case by earlier telling the Ministry inspectors that the "women concerned were used to factory conditions and had not adjusted themselves to the special needs of railway undertakings".

The above statement, incredible though it may be to the modern reader, might contain the kernel of the problem. 'Dilution' of labour had caused a problem in two wars, exposing women to working conditions that were not only uncongenial but highly dangerous, while male workers were often resentful at working alongside new colleagues who were being paid less for often doing the same job. This resulted in women not being properly trained in welding techniques at one major railway works, whose reputation suffered as a result, with overhauls on larger locomotives being transferred to other centres.

However, the workforce itself could not escape criticism on the question of a lack of statutory provision for railway staff welfare, with the Communist pamphlet *Full Steam Ahead* commenting that it was "an omission that is not unconnected with the failure to amalgamate the rail unions". It ended this broadside with a call for the current Factories Acts to be extended to the railway workplace so as to improve working conditions, particularly in motive power depots – and who could argue with that?

2

The British Transport Commission

A terrible winter of snow and flooding was followed by a baking summer. But if the sun was missing for all of the previous February, it seemed ever-present in the August of 1947. And it was on one of those stifling August days that five elderly men filed into a ninth-storey office above London's Broadway to decide the future course of British transport.

For this was the first meeting of the British Transport Commission – a unique, and ultimately futile, attempt by Government to bring together all aspects of internal transport on mainland Britain and make these directly serve the public need. Present in that stuffy room on that momentous – but surprisingly low-key – occasion were Sir Cyril Hurcomb, John Benstead, Lords Ashfield and Rusholme and Sir William Wood. At least one secretary must have been present to take the minutes of the meeting, but his or her details were not recorded, nor does the official record tell us who was in the chair at that meeting on 13th August, starting at 2.30pm.

These five – to be joined in weeks to come by one part-time colleague – were to decide the future of transport in one of the most densely-populated islands in the history of the developed world. They were to control the busiest railway system in the world, to say nothing of buses, long-distance lorries, Pickford's Removals, canals, docks, hotels and inns, more houses than could be found in many of Britain's cities and High Street shops operated by Thomas Cook Ltd.

They probably did not know it yet, but they would even be responsible for pleasure cruises on the Nile.

The 1947 legislation created a new stratum above the existing railway hierarchy with the establishment of the British Transport Commission, effectively creating a new tier of bureaucracy, but also bringing together all varieties of inland transport, except air traffic, under one Commission.

Under its auspices, there were now five separate executives communicating directly with the transport undertakings themselves, so joining the Railway Executive under the new BTC were similar bodies dealing with docks and inland waterways, hotels, road transport and London Transport – all gathered into what was intended to be a democratically-answerable organisation. It could of course be argued that all British transport matters were, in any case, within the sphere of influence, if not actual control, of the Ministry of Transport, whose head was an elected MP answerable to Parliament. While the Ministry would not be expected to operate transport services, neither, by its own definition, was the new BTC, although its remit was hardly clear-cut, as we shall see.

The new Commission was allowed a minimum of five and a maximum of nine members, but began its work with no more than six full-time Commissioners, including the Chairman.

No wonder it was described by the *Economist* magazine as "astonishingly small for the task". It appeared even smaller in the official photograph of BTC members, with the part-time Scottish representative, Sir Ian Bolton, missing. Board Minutes show that Bolton failed to attend the meeting in London on 1st January 1948, when *The Times* picture was possibly taken (although Lord Ashfield was absent also on that date, and Bolton could of course argue that New Year's Day was a holiday north of the Border, a habit the English have finally caught up with!). Unfortunately, with the death of Ashfield in November 1948, the Commission would become even smaller.

Effectively, only London and Scotland enjoyed any kind of 'partisan' representation on the Commission, which could have benefited from a regional allocation of commissioners and was also seriously lacking representatives of the marine shipping, canal and 'hospitality' industries. The next Transport Act, only six years in the future, addressed this inadequacy, increasing the Commission's size from nine members to fifteen, two of whom were required to be Scottish. This change also included the transfer of rail responsibility fully to the Commission by abolishing the Executives, but there was a subsequent passing on of power, in theory at least, to the Regions.

Northern Ireland was excluded from the 1947 Nationalisation process, the rail system there not coming under public control until 1st July 1948, with the establishment of the Ulster Transport Authority. This absorbed the N.I. Road Transport Board, along with the Belfast & County Down and Northern Counties Committee railways. Some cross-Border systems remained in limbo for the time being while inter-Governmental discussions took place.

The new Commission met frequently, but with no defined regularity. There were to be 30 meetings before the railways' 'Vesting Day' of 1st January 1948 – three in August, five in September, seven each in October and November, building to eight in the final month of 1947. By the following year, the meeting frequency had settled down at an average of eight per month. One of the five meetings in September 1947 was described as informal and another continued over two days. All these were held at Broadway, apart from one at Claridge's Hotel on 23rd December 1947 – a curious choice of venue when the Commission owned five hotels in the capital, and Claridge's was not one of them. It was at this meeting that the generous compensation payments (detailed in the previous chapter) were granted to the 'Big Four's' directors, about to be forcibly retired. Perhaps the sumptuous surroundings inspired the Commissioners to sympathise with anyone they perceived as losing out on existing riches.

The lifting bridge at the appropriately named Drawbridge Road, Shirley, on the Stratford-upon-Avon Canal which came to the BTC from the Great Western Railway.
(T.J. Edgington Collection)

In retrospect, the *Economist* comment, about the paucity of commissioners, was perfectly fair. Some meetings, such as the one held on 28th June 1949, were attended by only three Commissioners – the Act specified three as a quorum – and with three officials in attendance. On this occasion the BTC approved the purchase of £1.44 million-worth (£27.5 million) of Metro-Vickers equipment and the closure of two branch lines, one to passengers and one completely (from an area not yet covered by a TUCC). With none of the Commissioners having been democratically elected, it seemed a doubtful kind of progress in transport management, when the electorate had shown an enthusiasm for new ideas and new people to put these into effect.

Where were the members who could understand management problems likely to arise in running cross-Channel and British-Irish ferries, to say nothing of Thomas Cook's travel agency, hotels such as Gleneagles, Pickford's Removals and housing of which there were now 52,000 units in public hands? Who would be required to answer to those deprived of public transport options in the rural areas where railway closures had been rubber-stamped? To make matters worse,

Lord Ashfield, with his experience of administering London's transport, was not replaced for some time after his death on 4th November in the Commission's first year. He had chaired a meeting as recently as 7th October in Hurcomb's absence, but that was to be his last. John Benstead, the youngest BTC member, was appointed Deputy Chairman in the following January.

Sir Cyril (from 1950, Lord) Hurcomb was confirmed as Chairman of the BTC by the Minister on 8th August 1947, two days after the Act found its place on the Statute Book. As a career civil servant, Hurcomb was an almost inevitable appointment to run an organisation of this kind although, clearly, he had no operational railway expertise. Perhaps surprisingly, the new edition of the *Dictionary of National Biography* credits him with "negotiating" the 1923 Grouping. In fact, the 1921 Transport Act is usually attributed to Sir Eric Geddes who associated himself personally with such matters as the exact constitution of the 'grouped' railway companies and the attempt to introduce workers into the company boardrooms at that time. Admittedly, his involvement would not have excluded the creative contribution of such senior civil servants as Hurcomb, particularly with Geddes being unable to see the legislation through following his transfer to an economic ministry.

Hurcomb's entry in the *DNB* says of him: "without being an expert on any subject, he learned enough to be taken seriously by experts". However, this non-expert seemed to lack a grasp of technicalities, particularly in his assessment of rail safety measures, as will be shown.

Hurcomb was a 'safe' appointment and he was unable to make the BTC as much a part of British life as, for example, Lord Reith did the BBC. Significantly perhaps, when Hurcomb retired from the Commission in 1953, the *Railway Gazette* remarked that his greatest achievement had been not the launching of the BTC but in shipping control during both world wars. Yet despite his interest in marine matters, Hurcomb was not strong or influential enough to bring coastal shipping under the new BTC in its own Executive, as was arguably necessary. After retirement he was to become a major figure in nature conservation.

Dr. Bonavia considers Hurcomb's approach to this major organisational challenge as "tentative, almost amateurish", believing that it required a psychological adaptation "from a civil service to a managerial role". Nevertheless, Hurcomb can immediately be credited on one decision in 1948; he refused to allow the new nationalised rail system to be christened 'Great British Railways', even although the exclusion of the former LMS lines in Northern Ireland would have legitimised such a misnomer. (Northern Ireland is outside Great Britain.) For a misnomer it would have been – 'Impoverished BR' or 'Undercapitalised BR' would have been more appropriate.

Voted Deputy Chairman by the commissioners themselves was their 'host', Lord Ashfield. Before accepting a peerage in 1920, Ashfield was plain Albert Stanley, an Englishman whose family had moved to Detroit in the 1880s, where he began work as an office boy on the municipal tram system.

His career in transport thereafter was spectacular and in 1907 he arrived in London to oversee American investments in the new London Underground system. After a spell in Parliament, where he was appointed President of the Board of Trade, he rapidly became the supremo of London's transport, even although his attempt to establish a commercial monopoly failed. With legislation introduced in 1933 to institute the London Passenger Transport Board as a public corporation, Ashfield was the natural appointment to head it. He did so until invited to join the BTC in 1947. He was the Commission's only member who had served as an Able Seaman in the United States Navy during the Spanish-American War!

Apart from Ashfield, the Commission member with the most railway experience was undoubtedly Sir William Wood, until recently the President of the LMS – the nation's largest company before the Second World War. He had also been a member of the RE, as might be expected, and he must have been surprised to find himself as one of only two BTC members with administrative experience of railway operation. While Sir Ian Bolton had been a director of a railway company (coincidentally, also the LMS), he was a chartered accountant by profession, while both John Benstead and Lord Rusholme were trade union officials.

The Commissioners' salaries required referral to the Chancellor of the Exchequer, no less, and the incumbent of that post, Hugh Dalton, decreed that Hurcomb should receive £8,500 per annum. Although this equates to around £175,000 at 2005 prices, it was barely half what the former President of the LMS, or Ashfield at LTPB, had received in previous years. The *Railway Gazette* bemoaned this salary award in its issue for 22nd August – and the £5,000 per annum for the full-time commissioners – as "likely to make for difficulties in the promotion of some railway officers".

In reality, the situation was even more complicated. With Hurcomb entitled to a Civil Service pension, it was suggested by Treasury officials that the Chairman should draw only £6,500; Bonavia reveals that the Minister stepped in at this stage and that £7,000 was agreed. (£4,000 was to be made available among the BTC commissioners for expenses.) If the *Gazette* believed that it might prove impossible to pay BR staff more than the BTC commissioners, it need not have worried – the London Midland Region started its Chief Regional Officer at £7,500!

To support the work of the Commission, three professional appointments were made as early as possible. For its financial officer, the new body sought and obtained the release of Reginald H. Wilson from the Ministry of Transport, settling on him the military-sounding title of Comptroller of Finance, salaried at £5,000. Described as "a Scottish accountant", the 42-year-old Wilson's appointment was made at the first meeting, on 13th August; not until the second, on 21st August, was the post of Chief Secretary and Legal Adviser finalised, being offered to Miles Beevor, Chief General Manager of the LNER at a salary of £6,500.

Beevor was a lawyer with a keen interest in railways – and was also formally designated as Solicitor (England and Wales) to the Commission. He was described by his colleague, Dr. Bonavia, as subsequently frustrated at not being allowed to operate as a Chief Executive, although examination of the many documents he drafted for his commissionary superiors reveals a brilliant ability to sum up a problem, and suggest solutions for the board members to consider adopting. Meanwhile, Wilson was to be insured "in the event of his death during service", so highly was he thought of.

Beevor was quick to grasp the necessity to set up an efficient Public Relations department, pointing out in a confidential memo to BTC members on 16th October, the need – indeed, the right – for the public to know what was being done with the UK's transport in their name, while such a department would also improve 'esprit de corps'. He correctly adjudged that transport would always be a newspaper target for criticism "as soon as the Commission has assumed responsibility for the transferred undertakings [and] if only for political motives. The NCB, it is understood, delayed appointing a PRO until some time after they had commenced operations, with very unsatisfactory consequences".

He was absolutely right on this; nationalised industries quickly took on demonic status in the eyes of the right-wing press, blind to the fact that these bodies had been established by a Government given massive public support. By 11th November 1947 John Brebner had been appointed to start as Public Relations Officer on 1st December, from a similar post at the LTPB. He was on £5,000 per annum in this appointment and the Commission effectively took over his contract from the soon-to-be-abolished Board, even guaranteeing his 55% pension after the contract's end in 1960. Just before Christmas, Brebner was joined as Publicity Officer by Christian Barman, whose recent book about the Great Western Railway, *Next Station: a Railway plans for the Future,* was little more than anti-nationalisation propaganda, but a present-day collector's item for all that!

Beevor himself required a deputy and this would be a challenging appointment carrying a salary of £2,750. BTC papers show that three candidates were considered in November 1947, the chosen one being Sidney Taylor, a former GWR employee. One of those passed over was James Ness, then high in the LNER hierarchy and later to become a Regional General Manager on the nationalised system. The papers make it quite clear that he could not be appointed in case this suggested favouritism for the LNER – with Ness following his old boss, Beevor. Instead of selecting the best candidate and keeping an experienced partnership together, the new Commission was operating on the 'Buggins Turn' principle.

One lower appointment of interest to the railway historian was the candidate appointed to be Assistant Secretary, Development and Works Section of the BTC. The appointee was Michael Bonavia himself, fresh from the LNER HQ at the age of 38. Dr. Bonavia (as he became later, after completing a thesis for a PhD at the University of London) has written copiously and authoritatively on this fascinating period of transport history, and was an integral part of it all. He was described in the Commission minutes as having "given particular study to problems of post-war development" and was already the author of an important work on railway economics. His posting, at a £2,000 annual salary, was confirmed as early as 4th November 1947, but he must have been worth every penny. By the end of the year, Bonavia's workload was so severe that Beevor wrote to his masters "I urgently desire to obtain experienced help for him … Mr. Bonavia is being overloaded with urgent railway matters."

An organisation of such significance – it was potentially larger and more important than many Ministries – might have expected to have been allotted offices worthy of its almost unprecedented size and power. In fact, whatever civil servants were mobilised at the Ministry of Works to find a home for the

The prestigious hotel at Gleneagles (seen here in 1981) was opened by the LMS in 1924, though its construction had begun under the Caledonian Railway in 1913 before being halted during and after World War I.
(T.J. Edgington)

Commission, their work was done for them by Lord Ashfield. Before retiring as head of the London Transport Passenger Board, soon to become one of the five Executives under the BTC, Ashfield held, within his gift, office accommodation at 55 Broadway, near St. James's Park. Here, he offered two floors to the Commission, which received them gratefully, thanking Ashfield for providing them with "accommodation, and accommodation of such a character", as the BTC minutes record enthusiastically. This comprised 29 rooms on the eighth floor and 26 on the ninth. It appears that pre-war fire regulations had prohibited the LTPB from using at least one of these floors and the imposing clock tower, but this restriction seems to have been relaxed after 1945. Dr. Bonavia records that Ashfield declined the use of the office allocated to him by a harassed official and retained his own suite of two rooms on the seventh floor, depriving his successor at London Transport of an office worthy of his position.

While Hurcomb apparently felt that Broadway was sited close enough to Whitehall to maintain a link with Government, it should be said that this, the London Transport HQ, was not quite as celebrated a building as it had been when it was completed to the design of Charles Holden in 1929. Its exterior boasted ten pieces of statuary, by such artistic eminences as Epstein, Moore and Gill, although eight of them were located too high to be seen by the general public.

With an expansive attitude to staffing, the Commission was always going to have accommodation problems, as the Minute for the meeting on 15th September 1947 suggests:

"The numbers of office staff should, in the first instance, err if at all on the generous side, as it is obviously essential to make adequate provision that an efficient staff should be available at an early stage to deal with the immediate reports of the commission."

Here was fuel for any Opposition politician wishing to accuse the civil service of waste! So effective was the Commission in increasing its staff size that, by the end of January 1948, the Commission Minutes recorded that 55 Broadway was "already crowded...additional accommodation will certainly be required in the near future". An immediate attempt was made to secure the use of the former LNER office at 4 Cowley Street, SW1, to liaise with Parliamentary staff.

By the following month, and even with Cowley Street accommodation brought into use, there was still a shortfall. A document dating from 18th February 1948 shows that Comptroller Wilson had nineteen staff working in thirteen rooms on the eighth floor at Broadway, with the ultimate target complement of 40 occupying 25 rooms. Meanwhile, Beevor supervised no fewer than 53 staff – 36 at Broadway, seventeen newly installed at Cowley Street – but he saw 63 staff as his ultimate requirement. The former LMS Evacuation Centre at Watford was now firmly in the BTC's sights. All this, at a time when at least one BR Region was being urged to reduce duplication in office accommodation.

Others were less impressed with 55 Broadway than the Commission's members. Dr. Bonavia writes that Hurcomb's acceptance of this offer of somewhat Spartan premises at Broadway "reflected his own austere taste". Examination of the Commission minutes shows that its members were governed by an anxiety to "avoid any embarrassment [of being] housed at the outset at any one of the Railway HQs". Nevertheless, it hardly helped to establish the BTC in the public eye that it was effectively a tenant in someone else's building, with no entrance or receptionist of its own. Lord Reith, a would-be BTC Chairman, would never have stood for it!

As with many new organizations, the BTC felt it necessary to define its remit. The minutes of the first meeting record the conclusion that the Commission was to be:

"a policy-making and directing body acting collectively and not individually discharging executive functions".

Logical though this appeared, the BTC was soon executing its own policy decisions, in purchasing road transport concerns in 1948 and in operating ships and canals, often in parallel with its own Executives. It could be said that there was an unresolved contradiction here; it was unconsciously reflected in a speech given by Hurcomb to the Railway Students' Association in October 1948.

He announced that: "They [the BTC] can carry goods and passengers by rail, road, and inland waterway within Great Britain, provide port facilities, store and consign goods, and provide hotels for the passenger" but proceeded to contradict himself later in his oration when he added "The BTC are [*sic*] a small body, which makes policy but does not itself operate transport. In this sense they may be compared to a full-time Board of Directors."

Even describing the Commission as the top tier of transport administration was not strictly correct, as it was the Minister of Transport who was at the top of the tree. Gourvish records that Minister Alf Barnes, having asked the BTC to nominate a chairman for the Railway Executive, then went on to nominate committee members himself. Dr. Bonavia, in writing Hurcomb's obituary for *The Times,* pointed out that the BTC Chairman could hardly have expected ministerial interference in Executive appointments when these organizations had been set up specifically to carry out Commission policy. Admittedly, the Minister's position must have been a difficult

The BTC's shipping assets included Clyde steamers such as the LMSR's PS **Caledonia.**

one, and it certainly appears that in October 1945 Barnes favoured what would have effectively been an array of different Executives answering directly to his Ministry. But Herbert Morrison's London-inspired concept of an 'umbrella' commission prevailed and Barnes was later to face questions in the House of Commons on transport policy – something which was being forged outside his ministry and not always by Labour-supporting experts!

The reintroduction of Pullman services in 1947/8 was a case in point, offending many Labour backbenchers, although the expensive alternative would presumably have been for BR to have bought itself out of at least one binding contract with the Pullman company. Fortunately for Barnes, he had already given himself some elbow-room. In January 1948 he had relaxed the regulations forbidding special trains such as holiday excursions and Sunday School picnics. The railways were not slow to push at a slightly open door, securing permission to operate sporting specials as well, in this, the year of the London Olympics. By allowing nearly a million people to travel by special train in only three months, Barnes could at least look his political critics in the eye.

While it was undeniable that the railways had always hitherto been run on commercial lines, leaving behind in 1947 a pool of directorial 'talent', the media was not slow to criticise the choice of appointees to the new transport bodies.

"Mr Barnes's appointments [to the BTC] are so 'safe' they reflect such an obvious determination not to upset anything … one wonders more than ever what the Government thought it was accomplishing by its Act."

Fulfilling its election pledges, one might reply, and the final phrase above indicates that the organ concerned was hostile to

the Labour government from the start (this was the *Economist*). The magazine would have been doubly quick, one feels, to have reacted critically to any appointees to high office from the 'lower deck' of the transport world.

But the fact was that a number of appointments to both Commission and Executive appear to have had little, if anything, to do with transport administration. Even more controversially, many of the individuals were outspoken critics of nationalization and might have been astonished to be appointed to highly-remunerated posts by a socialist government. An example was Henry Dutfield, Chairman of the Road Haulage Association and described by Bonavia as "a doughty commander of the anti-nationalisation brigade", who accepted an appointment on the RTE. In contrast, Sir James Milne (General Manager, GWR) had been principled enough to decline a post administering an organisation in whose purpose and function he did not believe.

Unfortunately, it can be argued that Labour's generosity was misdirected and unappreciated. The BTC included a former Co-operative union leader (admittedly a possible Labour favourite) and a civil servant, in addition to an old Etonian with no technical expertise but who specialised in liquidating Scottish companies. The latter's appointment hardly augured well for Scotland's branch lines!

In some ways, it seems a surprise that the Commission lasted as long as it did, particularly with the Roads and Hotels Executives beneath it hardly forging much of an independent existence. The latter was an area which the railways had handled perfectly well for the previous century, and would again; road traffic simply represented an area too big for anyone to control without the direct power of legislation.

One inequality which an overall transport authority such as the BTC could have brought to Government's attention, but did not, concerned rating. Although legislation in 1930 – the Railways (Valuation for Rating Act) – had allowed railways and their canals up to 75% relief on the rateable value of premises "used wholly for industry or transport purposes", the railway companies were required to pass this financial benison on to customers requiring the transport of coal, raw materials for steel making, timber props for mining and agricultural goods. This was to have the unfortunate effect of reducing and minimising railway investment in freight transport, since the average return per train (and boat) was now reduced. While this legislation remained on the statute book until 1947, the unfitted goods wagon (without any continuous brake but with a hand lever) remained a transport staple and was effectively a handicap on new investments – larger wagons, fitted brake systems – necessary to modernize the transport of bulk cargoes.

In 1948 railways and railway-owned canals in England and Wales were assessed for £1.85 million (£37 million) in local government rates, following a revision two years earlier. Interestingly, the BR staff magazine commented at this time on the fact that the rates burden had been reduced from £8.25

million (£181.5 million) paid by the 'Big Four' in 1943, to £5 million (£100 million) three years later, "testimony to the efforts and valuable work of the Association of Railway Rating Surveyors", commended the magazine. The 1943 figure seems punitively high at a time when the companies were keyed into the war effort and were having to accept cargoes virtually under compulsion.

However, this was hardly a new problem; before World War One the Great Western Railway was claimed to be "the largest ratepayer in the Kingdom". While both railway and bus stations were rated to support local government finance, the railway also paid rates on its permanent way, while roadways were open to all, including commercial concerns.

Under the 1947 Act, the Commission itself was statutorily required to meet railways' and canals' rates burden, now payable in the form of "lump sum payments to local authorities", as the 1948 Local Government Act confirmed. And what did local government bodies spend much of their rates income on? Roads within their boundaries, of course! So bus companies and road carriers, while paying rates on their properties, gained an unseen subsidy, shared with the railway only in its road services division. This discrepancy was made worse with the railways losing their lucrative investments in commercial road transport, whether bus or truck-based, in 1948. Twenty years later, after new legislation allowed local authorities to offer financial assistance for unremunerative railway services, it was found that some authorities were spending more on roads than on council housing and certainly more than they were prepared to pay for a branch railway service.

If the BTC had been unable to persuade the Ministry to alleviate the railways' rates burden, particularly with the removal of rail investment in commercial road transport, the Commissioners could have demanded that future legislation should require local government to pay something back to the railways as a percentage of road investment. This could have taken the form of subsiding unremunerative rail services, much as the 1968 Act allowed and which came too late to save many a branch line.

Another area where the BTC could have shown some initiative in 1948 was in rail safety. As mentioned later, Hurcomb and his colleagues discussed Automatic Train Control (ATC) and track circuiting in detail during 1948, although reading 'between the lines' (no pun intended) of the chairman's comments, it can be inferred that he saw these as *competing* systems when in fact they complemented each other in being essential to the operation of a 20th century railway. Yet ATC was not adopted universally for a number of years, with circuiting only becoming commonplace as colour lights were introduced more widely. The BTC could surely have argued that the railways deserved support from the Treasury in making these improvements on a system where no profit was – or should have been – required.

Perhaps Hurcomb was too busy in the summer of 1947 to

The post-war reintroduction of Pullman services saw the return of named trains such as the 'Queen of Scots' between King's Cross, Leeds Central, Edinburgh and Glasgow. A3 4-6-2 No.60037 **Hyperion** *departs from Edinburgh Waverley with the up train on 9th June 1951. The locomotive is in the new 'express passenger' blue livery.* (Eric Bruton)

read the current *Monthly Bulletin of the Railway Research Service* which dealt with the decision of the French nationalised railway system to fit what was described as "Audible Warning Cab-signalling apparatus" to all its locomotives and railcars, triggered by ramps fitted beside each distant signal. So important was this AWS believed to be (and it lacked the control element of braking a train which passed a warning signal without slowing down) that even older locomotives were to be fitted with simplified apparatus as a matter of urgency. It was to be ten years before Britain followed this example and a large number of passengers was to die before then.

The first transport legislation produced by the Conservative administration succeeding Attlee's government at the end of 1951 was the Transport Act of 1953. This Act abolished the Executives, principally, it seems, to ensure greater independence for the road lobby, but also returned hotels to the railways. The Railway Executive was itself disbanded, with almost no thanks from a grateful nation – this organisation had operated with incomparable efficiency in two world wars – but, as suggested in the next chapter, the RE could be described as too steam-orientated for most politicians' taste.

Sadly, after 1953 the BTC was the legatee of the British railway network, with all its problems and faults. While attempting to decentralize system control – in a manner likely to appeal to a Conservative government with an acclaimed distrust of bureaucracy – by strengthening the Regions through the creation of six Boards, the BTC committed itself to an enormously expensive Modernisation Plan in 1955. This was to delight politicians and transport journalists, but would be the despair of economists. It may well have rung the death-knell of the Commission itself.

While taking the story of the BTC well beyond the time-frame intended for this book, it should be noted that the recapitalisation of Britain's railway system offered by the 1955 Modernisation Plan was doomed to economic failure, as long as identifiable areas of the network were known to be loss-making. Since those areas – mainly branch lines – were not scheduled to be modernised, they would predictably continue to make losses, thus acting as a deficit against capital. Logically, the future of such lines could be summarised with the imperative "Either close or spend". For example, the BTC was planning to electrify the Euston–Manchester service – which already made a profit, according to statistician Sir Christopher Foster – while failing to institute a Beeching-like programme which logic would suggest was necessary to eradicate those lines generating a deficit. Otherwise, these would offset and nullify the Plan's intentions of making BR profitable by 1960; the analogy comes to mind of trying to run a bath with the plug out.

Foster, writing in 1963, has pointed out in his book *The Transport Problem* that a modernised British Railways was expected to "break even in 1960 [but] that was the year of the greatest deficit so far". Perhaps this was the reason why one BR Regional board chairman – a chartered accountant – was looking in 1958 for "easier" (his exact word) ways to close the railways in his charge.

The Plan's failure was not lost on the Parliamentary Select Committee on Nationalised Industries, which reported in July 1960 that a decision would have to be made whether the railways should try to pay for themselves or address social needs. Unfortunately, a subsequent committee set up to examine the subject came to be dominated by a certain Dr. Beeching, with results we now know.

Even before the end of 1947, the BTC provided a forum for rail vehicle contractors to confront civil servants over the supply, or rather, non-supply, of enough steel to allow the completion of orders for the Shenfield electrification (of which, more later). It can be seen as a positive contribution by the new Commission; otherwise, the BTC began its life fighting off those problems on which existing ministries had given up. One such concerned Easingwold.

The existence of anomalies in vesting policy seemed to cause concern at 55 Broadway – as it did at Marylebone, where the Railway Executive carried out a review of independent systems in the autumn of 1948. In the summer of the previous year, the independent Easingwold Railway, near York, approached the Ministry of Transport for financial assistance with its operations and this request was referred, with the celerity that the Civil Service musters for passing on unwanted business, to the new Commission. As a result, BTC Secretary Miles Beevor found himself sitting down in York on 24th October with Henry Coates, the manager and secretary of the Easingwold line. Beevor soon wished that Mrs. Coates could be there as well.

Apparently, this good lady normally attended all her husband's business meetings, since Mr. Coates himself, at 79, was both frail and deaf. Coates had held the post of Easingwold GM since 1926, even when employed by the LNER, and his widow would follow him as Chairman of the company after his death in 1952; by 1956 she was the only Board member anyway.

In the meantime, it appeared the elderly manager objected to the LNER's charges for the hire of a locomotive for work which might take no more than 48 minutes per day. However, Coates was unable to provide Beevor with any information about the Easingwold's financial state, could not produce a copy of his original letter to the Ministry and had already run up £1,000-worth of arrears in locomotive hire. Beevor reported to the Commission that: "unless he was being deliberately obtuse, he appeared to be ignorant of the functions of the BTC and provisions of the Transport Act."

Beevor's proposed solution was, however, surprisingly mild, suggesting that the Railway Executive give Coates another four weeks' grace in which to pay and only then to authorise the withdrawal of locomotive supply. The historian can of course envisage a different solution, with the £1,000 (equal to £22,000 nowadays) being written off in exchange for Mr Coates's title to the near-moribund Easingwold Railway or as compensation for his shares in it. After all, some bus companies sold themselves directly to the Commission, although undoubtedly under the most favourable of terms – to their shareholders. While the Easingwold Railway closed to passengers within 14 months, an attempt to assimilate it would have appeared natural for the Commission set up to oversee Great Britain's railways. As it was, freight continued until the end of 1957, with the Assistant Commercial Manager at York administering the line in a nominal capacity as General Manager in addition to his Regional posting – something which simply intensified the anomaly.

North Eastern rail historian Richard Lacey writes: "it seems that such non-nationalised minor railways as the Easingwold had, of necessity, a very close relationship with BR – it was certainly the case with the North Sunderland as well."

Incidentally, in the BTC files regarding Beevor's meeting with Coates, which was probably not the kind of railway administration problem that Socialist politicians had in mind when they introduced their epoch-making legislation, there is only the barest of comments about the anomalous position of the Easingwold Railway, namely that "this railway does not vest". (See also Appendix I).

Three years after Nationalisation was accomplished, the magazine *Locomotive Post,* published by two railway engineers, commented in disappointment that "Nationalisation has lost its charm at lower levels, and a profound apathy has taken its place."

This was in January 1951, the year when the Festival of Britain was supposed to symbolise the nation's regeneration after suffering so much from World War Two and its aftermath. The same issue of the magazine reported on a visit to Carlisle by BTC Chairman Lord Hurcomb. Apparently an expectant audience of railwaymen awaited the Chairman, who arrived fifteen minutes late and left after only twenty minutes "with an abruptness that left many questions unanswered". Perhaps it was too much to expect a 67-year-old civil servant to present a bold facade of leadership to this tired industry. After meeting Hurcomb on a different occasion, canal enthusiast Robert Aickman said of him that he was "as old as the rocks on which he sat". Curious, with this meeting taking place in the comfortable surroundings of the Carlton Club; it nevertheless reinforced the suspicion that in Hurcomb's case, it was not so much apathy or indifference that was the problem, but fatigue.

3

The Railway Executive and the Transport Users' Consultative Committees

Although beneath the British Transport Commission in the new hierarchy, the Railway Executive had long pre-dated it – indeed, this was one of the UK's oldest Government-instituted organizations with a technological base.

Dating from 1914, the Executive had at its heart a central committee consisting of the most senior operational managers of the main British railways. In theory, the Executive took orders from HM Government and passed these directly to the General Managers of the lines. It was a fairly straightforward system and must have worked reasonably well – after all, both wars were won! In 1940 when the newly-appointed Minister of Transport, the aforementioned Sir John Reith, had bustled into his new post, expecting his supercharged organisational powers to be required to their utmost, he was immediately advised by both his predecessor and his officials that "the railways run themselves through the Railway Executive Committee". "Magnificent, if incredible" was Reith's verdict – and he was quickly on his way to a new appointment.

The Executive lasted in its first period of service until 1921, by which time compensation for war service, some £25 million (£600 million in modern prices), had been settled on companies which were having to face up to entirely new social and economic realities while recovering from the intensive demands of total war. Having 'bonded' through the existence of the Executive, the railway companies' officials found the concept of a Grouping imposed by Westminster to be less unacceptable than would have been the case before the recent war.

Nevertheless, and despite the longevity of the Executive, it was not without its critics, with Sir John Elliot describing it unkindly as "a collection of prima donnas with no conductor". Most of the criticism was to come in the last years of the Executive's independent existence and related to its perceived support for steam power on British Railways.

At the outbreak of World War Two, the Railway Executive was immediately reactivated, and was to continue until well into 1953. That it was quietly successful in its work seems indisputable whatever Elliot said; the railways' contribution to the war effort was of such a high standard as to render it taken for granted. Not only did the railways meet every demand placed on them, whether by the armed forces or by local authorities having to evacuate civilians from city centres, many of the companies' workshops went over to military production almost immediately. Shrugging off the direct effects of bombing – one destroyed bridge was reinstated in less than twelve hours – the railways put a brave face on a war-induced investment shortfall estimated by the Executive at some £179 million (£3.75 milliards) by the end of the conflict. But even the onset of peace barely lightened the railways' military burden.

Only days before Nationalisation, the 'Big Four' companies were ordered to lay on troop trains to return servicemen to their barracks from home leave over Christmas. On 28th December 1947 the LNER provided 50 special passenger trains in and out of King's Cross and Liverpool Street, the LMS 56 to and from Euston and St. Pancras, while 73 such specials ran on the GWR in and out of Paddington. On the following day the Southern operated 46 trains in and out of its three major termini in London. All this essential traffic was undertaken at the height of the Christmas holiday period, yet no-one in the transport or military professions thought it unusual.

Despite this impressive history, the BTC still seemed to find it necessary to define the Executives it controlled – although admittedly, the other four were new compared with the Railway organization dating back to 1914. As constituted from 1st January 1948, the Railway Executive comprised seven full-time and two part-time members. At its first meeting on 13th August 1947, the Commission had decided "the Executives will mainly consist of persons charged with functional responsibilities [but also] some persons of general experience".

At this initial meeting, the British Transport Commission was told by its acting chairman, Sir Cyril Hurcomb, that the Minister expected a recommendation to fill the chair at the

Old order and new order: 'Coronation' Pacific No.46245 City of London (photographed at Crewe in 1949) has gained its new BR number but still retains its LMS lettering on the old company's post-war black livery, while the carriages are of Great Western origin still in their chocolate and cream colours.

Railway Executive. By a unanimous decision, the BTC forwarded the name of Sir Eustace Missenden, General Manager of the Southern Railway, although Gourvish's suggestion that Missenden was not first choice deserves some credence. BTC minutes show that Hurcomb had to explain to his colleagues the "circumstances in which Sir James Milne's services were not available" and the GWR General Manager was clearly a favourite for the new post. It is not recorded if Hurcomb pointed out Milne's antipathy for socialist institutions – as well as an unacceptable desire to maintain his directorial appointments in other concerns – and it is probably unlikely that Milne's age of 64 was mentioned – this was Hurcomb's age as well!

All the former 'Big Four' were represented – Missenden from the Southern, Michael Barrington-Ward from the LNER, David Blee from the Great Western and, from the LMS, largest of the companies, Robert Riddles. While such measured representation was necessary at the top of the Executive, critics were quick to point out that a 'Buggins Turn' principle seemed to prevail in virtually *all* appointments to the Executive, with individual talent often ignored in the interests of ensuring that all the pre-Grouping companies were represented equally.

The three remaining full-time members of the RE were the appropriately-named Landale Train, Chief Engineer on the LNER, Bill Allen, a former ASLEF leader who was about to be honoured by having a new A1 Pacific named after him, and as Deputy Chairman General Sir William Slim. They totalled 242 years' railway experience among the seven of them, with Slim contributing none. Similarly, the two unpaid part-timers, Sir William Ayre and Christopher Nevile, had no such experience, being respectively a shipbuilder and a farming expert. Neither lasted more than three years on the Executive.

It could be argued that the Executive, which really should have been seen as dealing with the basics of rail operation, should not have included a soldier and two others involved in areas unconnected with transport – the BTC already had such an intentionally *randomised* approach to appointments. In any event, Slim resigned in November 1948, appointed more appropriately as the Chief of the Imperial General Staff – an

One of the London & South Western Railway's H16 Class 4-6-2 goods tanks, No.30520, has gained its third owner. Seen passing Clapham Junction 'A' signal box on empty stock duty, it carries full 'BRITISH RAILWAYS' lettering and the new lined black livery.

improvement for him on approving press releases about the pointless Locomotive Exchanges!

All Executive officials were linked to a particular committee member in a hierarchical relationship. Bill Allen, for example, with his remit to oversee staff matters, had only one assistant, H. Adams Clarke, formerly of the GWR and now salaried at no less than £4,500, more than was being officially but unsuccessfully proposed for the Chief Regional Officers of three of the Regions. Matching this salary, and the only RE official to do so, was C.M. Cock, who came from the Southern to take up the post of the Executive's Chief Electrical Engineer and reported to Robert Riddles.

Cock's appointment was requested by Riddles but was by no means automatic, with the BTC querying the need for such a high-profile posting, particularly when the 51-year old Cock was on £4,500 at the Southern. Beevor, however, argued strongly for this appointment, even although the Commission

minutes in December 1947 record that "there is likely to be little new electrification in the near future". Despite this disappointing, although realistic, assessment, Beevor reported to his colleagues that Riddles "wanted somebody to think out future standards". Within six months Cock was doing exactly that through his chairmanship of the committee which took his name (see the chapter on 1948), although it could be argued that he failed to anticipate the move to high-voltage traction; he had moved back into private industry within three years.

A curious criticism of the Executive can be found recounted in T.R. Gourvish's history of British Railways, where he points out that the Executive members and officials were regarded in Government circles as being "soft"! The RE's representatives apparently conducted themselves "with understanding and courtesy" when having requests for investment refused – in contrast to the ruffians of the nationalised electricity-generating and mining industries who fought harder for what they required. Unfortunately, a serious shortfall in the Railway Executive's expenditure proposals for 1950 did little, in the twin worlds of Westminster and Whitehall, to improve its reputation for professionalism.

As early as October 1947, the Commission was looking to convert the former Great Central Hotel into offices for three Executives at Marylebone – railways and road transport but not hotels at this stage, ironically, given the original function of the Marylebone building. £217,100 was requested for upgrading work for the former hotel, previously barracking Canadian troops, and an additional £44,554 for what was described as "hostel furnishings and equipment" for some 681 railwaymen "from the provinces". This was a reduced version of a Cabinet plan of March 1947 to have 1,020 men accommodated there, but the local authority had refused planning permission.

By the end of January 1948, the BTC was advised that the hostel plan should be abandoned, as the Executive was finding its two floors in the building "insufficient". A "whole" building was requested from the Commission, but in fact sharing was still to be necessary and, as it happens, with at least one unhappy co-tenant.

In Year One of Nationalisation, the newly-appointed head of the Road Transport Executive, General Russell, was concerned about sharing a building with the RE, in case the road haulage industry viewed this as "being overshadowed by the railways". The general was to be disappointed, however. Although the Railway Executive was complaining about the squeeze on accommodation in the former hotel, the new Road Transport Executive made it known that it required a minimum of twenty rooms immediately on constitution and "about 50" within two months, that is by the autumn of 1948. In January the hybrid plan for hostel and offices was abandoned, with the former Southern Railway's Craven Hotel taking 125 men immediately. In any event, Dr. Bonavia believed that the Marylebone building was superior to the BTC's Broadway from the start, although his description of "separate messes for senior and junior officers" reads strangely nowadays.

Towards the end of 1947, it was decided that the respective heads of BTC and Railway Executive, Hurcomb and Missenden, would issue a joint address to all British railway staff, designed to boost morale for the coming year. One inspiring passage reads:

"Railwaymen (and women) are rightly proud of the great tradition built up by their companies in the past. The Commission and Railway Executive desire not merely to maintain these traditions, but to strengthen and unite them under British Railways."

It was in fact the Railway Executive officials who returned their draft copy of this document to the Commission with the words "and women" very prominently scribbled in the margin opposite the BTC's encomium to the males in the railway industry! Appropriately too; the number of women working for the Railway and London Transport Executives at this time was approximately 50,000. Curiously, this New Year message had been preceded by a similar one in November. This was gender-specific, with the BTC and Executive noting "the difficulties which railwaymen of all grades are experiencing in the operation of the railways in this time of stringency and stress".

Matters sufficiently prioritized to be dealt with by the Executive in the first year of its existence were liveries, numbering and locomotive names. The first of these was important enough to be placed before the Commission (who fluffed a decision, as will be related), the second was left by the Commission for the Executive to deal with, while the third – locomotive names – was too important, it seems, for the Executive to leave to the Regions. With these processes being dealt with at different administrative levels, it will be

The Western Region carried on turning out GWR-type steam shunting tanks until 1956. Seventy of the '16XX' Class 0-6-0 pannier tanks – represented here by No.1653 – were built between 1949 and 1955.

appropriate to describe them in the later chapter featuring the work done by the new British Railways in its first year.

Another aspect of rail management which was dealt with less than effectively by the BTC was station catering. The LNER was out on its own in this regard, having appointed E.K. Portman-Dixon to organise canteens for stations in wartime, but he was so successful that he was put in charge of all the company's refreshment facilities and even introduced catering training. Station cafeterias were due to be taken over by the Hotels Executive once it was established, but the Commission must have felt that a temporary expedient was needed, so Portman-Dixon was assigned to the Railway Executive in December 1947, but as an 'Adviser on Refreshment Rooms' only and considered for staff purposes as an Acting Executive Officer.

Dr. Bonavia shows a high regard for this temporary official's work and believed that the Hotels Executive's structure later failed to draw the best from him. Perhaps the failure of the new nationalised structures to accommodate and promote the skills of individuals such as Mr. Portman-Dixon should have indicated that the structuring deserved reappraisal. In particular, the lumping of station and restaurant car catering with hotels was to expose the Hotels Executive to relentless press scrutiny and it might have been better had this area of work being assigned to the Railway Executive as the new era dawned.

While Labour's 'Morrisonian' policy of leaning towards administrative experience was understandable, particularly on the Railway Executive, it had the unfortunate result of maintaining something of the *status quo* in the railway industry's upper echelons. Through the appointment of Commissioners with no sympathy towards the idea of public ownership in general or of railways in particular, managers continued to assess the success of rail operations by examining the 'bottom line' of profitability – or the lack of it.

Not surprisingly, there was disappointment at the time at the apparent lack of workers' representation in the nationalization process and this did not change as the years went on. In March 1947, E.J. Doody of Willesden was quoted as saying:

"Nationalisation does not give the workers control of the industry ... was I wrong to look for an indication that we shall not be supervised by incompetent position-seekers?" while E.W. Jackson of Neasden was recorded as complaining "We have been completely fooled". Both these ASLEF members were quoted by Brian Murphy who wrote in 1980 in his official history of the union:

"For the members of ASLEF who greeted the coming of Nationalisation as a new dawn, their hopes were sadly tarnished".

We have already seen that the leading candidate to head the Railway Executive was Sir James Milne, the GWR's General Manager, but he refused this £150,000 post (adjusted to modern figures), no doubt because of what Gourvish calls his "well-publicised antipathy for nationalisation". Such men were unlikely, for example, to look kindly on unremunerative, but socially significant, train services in rural areas. Almost as if anticipating this forensic approach to rail economics, the Transport Act also set up the Transport Users' Consultative Committees and it is appropriate to examine these well-intentioned but highly-flawed bodies before proceeding further.

Transport Users' Consultative Committees

Established under Section 6 of the 1947 Transport Act, the Transport Users' Consultative Committee (TUCC) system had two roles – to make appropriate recommendations to the Minister of Transport on rail and other services provided by nationalised transport undertakings, and to offer an impartial process for considering complaints from the public and local authorities about passenger train withdrawals and line closures. The Committee could make representations direct to the Minister on either of these points and in particular concerning any possible hardship caused by a closure proposal. Each committee had to include a BTC member and the Minister could appoint representatives from a number of directions, although the obvious source – members of local government associations – was well down the list displayed in the Act's clauses and below possible appointees from rival transport organisations.

When originally launched in 1947, this (supposed) travellers' charter consisted of a Central Transport Consultative Committee. Although both Commission and Executive wanted this up and running by January 1948, it was in fact April before it was formed, with its Scottish and Welsh counterparts not following until 22nd July 1949. Curiously, the Minister had the power to abolish the central TUCC, but not the Scottish and Welsh committees.

*Former Great North of Scotland D40 4-4-0 No.62278 **Hatton Castle** arrives at Macduff with the branch train from Inveramsay. The future of rural branch lines like this would be for the Transport Users' Consultative Committees to consider – and the Scottish TUCC included representatives of the road transport industry! The Macduff branch closed in 1951...*

English transport problems were to be dealt with by a sub-network of eight Area Committees from 1951. England and Wales had previously benefited from an informal consultation network which had sprung up in the 1920s. At that time 28 joint committees had been created after the 1921 Transport Act, allowing discussions on localised transport needs between the 'Big Four' railway companies and local authorities. While not perfect in its execution – and the number of committees was allowed to decline to only four by 1952 – this exchange of transport ideas in some ways anticipated the 1968 Transport Act which made local authorities direct participants in transport provision, as they should have been earlier.

Unfortunately, the TUCC's remit was so narrow that it had no powers to recommend alternatives to closure – for example, allowing a branch line to run at a manageable loss if it served a public need – nor could it make suggestions for more economical operation. After October 1968 the committees received the power to assess the *quality* of possible alternative transport facilities, but that sensible alteration came too late to save many railways.

It is significant that a court challenge to Section 6 of the Act came about early in 1950, when a county council disputed BR's right to withdraw passenger services on a particular branch line. Surprisingly, the council effectively won an immediate injunction postponing withdrawal, with the judge commenting that "a nationalised undertaking could not take the law into its own hands", although he conceded that BR could still lodge a defence. The report on this is incomplete, but the resulting defence was obviously based on recent legislation and the line closed within a year. However, it says little for the new TUCC system that it should be challenged so soon by the very section of the community – local government – which it was arguably intended to benefit.

Regrettably, the TUCCs were not always seen as impartial. Tom Rolt, famed as one of the leading lights of the post-war heritage movement, attended a meeting to object to the withdrawal of passenger services on the former GWR line between Cheltenham and Honeybourne, only to observe "the members of the [TUCC] committee, and the local officials of the Western Region coming in together, laughing and joking among themselves ... It struck me then that we were wasting our time ..."

He was. Nor was this a purely English problem; the Association of Scottish County Councils was to appeal to British Railways in 1956 to assess transport alternatives itself in the event of proposed closures, although a local government

LNER B1 4-6-0 No.61050 at Liverpool Street with the 'Broadsman' to Norwich and Cromer. Although this example was built by the LNER, construction of these mixed traffic locomotives continued under the Railway Executive until 1952. Also in view are the overhead wires of the Shenfield electrification, an LNER project completed by the RE in 1949.

body must have known that this was the TUCC's prerogative. In one particular closure controversy (Peebles, a few years later), the presence on the committee of the manager of Scottish Omnibuses was seen – quite reasonably – as evidence of a lack of impartiality. The company had already complained about the use of diesel multiple units on the railway under threat, as these had (temporarily) eaten into the road company's profits. Needless to say, the line closed anyway, leaving the entire county of Peeblesshire without a passenger rail service. How anyone could regard this Committee as a fairly-run organ of government seems unbelievable.

In his detailed appraisal of rural transport options (see Bibliography), David St. John Thomas was kinder in his summing-up of TUCC failings:

"TUCC staff are of course answerable only to the committees, but it would be scarcely surprising if they had greater sympathy with railway officials than with people they represent but with whom they are less closely in touch."

He added the criticism that those serving on such committees, or servicing them in a clerical capacity, need not have any transport expertise, or personal knowledge of alternative transport services available in the event of a rail closure. In practice, there was perhaps *too much* expertise and personal knowledge. The Scottish TUCC included rail officials – representing those proposing the closures – and officials from the road industry – those most likely to benefit from them!

When Dr. Bonavia wrote in his book *The Nationalisation of British Transport* that the Scottish TUCC included Sir Ian

Bolton of the BTC, Tom Cameron, Chief Regional Officer of Scottish Region, and James Amos of the principal bus company north of the Border, he cited these appointments as evidence of "the importance of Scottish opinion". It is difficult to discern quite what he means by this. While the Act required a BTC member to be delegated to each of the three TUCCs, Bolton is believed to have instituted a controversial (to say the least) accounting procedure in Scotland which appeared to grossly overestimate the recovery value of equipment from closed lines – the closure of the Lauder Light Railway, with its minimal earthworks and corrugated iron buildings, was described as the second most lucrative closure in Scotland – while the presence of Mr. Amos would appear to be quite inappropriate.

In the event of closure, not only would the bus company in the area begin trading in a transport monopoly, it could claim grant assistance from the railway authorities who had just closed their own line! This apparent maladministration of Scottish transport in the 1950s and 1960s is examined by this author in the book *BR Region by Region: Scottish,* based on an analysis of official records.

The TUCC system, with its many faults, outlived both BTC and Railway Executive. In 1968 the committees were authorized to assess the *quality* of replacement services, which gave their existence greater meaning, and passengers greater protection. Indeed, it is arguable that, until this assessment process was undertaken, the TUCCs had no point to their existence and the appointments policy which led to rail and bus operators appearing on such committees was never free of 'conflict of interest' charges.

Abolition

The existence of the Railway Executive was ended with the passing of the 1953 Transport Act which "shall provide for the abolition (if it has not already been abolished) of the Railway Executive".

This formally happened in October 1953, but the Act's wording was a less than grateful farewell to an organisation which had served the country effectively in peace and (particularly) in war, and had given senior management the experience of working together for the good of the nation long before Nationalisation became a reality.

If such a disparate group, representing so many companies and Regions over the years and involving so many differing personalities, can be considered to have exhibited a particular *corporate* failing it must have been its apparent loyalty to steam power on British Railways. As will be revealed later in this volume, both Missenden and Riddles championed the steam engine against the twin threat to its supremacy from diesel and electric traction. Missenden went on record in 1951 to argue that plentiful coal supplies alone justified a renewed faith in steam power, while suggesting that the physical constraints on generating more than 1,600 horsepower of electricity from a single unit diesel locomotive were effectively insuperable, necessitating double-heading for heavier trainloads. Perhaps not coincidentally, Missenden's comparative figures for first cost of the rival forms of traction were weighted in favour of steam to what appears an unfair degree.

Riddles meanwhile simply got on with the task of introducing the 'Standard' classes, supplementing orders for existing types such as the 'Black 5' and the B1 emerging from (mainly) commercial manufacturers in a ratio to 'Standard' types of three to two. His attempt to place orders in 1953 for new push-pull passenger stock for steam power in preference to DMUs ignored, as Gourvish has pointed out, the traffic-stimulating effect of the new motive power through its sheer novelty. Not surprisingly, he was blocked by the BTC. Meanwhile, the Western Region cheerfully went ahead with the construction of new steam shunting engines – nearly 350 of them in the years of Nationalisation up to 1956. To be fair, the BTC itself approved 150 0-6-0 tank engines for the GWR in December 1947, but only after being told that diesel shunters, minuted by the BTC as more efficient, would not be appropriate as the steam locomotives were needed "for specialised trip working". No wonder that the Railway Executive could easily be viewed, whether by Commissioner or Minister, as wedded to steam!

The RE's abolition was, in any event, a political inevitability with the Conservatives once again in power at Westminster. The freeing of commercial road operations from the supervision of the two road Executives reintroduced an almost *laissez faire* degree of freedom to the industry and it was felt that rail operations could be transferred to an enlarged BTC, with a stronger element of Regional decision-making. This satisfied the conviction that there was over-centralisation in the world of transport and the Railway Executive had been seen as a prominent example of this.

To a very major extent, Britain's railways would be run by the Regions from now on until privatisation, or at least until 'sectorisation'.

4

The Regions

Regional administration on the new British Railways was a subject deemed important enough to be announced at a press conference, on 26th November 1947. The six Regions revealed to journalists, were, in order of mileage:

London Midland: 4,993 route miles
Western: 3,782
Scottish: 3,730
Eastern: 2,836
Southern: 2,250
North Eastern: 1,823

This list contained no surprises, although Sir Cyril Hurcomb hinted intriguingly that "others may be created later". Three months on, the *Railway Magazine* was still reporting on rumours of "fresh Regions being set up".

The *Railway Gazette*, in contrast, wanted no Regions at all and pursued the point editorially long after the organisational die was cast. In October it had urged the retention of the 'Big Four' companies reporting to the Railway Executive, with the BTC above, and the Ministry above that, just as railway companies in India had maintained much of their corporate identities during the government takeover there.

"Railway systems, not railway regions, should be the basis. A geographical distribution is not a practicable proposition."

In a later editorial, the magazine was prepared to allow sub-company systems to develop, breaking up the Southern into electric and steam-hauled networks, with Scotland divided into former Caledonian and North British lines (a reference to former LMS and LNER systems north of the Border would have been more tactful!). The irony about all this lies in the fact that Transport Minister Alf Barnes had also believed in a 'systemic' approach to rail reorganisation, with the considerable difference that each of the four networks would operate road and canal transport as well in their areas of influence.

By the end of November, after reporting on Hurcomb's public presentation, the *Gazette* commented "We still think that these geographical regions will not be a success". In particular, the decision not to publish separate Regional accounts was deplored and this was perhaps a more reasonable complaint, since such accounting did in fact take place internally. However, by the following year, the magazine found that the BTC was publishing as much statistical data as anyone could possibly want. As well as revenue figures, the accounts included coal consumption on the six Regions and the second issue, in March, disclosed that the speed of the average goods train on the new nationalised system was precisely 8.69mph! That particular statistic was soon dropped!

According to BTC Minutes, the decision to publish monthly statistics, whether Regionally or centrally, was by no means automatic. The 3rd February 1948 meeting was told that "although publication of traffic receipts is no longer necessary for the information of shareholders as formerly, it may be considered that the general public should be given some indication as to how the main business of the Commission is progressing".

The transport media certainly thought it was necessary and it was natural that Comptroller Wilson, the author of this memo, should think in terms of traffic receipts. Yet this provided data which could just as easily have taken the form of line occupation, traffic-miles for passenger trains and ton-mileage for freight. Did the taxpayer need to have a month-by-month index of *financial* performance, or would an index of traffic intensity not have done just as well and avoided the kind of ruthlessly fiscal approach to railways more appropriate to a commercial concern?

Hurcomb's hint about possible new regions was probably an allusion to concern shown by both Commission and Executive about the size of the London Midland Region, nearly one-third as big again as the second largest. Discussions appear to have been held in BR's earliest days about breaking it up, but by 1st July 1948 the BTC had formally agreed with an Executive suggestion that the LMR "should not be divided" and that applied to the Western as well. In the latter's case, there was some discussion about the administration of the lines west of Exeter as late as July in that first year, although the dual workings of Southern and Western Regions in the area was to continue into the 1960s.

But the "consolidation" of the Scottish Region seemed to be causing concern by then and Commission documents made it clear that substantial savings were expected from the elimination of duplicated facilities. In December 1947 the BTC approved a list of salaries for 24 Scottish Region officials below CRO and Deputy CRO level. Far from showing a reduction in staffing for a united Region, Miles Beevor reported that this represented an annual increase of £5,191 (£103,000) on 1947, but commented that "it is understood that some reduction of the number of District Officers is planned". However, when the BTC was subsequently informed of the resulting divisional changes on 23rd September 1948, its members must have been unimpressed, the Commission's

minutes commenting that "the Executive to be asked to report periodically on their progress in securing early and substantial economies in Scotland, for which, in the Commission's view, there must be ample scope".

Interestingly, BTC Chairman Lord (then Sir Cyril) Hurcomb seemed to hold a more relaxed view of Scotland's potential economies than his own commission, telling the Railway Students' Association on 20th October 1948 that "it will take time before the full effects and economies of the change [in Scotland] can be worked out in detail".

Sir John Elliot, when RE Chairman, was later to claim spectacularly substantial savings resulting from the reduction of duplication north of the Border, despite the fact that office buildings were kept on in both Glasgow and Edinburgh city centres in 1948, with the staff given assurances against redundancy, and with no large-scale closure of termini, yards or depots – only harmless rural branches were ruthlessly purged, no fewer than seventeen of them in a single year, 1951. Yet Elliot boasted of annual savings of £12 million in 1951 – equivalent to one-third of annual revenue – and subsequently claimed £3 million saved annually for five years to 1953. He did not specify where such colossal savings were achieved, or

In March 1948 it was reported that the average speed of goods trains on the new nationalised system was just 8.69mph. Loose-coupled pick-up goods such as this no doubt helped to achieve this dismal statistic: on the Western Region 1897-built 'Dean Goods' 0-6-0 No.2538 potters along the Mid-Wales line near Rhayader on 9th October 1950.

London Midland Region: a pair of LMS 'Jubilee' 4-6-0s, Nos.45705 Seahorse *and 45576* South Australia, *storms away from Leeds City with an express from Newcastle to Manchester and Liverpool. In 1957, in a rearrangement of Regional boundaries, ex-LMS lines in the Leeds area were transferred to the North Eastern Region.* (Eric Treacy)

why there was an apparent contradiction in the figures he supplied – to a media clearly too indifferent to query them.

However, there may have been genuine doubts about the viability of a Region as small as the North Eastern in 1948; Dr. Bonavia records that "the creation of a North Eastern Region had hung in the balance", although BTC documents record that the Commission's Secretary, Miles Beevor, argued strongly for an autonomous NER. He was right do so; it

turned out to be one of the most successful! The new NER went on to produce the best economic performance of all six BR Regions in the next thirteen years.

In that first year, when a working paper declared that "the North Eastern is too small", changes were made within six months, but these were effectively boundary alterations and localised in extent, apart from the 'retreat' from the Irish Sea at Silloth. At the 1947 press conference, Hurcomb had paid particular tribute to the LNER's decentralised structure, which had facilitated the creation of no fewer than three of the six BR Regions. This had effectively allowed the launch of the NER as a self-contained entity and its absorption by the Eastern in 1968 is something of a surprise. The latter Region was less successful economically and had an awkward management structure, incorporating three mutually-exclusive systems (from west to east, Great Central, Great Northern and Great Eastern), each with its own London terminus. In this respect,

Hurcomb's comment was less appropriate; indeed, there might have been a case in late 1947 for setting up an 'East Anglian' Region to incorporate the former GER system and the one-time Midland and LMS-owned London Tilbury & Southend.

The BTC was determined to limit the new spirit of devolution by insisting that the six officials in charge of the new Regions could not be described as General Managers, but as 'Chief Regional Officers' (CROs). Miles Beevor, BTC Secretary, suggested in October 1947 that the Commission should consider looking outside the present rail company structure for CRO appointments, "there being scope for the employment [appointment] of men with some knowledge of railway working who have shown distinction in the fighting services or elsewhere".

Significantly perhaps, Beevor was an RAF reserve flight lieutenant until as recently as 1942. More obtusely, *The Times* published a leader late in 1947 showing concern about the resulting hierarchy:

The Scottish Region possessed a considerable mileage of rural branch lines. J39 0-6-0 No.64843 brings the Eyemouth branch train into its ECML junction at Burnmouth, a service which survived until 1962.

"The position of the Chief Officers does not appear inviting, and the dual responsibilities of departmental officers are likely to prove embarrassing … could the departmental officer appeal over the CO's head to the Executive?"

Whether any such officials – mechanical or civil engineers, or marine superintendents, for example – were ever "embarrassed" is not immediately clear from the records, but this point also exercised the *Railway Gazette*. Even worse, *Modern Transport* decreed that the CRO "seems destined to become a figurehead" – yet the LNER had operated perfectly well with a 'regional' system by dividing its network into three Areas, while maintaining 'all line' functions such as mechanical engineering which transcended such divisions. But in concluding that the CRO appointments would prove unworkable, the *Gazette* opined that "press scepticism has been remarkable for its unanimity".

Executive plans for a two-tier Regional system, grading the Regions by size with the senior staff being paid accordingly, did not find favour with the BTC in December 1947, with regional identities already made public. The Commission's documents of the time dealt confidentially with the salaries of the "figureheads" and all other senior rail officials, but attempts to impose a standard system of remuneration seem to have failed. As late as April 1948, a scale of CRO salaries was circulated, with none higher than £4,100 per annum, this for the LMR chief.

This document – not seen below Commission level – may be misfiled in the archives, as Beevor is recorded as early as 20th January 1948 indicating that the scale for the Regions would run from £2,250 to £7,500. Top of the tree was the newly-appointed head of the LMR, G.L. Darbyshire, who retained his existing salary of £7,500. Historian T.R. Gourvish describes Darbyshire as having been a Vice-President of the LMS, although media reports in December 1947 refer to him as Acting President, as does archival correspondence. After all, to be head of the UK's largest company conferred a certain prestige and Darbyshire's predecessor, Sir William Wood, had been elevated to the BTC itself.

The CROs of the new Southern and Western Regions were salaried at £6,700 and £5,500 respectively, considerably higher than in the BTC's recommendations. In contrast, the Scottish chief received £3,750, despite uniquely requiring to integrate former LMS and LNER staff and practices. Indeed, so challenging was the Scottish post thought to be that in September 1947 Hurcomb had sounded out Sir Robert Inglis "on his position". This suggests that the appointment of someone like Inglis – a Scot occupying a major position in transport in the Control Commission for Germany (British Element), as it was curiously called – would reflect Beevor's advice about the need to go 'outside the tribe' for outstanding candidates. (Inglis's response is not recorded). The NER's CRO, C.P. Hopkins, was the youngest and also, with an annual salary of £2,250, the least-well paid, although he was awarded annual expenses of £750.

In the event, there was a major reshuffle in 1950, made inevitable by Darbyshire's veteran status. The head of the LMR stood down within three years of taking charge of BR's largest Region and was succeeded by Elliot of the Southern, despite, as Gourvish observes, the latter's lack of familiarity with the network north of the Thames. Elliot took his existing salary level with him, thus saving BR £800 a year, and he was succeeded by Hopkins, whose new salary of £3,750 gave him a handsome increase, while saving BR £1,750. The NER's new CRO, H.A. Short was salaried at £3,500, almost equal to Cameron's salary on the much larger Scottish Region.

Miles Beevor pointed out that the proposals from the RE for a two-tier Regional system meant that Chief Regional Officers (CROs) in Group A would receive only £500 more per annum than those in the Group B classification and believed this to be administratively inconvenient and unnecessary. His chairman agreed and in the event the CROs were paid on a fairly arbitrary basis, with those already bearing great responsibility – such as Darbyshire of the LMS – being translated into a new post at the same salary, no doubt to avoid another embarrassing refusal (like Milne's) to accept a new post.

But the 'two tier' idea lived on at Marylebone. In April 1948 Bill Allen presented a paper to the BTC on Regional appointments and salaries, although his concern about the viability of the LMR would seem to be expressed a little late in the day. He had "doubts as to the future of this Region … if the LMR remains unaltered it will be necessary to consider some increase in the scale of salaries prepared for this Region".

For the record, the 'Big Three' Regions were to have been LMR, Eastern and Western, although it should be pointed out the Scottish almost equalled the Western in mileage and the Southern would better any of them for modernity and revenue performance – not surprisingly, considering that in its Southern Railway guise it had been by far the most profitable of the 'Big Four'. In the event, the Eastern CRO received a 'Group B' salary, while his counterpart on the (smaller) Southern Region was second only to Darbyshire of the LMS in the payment hierarchy. The array of CRO salaries in 1948 is summarised below.

Region:	RE tier designation	Actual CRO pay status
LMR	A	1st
WR	A	3rd
ER	A	5th
SR	B	2nd
ScR	B	4th
NER	B	6th

The future of joint railways was thought complicated enough to be the subject of a later press announcement. This was made on 8th December, consigning, *inter alia,* the Great Central to the Eastern Region, along with the Midland & Great Northern Joint, while the LMR took over the Birkenhead Joint lines, and the Southern the Somerset & Dorset. The Cheshire Lines Committee was to live on for the time being, its continued 'independence' the apparent result of an administrative misunderstanding (on which Gourvish is truly scathing!). These arrangements were not cast in stone; in particular, the former GCR system was destined to have more than one master over the years.

The 1947 legislation did not include a specification for Britain's railways to be administered on a Regional basis, but this working concept seems to have been a matter of consensus among railway managers and was not seriously challenged at the time. Interestingly, it was left to the Acts of 1953 and 1962 to legitimize such a 'federal' structure, with the latter statute specifying the Regions' operational and financial powers. However, in the autumn of 1947 a draft for six Regional remits was drawn up by Miles Beevor and approved by the BTC for forwarding to the Railway Executive, which would publish them.

These 'Holy Books' were typewritten and surprisingly sparse. Each one was typed from scratch, even for those

On the South Devon main line, GWR '43XX' 2-6-0 No.5397 trundles four vans and a brake along the sea wall at Teignmouth on 11th June 1949 at a speed described by the photographer as "about cycling pace". (Eric Bruton)

clauses and definitions common to all Regions – the NER issue (alone) has a prominent spelling error in this section. In contrast, nowadays they would be produced from a single, adaptable, template on a word-processor.

With a publication date of New Year's Day 1948, this numbered series, entitled *Instructions,* began in the north with Scottish Region, with the LMR second in the series, followed by NER, ER, SR and with Western bringing up the tail. The colour of their pages within a buff cardboard cover may appear to represent bibliographical details too trivial to mention, although the modern researcher is tempted to wonder if this symbolised rail administrators' thinking, giving each Region a liveried identity. The LMR was treated to pink pages in its booklet, with the NER in tangerine, Eastern in light blue, Southern in green, and the Western in a bright daffodil shade as No.6! Scottish had to make do with white. The *Instructions* included location of HQ, posts peculiar to the Region and Regional boundaries, illustrated by map where thought necessary, namely in No.1. The map was noticeably vague about inter-Regional boundaries and it is no surprise to find that many of these changed within six months and again two years later.

The largest of the regions was the pink-tinged **London Midland.** Comprising nearly 5,000 route miles, the LMR had its HQ at Euston and stretched some 300 miles north to Gretna, comprising both the West Coast Main Line and Midland routes. While easily the largest Region – and there were suggestions at one time that it should be halved in size – it was still considerably smaller than the former London Midland & Scottish Railway, which had stretched as far north as Wick and Thurso and had taken in the railways of Northern Ireland as well. The new Region also lost lines in Wales to the Western and the London Tilbury & Southend to the Eastern.

One system taken over in its entirety was that of the Cheshire Lines Committee, although this was by no means automatic, the CLC maintaining its nominal independence until 1st December 1948. Civil servants seem to have treated this system with kid gloves, much to Gourvish's subsequent scorn; he points out that at one time rolling stock was being labelled 'British Railways (CLC)'. Also, initially, the London Midland Region was responsible for administering the Northern Counties Committee and Great Northern Railway systems in Northern Ireland until the Ulster Transport Authority was formed. This was temporary, but the Region was responsible for the ferry facilities at Belfast and, from 1952, at Larne as well.

Despite its shrinkage from its LMS embodiment, this was an administrative unit of formidable aspect, its chief executive commanding a salary twice that of three of his Regional counterparts and some 40% more than what the BTC had considered for the post. Interestingly, Lord Ashfield had suggested to his Commission colleagues in October 1947 that this should be called the 'North Western Region' – in the event, the title 'London Midland' shared nominal aspects of both the gone-but-hardly-forgotten London & North Western and Midland companies.

Despite its might, the LMR was revealed in 1948 to be operating its freight trains at an average speed of 6.61mph, the lowest on BR.

RE definition: Group A   HQ: Euston
CRO: G.L. Darbyshire, £7,500 pa.

The **Scottish Region** – what was described in a RE document as the 'railway region of Scotland' – presented a unique challenge to rail administrators. No other Region involved the merging of major geographical areas of two former companies, in this case the Scottish Area of the LNER, running from near Berwick-on-Tweed north east and north westwards respectively to Lossiemouth and Mallaig, and the mainland section of the previous LMS's Northern Division, spread from Carlisle and Stranraer to Oban, Kyle, Wick and Thurso. That such a merger was made efficiently was to speak volumes for the diplomacy and administrative talents of Tom Cameron, who moved from his former LNER office in Edinburgh to the erstwhile LMS premises in Glasgow. Ironically, the BTC appears to have been prepared to go outside either LMS or LNER in making this appointment, as has been explained, although Cameron handled the job perfectly. Until 1952, Scottish was responsible for operating ferry facilities at Larne.

RE definition: Group B   HQ: Glasgow Buchanan Street
CRO: Tom Cameron, £3,750 pa.

In his 26th November press conference, Hurcomb had complimented the LNER on its devolved structure and this led to a comparatively painless division into two and a half BR Regions. As we have seen, half the Scottish Region was based on the LNER's Area set-up there, while the **North Eastern Region** constituted the former North Eastern Area. This stretched south from Berwick-on-Tweed to Shaftholme Junction, just north of Doncaster. Miles Beevor argued strongly for an autonomous North Eastern Region, memoing his masters in October 1947 that "the North East Area of the LNER is in fact a homogenous region which has always been efficiently workable from its York HQ".

The Region included electrified lines on Tyneside, but was also noted for its heavy mineral traffic – so heavy, indeed, that Hopkins was later to claim that nearly one-fifth of all coal movements by rail in the UK originated on his Region. For the first five months, the NER reached the west coast of England, taking over the Silloth branch along with Carlisle Canal shed, although both soon passed to the LMR. Carham and Sprouston stations, west of Berwick, were listed in the remit as "deleted", falling into an organisational limbo as the Scottish Region failed to include them – in fact, they would stay with the NER.

This was the only Region without a marine presence – while it nominally took over Goole shipping in 1951, this was then operated by contractors. The Region's Continental business was conducted on its behalf by Eastern Region.

RE definition: Group B   HQ: York
CRO: C.P. Hopkins, £2,250 + £750 expenses

The **Eastern Region** comprised the former LNER Southern Area although this had not been a particularly happy administrative unit. With its HQ at Liverpool Street, the one-time Great Eastern terminus, the area encompassed also included the former Great Northern and Great Central lines north from the capital and these were virtually mutually-exclusive railways. One concession to reality was the transfer to the Eastern of the former London Tilbury & Southend line within 25 months. It was believed that the Midland had snatched this line away from the nearby Great Eastern in 1913 by promising to electrify it, something which had still not happened.

RE definition: Group A   HQ: Liverpool Street
CRO: C.K. Bird, £3,500 pa.

The **Southern Region** took over the lines of the Southern Railway without major complication. Territorial additions included the North Devon & Cornwall Junction and the somewhat better-known Somerset & Dorset, as well as the East Kent Light and Kent & East Sussex, which Rolt pointed out had been considered too obscure to be included in the 1923

Grouping. The Southern Region was classed initially as a Group B Region, although having enjoyed electric traction since the mid-1920s it already exhibited a level of modernity in its traction operations which would leave its larger rivals far behind. If unpowered electric multiple unit carriages are included in the traction equation, Southern enjoyed a level of 64% of its transport stock modernised by 1948.

RE definition: Group B   HQ: Waterloo
CRO: John Elliot, £6,700 pa.

The transition of the Great Western Railway into the **Western Region** was comparatively painless, with little territorial

change. Some Welsh lines passed to the LMR, but the new Region gained the Shropshire Railways, the Shropshire & Montgomeryshire Light ("subject to WD possession"), Easton & Church Hope, Weymouth & Portland, West London Line and Extension and the GW/GCR Banbury Junction line.

The Railway Research Service (published out of an LNER office and printed by that company's printer) was highly complimentary towards the GWR in 1946 for its carriage livery, describing it as "the only British company to have retained the practice of having a lighter coloured upper panelling contrasting with a darker colour below the waistline". This summed up the spirit of the former company, a spirit which never quite dissipated in the south and west of England, or in the minds of its admirers everywhere. More examples of this independence were to be seen in the years to come, with the new Region's signalling engineers persisting with lower-quadrant semaphore signals when the rest of BR adopted upper-quadrants, and its motive power department eschewing diesel-electric power for diesel-hydraulic.

RE definition: Group B   HQ: Paddington
CRO: K.W.C. Grand, £5,500 pa.

The North Eastern Region inherited the Tyneside electrification begun by the North Eastern Railway in 1904 and extended by the LNER in 1938. A North Tyneside train of LNER-built stock approaches Newcastle Central, with the lines across the High Level Bridge to South Tyneside going off to the right.

Overall, Nationalisation created no redundancies at senior managerial level; quite the opposite. Where the 'Big Four' companies (and the Cheshire Lines Committee) had been administered by 182 officials earning more than £1,750 (£35,000) in 1947, fifteen *more* were now required, 44 of them in the offices of the BTC, as we have seen, as well as the Executive. Another sign of centralisation was that the overall salary bill for such posts increased by some £11,000 to £550,996 (£11 million) as 1948 got into its stride.

This largesse was given out at a time when the United Kingdom hovered on the brink of bankruptcy. Stringent conditions qualifying a loan from Washington meant that the pound had to be allowed to 'float' against the dollar, resulting in a rush by investors to rid themselves of British currency and eventually to a sterling devaluation. The Americans almost immediately were to introduce the Marshall Plan for aid to Europe, although the UK was not informed officially about the Plan at first, even although the British became its principal beneficiary. It all added up to a humiliating time for the British Government; when one Government minister referred to 1947 as "annus horrendus", he was not talking about the weather (although he could have been!). However, the jobs and directorial bonanza of 1947/8 would have suggested otherwise to the casual reader.

One interesting aspect of the appointments policy is that the BTC approved at least two appointments of over-60s to senior management "contrary to past railway practice" as the Board Minutes put it. This was "thought to be justified under present circumstances"; not least the fact (although not stated) that the BTC Chairman himself was 64, as was Sir William Wood, while their colleague Lord Ashfield was nine years older!

How were the new Regions faring as 1948 opened out? Documents circulating between Executive and Commission, in that first summer of British Railways, analysed all the Regional performances for the months of March and April, both in terms of profitability and punctuality. As far as the former concept was concerned, normal accountancy rules applied; there was no nonsense about running services for the good of the people! (These results were not made public.)

All six Regions took £9.76 million (£195 million) in gross passenger revenue, out of a total national income of £28.29 million (£565 million) from all rail operations in four weeks to 21st March, including ships and hotels. These figures showed increases, both in forecast and compared with the same period in the previous year. In the four weeks to 18th April, rail operations showed the heaviest net loss in Scotland, the system losing no less than £369,000 north of the Border. Nearest to Scottish was the Western, with a loss of £306,000, while the London Midland and Southern lost only £28,000 and £18,000

respectively. In contrast, both the Eastern and North Eastern showed a profit of at least £70,000. The Scottish and the Western could argue that large parts of their systems were dependent on holiday revenues and this appeared to be supported by the returns from hotels and restaurant cars, which made a loss in all Regions. (The Hotels Executive, which would take over these aspects of "railway" operation, did not begin operations until July.) On the LMR, the loss on hotels was much greater than that on rail services, no less than £34,000.

Punctuality was, however, something else again; in the four weeks to 20th March, Southern express trains showed the best 'on time' statistics in the six Regions. While only 60.6% of its electric services arrived at their destination punctually, this was half as punctual again as the national average of 40.7%, with the Eastern at the bottom of the table with 22.9%. Southern steam only managed 55.8% punctuality, bettered by Scottish with 58.4% and despite the latter having to operate with the LMR (34.1%) and NER (39.1%) as its immediate partners in Anglo-Scottish express operation.

For passenger services overall, the Southern recorded 82.5% punctuality with its steam services and 68.7% with electric but, with the technical press commenting frequently on the poor quality of locomotive coal available, this makes the all-steam Scottish Region's figures of 79.6% appear all the more impressive. This compared with 89% and 78.4% for electrics on the LMR and NER respectively.

Bearing in mind that the unique problem facing the Scottish Region – namely, the amalgamation of two rival systems – was sufficient for the BTC to have considered requesting the release of a high-ranking military transport officer from occupied Germany, it can be argued that Cameron and his management team had achieved a considerable amount in a short time.

At no time did the BTC seem to consider assigning individual liveries to the Regions, despite the colour coding shown in their remit documents, implying the germ of such an idea. According to the *Railway Magazine,* such Regional variety would reduce scope for the interchangeability of rolling stock, although in practice there were often technical reasons why, for example, stock could not be redistributed.

The BTC did not concern itself with the numbering of rolling stock, which was partly arranged by Region, partly by type of motive power. This will be examined in the chapter on 1948, the first year of operations.

However, the Commission really should have been more dynamic on such matters as livery and insignia for the new British Railways. Even the numbering scheme was not published in the technical press until nearly a quarter of BR's first year had gone. Enquirers telephoning railway booking

The Cheshire Lines Committee, which had been joint LNER/LMS, was placed in the London Midland Region. LMS 8F 2-8-0 No.8089 passes through Cheadle station with a train of ICI hopper wagons.

offices in January 1948 heard telephonists answering 'Railway Executive'! BR ships even had no corporate flag for the whole first year of nationalised maritime operations.

The transport community would have been spared a lot of confusion if a more PR-orientated approach had been adopted towards this massive reorganization of Britain's transport and the chance of engaging public support and interest was lost. (This was despite Miles Beevor moving as quickly as he could to secure a PRO for the new organisation, but he was clearly too late.) The fudged introduction of BR's corporate state will be examined in the account of the year 1948, later in this volume.

When, in October 1950, the magazine *Locomotive Post,* published by two engineers, reported that "Undoubtedly there is considerable disappointment with the outcome of Nationalisation. The respective regional administrations carry on in the same way as under private ownership".

It seems entirely possible that rail managers at Regional level would have taken this as a compliment.

5

The other Executives –
canals, hotels, road transport and London

One element all the above had in common before 1948 was – railways. The 'Big Four' railway companies ran all but the most important canals, owned hotels from Dornoch to St. Ives, while 'earning' – through apparently shrewd investment – millions annually from commercial bus services and even such firms as Pickfords. At the same time, London Transport was such a major undertaking that its designation as a self-standing Executive was never questioned.

It seems curious nowadays to observe that the heads of the Executives – particularly of commercial road transport – were salaried at a lower rate than three of BR's Regions! Two aspects of the transport scene left with railway administration comprised ferries and coastal shipping sailing on fixed routes between ports and these omissions from the assignment of Executive status are discussed below.

London

London's transport holds a seminal place in the history of nationalisation. As early as 1931, when there were only two technology-based public corporations operating throughout Britain – the Central Electricity Board and the BBC – a unitary body was proposed to administer the capital's transport. Minister of Transport at that time was Herbert Morrison, a Labour MP dedicated to promoting London's interests and who, after declining to follow Ramsay Macdonald into a national government dominated by Conservatives, resigned office and proceeded to write a book (*Socialisation and Transport*) about London's internal communications.

Its statistics are interesting. By March 1933, when Morrison's proposed legislation for a centralized transport body were revived by the subsequent minister, London had no fewer than 307 miles of track electrified by the main line railways and 132 route miles of Underground, all part of a total of seventeen railways comprising the 'Big Four', four 'Underground' companies, the Metropolitan and eight joint lines. On the roads there were sixteen tramways – thirteen of them municipally-owned – 62 omnibus operators, of whom 54 were independent, and 21 coach lines. Morrison argued that their very multiplicity made essential a unitary supervisory or controlling body, although in passing it must be said that many cities today would envy Londoners their huge choice of transport options! Interestingly, even Thatcherite measures like the deregulation of Britain's bus industry in 1986 left London unscathed, so established was Morrison's vision of an integrated transport system in the capital.

With the setting-up of the London Passenger Transport Board (LPTB) by Morrison's successor, the bonding of capital transport into a *commercial* monopoly, probably controlled by Lord Ashfield, was prevented. According to his entry in *DNB*, Ashfield took this setback in good part, accepting the chairmanship of what became the LPTB, a public corporation not dedicated to profit-making. With his seemingly Midas touch, Ashfield made a great success of the new corporate body, thereby creating a model for the BTC, which he was invited to join at its outset.

London Transport, in whatever nominal form it is considered, was fortunate in its administrators. While Frank Pick gained fame for his stylized maps of the capital's underground – and they were only part of his contribution to the successful branding of LTPB and its successors – Lord Ashfield was also widely praised. We have already met Ashfield donating two floors of an office building to provide a home to the fledgling BTC, but he also received an unsolicited testimonial from Lord Brabazon of Tara, a former wartime Minister of Transport speaking in the House of Lords on 20th May 1947. It is worth quoting Brabazon's words when he recalled the early development of the LPTB:

"The great Lord Ashfield early saw that there was going to be competition between the Underground and the buses ... and made a common pool of their receipts. In early days, the tubes paid for the buses, and later the buses have paid for the tubes."

Brabazon argued that a common receipts pool should be adopted for all nationalised British transport, which although it might appear to the modern reader as impracticable to the point of fantasy, nevertheless shows the seminal effect of

London Transport's rail activities were not confined to the tube but also included loco-hauled trains out along the Metropolitan Line to Rickmansworth and Chesham. One of the former Metropolitan Railway's electric locomotives, No. 3 **Sir Ralph Verney**, *passes Neasden with a train from Baker Street to Chesham.*

London's transport unification from 1933 on the minds of transport administrators; Brabazon was the last civilian Minister of Transport in Britain before that ministry was taken over by its wartime equivalent in 1941.

It is not the purpose of this book to discuss London's transport at length; it is too complex a subject and has been well documented over the years. However, the reader should be in no doubt about London's inspirational example on the development of public transport on a national scale.

Southampton was pre-eminent among railway docks and was described as "The jewel in the crown of the Southern Railway" by its General Manager, Sir Herbert Walker. It hosted such legends of the seas as the RMS **Queen Elizabeth**, *seen here in front of the Ocean Terminal, a project begun by the SR and completed by the British Transport Commission. It was opened by the Prime Minister, Clement Attlee, in 1950.*

Canals and docks

Inland waterways should have no place in the railways' story after 1st January 1948. Allocated to a new Executive shared with Docks, they were intended to be divorced from their former railway owners, who were probably glad to wave goodbye to a transport system which had caused them considerable irritation and inconvenience, in return for little in the way of income.

For the record, the railway canals nationalised in 1948, and tabulated here in terms of the 'Big Four' companies, were:

Owners at Nationalisation	Owners before 1923 Grouping
LMS	
Ashby-de-la-Zouche	Midland
Birmingham & Liverpool Junction	Shropshire Union Rlys
Birmingham Navigation	LNWR
Cromford	Midland
Ellesmere & Chester	Shropshire Union Rlys
Forth & Clyde	Caledonian
Huddersfield	LNWR
Lancaster	LNWR
Manchester, Bolton, & Bury	LYR
Monkland	Caledonian
St. Helens	LNWR
Shropshire Union	Shropshire Union Rlys
Trent & Mersey	North Staffordshire
Ulverston	Furness
LNER	
Ashton-under-Lyne	Great Central
Chesterfield	Great Central
Edinburgh & Glasgow Union	North British
Fossdyke	Great Northern/then leased to LNER
Grantham	GNR
Macclesfield	Great Central
Norwich & Lowestoft	Great Eastern
Nottingham	GCR
Peak Forest	GCR
Pocklington	North Eastern
Ure & Ripon Navigation	NER
Witham	GNR

Owners at Nationalisation	Owners before 1923 Grouping
GWR	
Brecknock & Abergavenny	
Bridgwater & Taunton	
Grand Western	
Herefordshire & Gloucestershire	Leased to GWR
Kennet & Avon	
Monmouthshire	
Stourbridge Extension	
Stratford-upon-Avon	
Swansea & Trewyddfa	
SR	
Gravesend & Higham	South Eastern & Chatham
Joint	
Kensington	West London Extension [1]
Lydney	GWR/Midland

1. Taken over by BR Western Region in 1948

To put all this into perspective, in January 1947 Britain's railways generated revenue of close to £20 million, nearly 400 times what 34 railway-owned canals, totalling 976 miles, earned in the same month in tolls and freight charges. On the other hand, as Tom Rolt had pointed out, the privately-owned railways had failed to set up a clearing house which would have standardised tolls and freight charges on the canals they owned and thus centralised inter-company paperwork. Nor had the railways exerted themselves on such matters as dredging and maintenance; indeed this decade saw the urgent establishment (by enthusiasts) of the Inland Waterways Association, so dire did the future of many canals appear. The writings of Tom Rolt and Robert Aickman leave the reader in no doubt of the seriousness of the decline in probably three-quarters of the canal network, although possible exaggeration because of the authors' political beliefs and affiliations have to be borne in mind when reading such books as Rolt's *Narrow Boat* or Aickman's *The River runs Uphill*.

The actual process of absorption into public ownership was hardly smooth, a BTC document advising in December 1947 there would be a delay in establishing a canal administration and "existing arrangements on [railway-owned] canals and docks will continue for the time being". Reading the BTC files nowadays gives the historian the unmistakable impression that the commissioners saw no pressing reason to take their waterways away from railway managements, presumably under the impression that they were being well looked after. This is perhaps just one interpretation, but it is noticeable that, of the 25 canals designated for the five Docks & Inland Waterways Executive areas delineated by November 1947, only nine came from the railways and a number of those were only partly taken over for navigational purposes.

Heading the new organisation was Sir Reginald Hill, a former civil servant at the Ministry of Transport. Of him Aickman said "it is impossible not to like him [but] he was unfortunate in being set at the head of an enterprise which the gods scarcely intended to prosper". The supposedly-doomed DIW Executive only got under way on 1st July 1948.

Just as there was surprise among railway enthusiasts at the number and variety of railways not 'vested' in BR, so the supporters of the canal network were baffled by a number of waterways omitted from the 1947 Act. Rolt and Aickman visited the Ministry of Transport to query the omission from Nationalisation of the Manchester Ship Canal, and the reason given the enquirers was that it was regarded as virtually public property anyway through the local authority's ownership of such a large proportion of the share capital. A number of unspecified canals in eastern England was also excluded and in his book Aickman does not name them; he and Rolt apparently received no satisfactory explanation for their exclusion. Finally, a senior civil servant astonished Rolt and Aickman by expressing surprise that railway-owned canals would be taken over ("You mean, we get these as well?"), although one wonders if the Ministry official was 'winding up' these upright and undoubtedly sincere gentlemen.

Categorising canals with docks, nearly of all them marine, hardly seemed logical and, according to historian Charles Hadfield, "the 'Inland Waterways' component was very much the junior partner". (Interestingly, the short title for the new Executive was minuted as 'British Waterways' by the BTC on 21st October 1947). Matters were then made even more complicated by the earliest administrative structure for inland waterways proposing the setting-up of two regions (later, five area groupings), but excluding Scottish canals altogether. Two Scottish canals already publicly-owned through trust organizations, the 69 miles of the Caledonian and the Crinan, had been controlled by the Ministry of Transport but were now placed directly under the aegis of the BTC, much to Hurcomb's reported irritation. Nevertheless, the public directories advised that the two waterways were "administered by the Executive under the direction of local officers".

The new Executive found its home at 22 Dorset Square in Marylebone in early 1948. Previously, its embryonic staff was accommodated in what was officially described as "entirely unsuitable quarters" in a Transport Ministry building in North Gate, St. John's Wood. Considering that no structure for the administration of waterways had been decided even as late as October 1947, it was hardly surprising that the new Executive embarked on a nomadic existence to begin with. Meanwhile, BR's Regions were expected to administer existing railway canals for at least six more months, although they were warned that no closures could be carried out without permission from the Executive – the *Railway* Executive, naturally!

In any event, the new Docks & Inland Waterways Executive was an unhappy hybrid, the product of what Dr. Bonavia called "administrative convenience". During 1948 railway docks generated five times as much revenue as the canals previously owned by the 'Big Four' and the latter had a considerable accumulated debt. Bonavia quotes informal notes from Hurcomb's own private secretary to the effect that the Government's approach to docks was muddled, to say the least, but that was not likely to cause the transport media much surprise at the time.

Approximately one-third of the nation's docks was now nationalised from railway sources, the outstanding examples being Southampton, Barrow-in-Furness, Cardiff, Swansea, Plymouth, Grangemouth, Hull and Goole, to say nothing of 'packet stations' at Fishguard, Folkestone, Harwich, Heysham, Holyhead, Stranraer, Larne and Belfast.

So pre-eminent was Southampton among railway docks that Missenden, former Chairman of the Southern Railway company which owned the complex, argued that the railways should continue to run it, not least because the RE had persuaded the BTC to allocate £775,000 for work on berths 43 and 44 in December 1948. In this, Missenden was supported by one of the rail unions, the NUR, while the TGWU took an opposing view. Absorption by the new DIWE was delayed while this was sorted out – with defeat for the Railway Executive in September 1950 – and the Hampshire port became the site of one of three regional HQs of the new Executive, the others being in South Wales and Humberside. Interestingly, the regional head of the South Wales Division was A.E.H. Brown, formerly of BR Eastern Region and, for a short time before his untimely death in 1955, General Manager on the Scottish Region: an illustration of the close relationship between railways and docks (which was, of course, Missenden's and the NUR's point).

The year 1948 was only seven months old when the BTC was offered – and declined – control of two new dock areas. These were Military Ports 1 and 2, respectively at Faslane (Loch Long) and Cairnryan (near Stranraer). These had been constructed in wartime in case existing west coast docks, particularly Liverpool's, had been bombed out of commission, although neither had, mercifully, to be used to full capacity in transshipping material between ship and train. On 15th July, the Commission minuted that its members "saw no prospect of these bases ever becoming commercial ports and it would not be proper to take them over from the government".

The lack of a commercial future would come as a surprise to P&O, which uses Cairnryan nowadays – indeed, it is understood that this will soon usurp Stranraer as a terminal for all Irish traffic from this part of Britain. Meanwhile, Faslane has become the most important naval base on the west coast.

Hotels

Although the spread of the railway network had inspired the construction of some of the UK's finest hotels, there was a conviction abroad in the late 1940s that these should be separated from the transport sector. Sir Cyril Hurcomb explained it to the Railway Students Association in March 1949:

"Hotels had been separated from the railways at Executive level [in 1948], because they were a specialized industry and required individual management, but the excellence of the hotels would be a means of increasing traffic". However, the last part of his comment would appear to contradict the first part, by emphasising the relationship between train and hotel.

As with docks and canals, the establishment of a separate Hotels Executive was clearly not keeping pace at that time with its railway counterpart, with its history going back to 1914. Not until 1st July 1948 was the Hotels Executive formally established, although it appears that Lord Inman, with a lifetime of hotel administration experience, was chosen as a suitable head for the new Executive as early as February.

Unfortunately, with delays resulting in the establishment of the new body – an immediate challenge was finding accommodation for it – a question was asked in Parliament about whether Inman was being salaried during this interim period. Transport Minister Alf Barnes was able to assure the Member concerned that his lordship was accepting no remuneration until the new Executive was in existence – a gallant gesture by Inman considering the delay was hardly his fault.

The first railway hotels were at Euston in 1839 and its two buildings were linked in 1881 by a new block which included access for the station approach road. The Euston Hotel closed in 1963 as part of the complete rebuilding of the station. (T.J. Edgington Collection)

The art deco Midland Hotel at Morecambe, opened by the LMS in 1933, the future of which exercised the Hotels Executive in the first year of nationalisation.
(H.N. Twells Collection)

Accommodation was being prepared for the Executive at 222 Marylebone Road, sharing with its railway and road transport counterparts, although this was not ready initially, the new organisation starting life as a lodger at Euston. The media's welcome was perhaps less than effusive, with press demands for an investigation of alleged food poisoning on the 'Flying Scotsman' in August when four passengers were reported to have been taken to hospital. Transport periodicals, reporting this mishap, tried not to suggest that these socialist fellows had, to coin a phrase, bitten off more than they could chew.

Archival documents reveal the Railway Executive, from the preceding April, reviewing its complement of 33 active hotels in time for the coming summer season. This was a reduction on the number originally involved in the Government's haul. BTC documents from September 1947 number these at 62, with Hurcomb, curiously, questioning whether Gleneagles "should be retained". This prompted the Chairman, who may just have been under the impression that Gleneagles was not rail-connected, to suggest a complete appraisal of hotels to be administered by the BTC, telling his colleagues on 23rd September:

"We should call for reports on all the hotel properties, with full information as to the purposes they serve and the class of persons for whom they cater".

Those which failed to impress the Commissioners could then be sold off, something which (although permitted by the Act) strikes the modern reader as completely contrary to the spirit of converting British transport to public ownership – as indeed does the uncomfortable reference to the "class" of people served in the hotels! More seriously, there was a blurring of responsibility of hotels between BTC and RE, to say nothing of the supposedly superseded 'Big Four' companies, until well into 1948.

The *Instructions* booklets issued to the BR Regions were less than clear when dealing with the hotels network. These remits were drafted by Beevor at the Commission and he was aware that the new Executive was nowhere near ready to begin operations. The resulting RE document informed the Regions that the hotels would continue to be administered by the former company officials of the pre-Grouping companies, LMS, LNER, GWR and SR – and these companies are named in the documents, as if the 'Big Four' continued to exist! Certainly, their four final AGMs were not held until around the close of the 1947-8 tax year, but it remains a curious anomaly in the files of the nationalised railways and one wonders what kind of 'job security' could be expected by the officials burdened with the responsibility of running major hotels and all station refreshment rooms. Additionally, the RE placed David Blee, former GWR Chief Goods Manager, nominally in charge of hotels, although there are also two references to these being run by the hotel managers of the 'Big Four'.

Even while wrestling with the general concept of owning hotels – of which only Sir William Wood among the BTC members could possibly have had much experience, since the LMS had been the biggest railway hotel-owning company in the world – the question of one particular hotel occupied the Commission in the meantime. As mentioned earlier, this was the Midland Hotel at Morecambe, famed for its futuristic outline and Art Deco interiors. It very nearly lost these, and its very existence, in 1947, with the local authority pressing for conversion of the building, dilapidated following wartime use, to housing. Darbyshire, Acting President of the LMS writing to the Minister, urged disposal of the hotel on the (perhaps) surprising grounds that it required "conversion into an Hotel more in keeping with the type of business at this Lancashire holiday resort".

The question of restoration was postponed pending discussions with the Post Office, which was interested in hostel use of the Midland for its employees, but when this fell through the BTC agreed to full restoration, provided that the building would be ready for summer use in 1948. Unfortunately, this timetable proved impossible to fulfill and the Commission was asked to make no hasty decisions until Lord Inman had visited the building. With the Hotels Executive not formally instituted until 1st July and Inman only nominally appointed as its Chairman on 8th June, it remains to the BTC's credit that it continued to resist local pressure for a short-term solution, authorising a £27,000 rehabilitation programme on 1st June to be completed as soon as possible.

An architectural jewel was saved, although the taxpayer did not enjoy its benefits for long; it passed out of nationalised hands in 1952. At the time of writing, the building is derelict once more, once again being promised restoration from public funds. Morecambe's Midland Hotel almost exemplifies the UK's railway system – operated and largely mismanaged in private hands, awaiting public funding to rescue it from the wreckers' ball. Like Darbyshire, this author wonders if this hotel is right for its location. If it were to be converted into, say, a 'Museum of the 1930s', one could envisage people travelling to Morecambe to see it, but not visitors residing in it to see Morecambe.

Lord Inman – on £5,000 a year (at last), equal with General Russell who was theoretically in charge of Britain's entire commercial road network, both passenger and freight – was one of only two full-time members of the new Hotels Executive, the other being Francis G. Hole, one of the leading lights in the hospitality industry. The three part-time members actually included one woman – Mrs. Ella Gasking – the only member of the fair sex making an appearance in transport documents from the late 1940s.

Mrs. Gasking had built up Batchelor's Peas into a major canning industry from the age of 22 and was the company's Managing Director for 30 years. She became a full-time member of the Executive in 1950. Such an imaginative appointment probably needs explaining in a civil service atmosphere not noted for imagination and it seems probable that her appointment came about as a result of the Board of

Trade being consulted, as it was as early as the previous September, about the membership of the new Executive. Mrs. Gasking had served on a Board of Trade committee regulating retail pricing.

Like its railway and road counterparts, the new Executive had its headquarters at 222 Marylebone Road – although the last organization to find accommodation there.

Hotels were now classified into three categories according to size, with ten in Category A (and these were among the top establishments in Europe), thirteen in B and nineteen in the lowest classification. Morecambe, Saltburn and some of the Scottish hotels were not included in this list – effectively, a 'stocktaking' handover from the Railway Executive.

Category A comprised (in no particular order): Great Eastern, Great Western and Charing Cross in London, Manchester Midland, Liverpool Adelphi, Leeds Queen's, Glasgow Caledonian, Edinburgh Caledonian and North British, Gleneagles.

B: Great Northern and Euston in London, Birmingham Queen's, Royal Station Hotels in Newcastle, Hull, Sheffield and York, Liverpool Exchange, Glasgow St. Enoch and North British, Stratford-on-Avon Welcombe, Tregenna Castle at St. Ives, Felix at Felixstowe.

C: Leeds Great Northern, Bradford Great Northern Victoria and Midland, Derby Midland, North Staffordshire at Stoke-on-Trent, Station Hotels at Perth, Inverness, Ayr, Holyhead and Dumfries, West Hartlepool Grand Preston Park, Great Eastern Parkeston Quay, Sidmouth Knowle, Crewe Arms, Grimsby Yarborough, Goodwick Fishguard Bay, Moretonhampstead Manor House and hotels at Kyle of Lochalsh and Dornoch.

By April 1949 the new Executive was able to look back on its first nine months of existence, administering (and here the figures differed again from those quoted by the Railway Executive) 65 hotels, with approximately 5,000 bedrooms. 'Bednights' booked in the previous calendar year came to 1.3 million, with 6.5 million meals served. There were 476 refreshment rooms in the Executive's care and 483 restaurant cars on the railways, serving ten million meals in 1948.

The last-named were a curious inclusion in the Hotels brief, although, since these facilities were notoriously unprofitable, railway chiefs may have been quite happy to see these administered by non-transport experts. Within three years, it was Inman's turn to want rid of them, as he came to believe that they were integrated into railway operational matters. At one time, the Commission felt it would be logical for these vehicles to have a distinctive livery, although this was not pursued. Interestingly, it was rail-borne catering which seemed to come under the strictest media scrutiny, doubtless giving cause to Lord Inman's willingness to return these to rail managers.

The *Railway Gazette* in particular provided a platform for long-distance rail travellers to comment about the quality of rail-borne meals. By mid-1949 the consensus seemed to be that Eastern Region trains offered the best meals and the LMR, the worst although, as one retired colonel thundered, "there should be no material difference". The LMR's poor performance apparently surprised nobody involved in rail catering and the vehicles used on the Midland main line expresses were regarded by the staff as the oldest and most difficult to work in. Scottish recorded a faint cheer by being complimented on the excellence of its fare at Edinburgh Waverley despite the alleged scruffiness of the restaurant.

Lord Inman would have time and cause to consider that the popularity and prestige of the major hotels he administered were invariably at contrast with the apparently incessant press criticism of BR restaurant cars and refreshment rooms.

Road transport

As observed earlier, roads were developing as an area of transport which was simply too big to manage, unless through the Road Traffic Acts. Quite early in the drafting of transport legislation, Minister Alf Barnes relaxed the controls on certain aspects of freight transport, thus effectively ensuring that there was no question of the highly-regulated railways system being able to compete with road equally.

In fact, railways before 1948 had played an important part in road services, even if their involvement with bus and trucking companies had not worked out quite as intended in the board-rooms of the GWR, LMS, LNER and Southern.

In 1928 the Railway Road Powers Act had settled an unusual benison on the railway industry by allowing the 'Big Four' to invest in such road concerns as Pickford's, British Automobile and Northern General. Some of the share proportions taken were, or were supposed to be, as much as 50% of existing capital, although there is evidence that some rail managers were outwitted by bus operators more accustomed to fight for their market share than railway administrators who had enjoyed a monopoly on public transport for all their working lives.

At least one deal which should have given both LNER and LMS a major say in the running of a regional bus concern was mysteriously delayed while the bus company quadrupled its existing capital, presumably through the kind of informal dealing now frowned upon, if not downright illegal, to benefit existing shareholders, thus downgrading rail's influence in the boardroom. Yet the archival papers show how blissfully

AEC bus operated by the LNER, with 'Gainsborough' shown on the destination blind. (T.J. Edgington Collection)

unaware the railway officials were that they were dealing with transport professionals living on the edge of an expanding market. In this particular case, the LMS negotiators were memoing each other about the background of one of their LNER counterparts, while the bus owner, who had built up the company from a single vehicle, was busy securing his own position and doubtless that of his friends and relatives as well. Not surprisingly, the file closes with a comment from the LMS solicitor criticizing the way both sets of railway officials had allowed themselves to be bettered.

In the long run, it scarcely seemed to matter. Dividends from bus companies provided a handsome bonus to the pre-nationalised railway companies. In 1947 the dividends of the 'Big Four' from the bus companies were as follows:

LMS: £1,325,773
LNER: £1,159,966
GWR: £585,017
SR: £417,946

This was unadulterated profit and the figures above should be multiplied by twenty to give a modern equivalent. Bus revenues (as well as rail's) blossomed in the immediate post-war years as people attempted to return to pre-war normality in terms of commuting to peacetime employment and taking what trips they could, while car drivers were subject to petrol rationing and hire vehicles could only be driven within a 20-mile radius. This was a golden time for public passenger operators!

LNER 'earned' the equivalent of £3.5 million from one company alone – United General – while north of the Border, investment in Scottish Motor Transport provided the equivalent to £11 million to the LMS and LNER in the same year. Of course, such income was abruptly removed after the bells had hanselled in 1948.

Consider that in its first year Eastern Region made a profit of only £800,000 and Scottish (including former LMS lines) £200,000. In its previous year the LMS and LNER had received more than £450,000 in dividends from one bus company in Scotland alone. Yet North Eastern Region, despite the loss of road investment, recorded a profit of nearly £8 million in 1948.

Freight road transport investments included Curries of Newcastle, in which the LNER had no less than £84,806-worth of shares in 1944. Nationally, the 'Big Four' had £3.1 million invested in Hay's Wharf Cartage in 1944, thus controlling Pickford's. If any other proof were needed of the railway companies' interest in Hay's, curiosity can be satisfied by a glance at the names of four of the Cartage directors – such railway 'aristocracy' as Milne, Newton, Missenden and Darbyshire, no less.

BTC Minutes record the rushed, indeed almost reckless, acquisition by the Commission of the road carriers H. & G. Dutfield in January 1948. Henry Dutfield was an outspoken opponent of Nationalisation, a point of view to which he was perfectly entitled as Chairman of the Road Haulage Association but which, curiously, seemed to guarantee him a place on a State-owned transport organisation. (The official reason for his appointment was, of course, to take advantage of his knowledge of the business, but it was also an effective, if expensive, way to silence a critic.) Dutfield was to join the Road Transport Executive, but the announcement of his appointment seemed to catch the BTC by surprise, with his company not yet absorbed. Archival papers show that Comptroller Wilson suggested to the Commission that it should immediately pay £137,500 (£3 million) to Dutfield for his shares, although Wilson advised that the total cost to the BTC might come to £200,000 (£4.4 million). However, Wilson memoed "we are satisfied that the price is reasonable and defensible" – an interesting turn of phrase, to say the least – but warned that "the approval of the Commission must be given today".

Needless to say the railway companies also operated their own goods transport networks, the four owning more than £4 million-worth of vehicles at the end of the war, with garages and stables valued at £2.7 million. Under nationalisation, the railways were able to maintain their road presence, while obviously losing their investment in commercial companies, whether passenger or freight.

The 1947 Act brought some 20,000 long-distance road freight vehicles under the jurisdiction of the new RTE (the figures, perhaps not surprisingly, vary depending on which document is consulted), although this was dwarfed by the 53,000 vehicles which the 'Big Four' operated on the roads. Within two years the RTE was renamed the Road Haulage Executive, dealing with freight only. A Road Passenger Executive was then formed from June 1949 but, despite its title, had no executive functions.

Like the hotels and canals, road transport was not so readily brought under national control as the railways and only came under the BTC umbrella in mid-1948. Office accommodation was, as always, a contentious subject, with the Executive's first Chairman, General G.N. Russell, advising the BTC in January that it would not be appropriate for the road transport to share offices with the Railway Executive "so as to allay in the minds of the Road Haulage trade any possible suspicion, however far fetched, that they are being overshadowed by the railways".

Despite Russell's advice, a shared building was the outcome, with the RTE accommodated with the railways and (later) the hotels at 222 Marylebone Road. As we know, the location of the new road authority was already fixed, but the Commission officials seem to have reined in Russell's ambition for a separate building. He had an eye on Thomas Cook's offices in central London, but was apparently advised that these were out of his reach.

The free-wheeling world of road freight haulage may have experienced difficulty in accepting a panoply of ordinances beginning to fall on its members. In September 1948 those firms acquired by the state were ordered to resign their membership of the Road Haulage Association, as their subscriptions were effectively subsidising the Executive's – and the Government's – critics. (Curiously, the Association's former Chairman was now a member of the Executive!) RTE vehicles were to be made available to members of other executives as required although, in return, the road hauliers were assured that they would be kept informed of railway closures, so as to ensure that they could pick up any ensuing business, whether passenger or freight. Such an assurance was hardly necessary; one TUCC already included a representative of the road haulage industry – an appointment which was hardly going to offer much of a lifeline to rural railways.

Meanwhile, General Russell was advised that his car registration 'BRS 1' was not perhaps such a good idea – it made it almost impossible for him to pay a surprise visit to any haulage depot!

Cook's Travels

A more distant waterway where the BTC organized sailings, theoretically anyway, was the Nile. This was because the famous travel agency firm of Thomas Cook & Son passed into the Commission's hands on the first chime of the clock in 1948 and it is interesting to see how and why this happened.

Established in mid-Victorian times, Cook's suffered its first real setback when the First World War closed so many borders and virtually wiped out the tourist trade for nearly five years. As a result, the company was vulnerable to takeover and in 1928 became part of the Belgian-based International Wagon-Lits company.

To avoid its assets falling into German hands in 1940, the company was seized by the UK's Custodian of Enemy Property, but the war had pitched the company into the red anyway. The four British railways agreed to step in and take over Cook's, with losses being guaranteed by the companies for three years, and this was sealed by an Act of Parliament in 1942. The share capital of Cook's was vested in the road transport firm Hay's Wharf Cartage – which also administered Pickford's – so the travel company remained a subsidiary of the railway companies.

With 142 High Street outlets, Cook's remained a well-known travel company and the BTC members soon found themselves reading reports not only about the organising of foreign and group travel but also about the administration of the company's two holiday camps, at Prestatyn and on the Isle of Wight. They also learned about Cook's Egyptian subsidiary, which operated an engineering works and ran pleasure trips on the Nile.

Ships

One facet of transport not granted its own Executive, but left with the railways, was the ferries and pleasure vessels operating throughout the UK, from the White Cliffs of Dover to as far north as the Isle of Skye. These even included some cargo ships, although only operating on fixed routes, as opposed to 'tramping' – travelling anywhere where cargoes were available.

The ferries came into two categories – train ferries, which transported rail vehicles and were only operating out of Harwich and Dover – and road ferries, found almost everywhere around the British mainland, the northernmost railway-administered example being located at Kyle of Lochalsh. These were effectively ferries for pedestrians with cargo loaded and unloaded by crane; demand for vehicular 'roll-on roll-off' services was to become increasingly insistent.

Addressing his BTC colleagues on 29th September 1947, Hurcomb was recorded as saying: "The operation of existing steamer services should continue to be linked with the Railways, of which they are in effect a projection across the narrow seas."

All but the North Eastern Region appointed a Marine Superintendent to undertake the operation of the railways' maritime services, although that Region nominally took over services out of Goole in 1951. Freshwater operations were also included, at Windermere and on Lochs Awe and Lomond. In his 1947 summary, Hurcomb had added that he believed that Clyde services would offer no problems in assimilation, "but there remains the troublesome matter of MacBrayne services, in which we shall become half-owners in succession to the LMS and in partnership with Coast Line."

What was troublesome about this was the promise made by the LMS to purchase half the shares in a new £100,000 issue, designed to pay for new tonnage. In April 1948 the BTC Comptroller recommended that this transaction should be proceeded with. Taken with a 1950 Modernisation Plan for seven new railway-owned Caledonian Steam Packet vessels, this represented a major investment in Scottish shipping, of a kind that the corresponding Scottish Region rail network could only dream about.

So disparate were the types of shipping involved, and so high the risks of marine operation in all weathers, that it is doubtful if the best interests of the travelling public were served by the

One of the newest ships to enter BTC ownership was the Great Western's TSS St. Patrick, built by Cammell-Laird & Co. and launched in May 1947 for the Fishguard–Rosslare and Weymouth–Channel Islands routes. She replaced an earlier vessel of the same name sunk by enemy action in 1941.

Government's failure to establish some kind of Inshore Shipping Executive. While the BTC did operate a Coastal Shipping Advisory Commission, this had no executive function despite being established by statute in 1947. Nevertheless, it was well constituted, its members in October 1948 including Messrs. Darbyshire, Elliot and Cameron – heads of the LM, Southern and Scottish Regions respectively – as well as representatives of the Railway and Docks Executives.

In early March, the Minister was tackled in the House of Commons by MPs concerned by the lack of any corporate identity for the vessels once owned by four mutually-exclusive rail companies. Minister Alf Barnes promised to refer a request for a 'house' flag to the BTC and it comes as no surprise that the organisation, which had launched British Railways with no national livery and no publicly-announced numbering scheme for rolling stock, had not covered this point either. What started as a sensible Parliamentary debate on this occasion about hull and funnel colours soon degenerated into a political brawl, with Conservative members suggesting, for a suitable masthead flag, either a 'hammer and sickle' design or the 'Jolly Roger'.

Not until April 1949 was BR's shipping flag unveiled. It constituted a saltire with lined diagonals and a lion at the centre. Interestingly, it was to be flown by BTC-operated and Executive-run vessels alike.

The comparatively-generous investment in shipping in the ten years after the war must have made railway managers turn green with envy and – worse – the figures would suggest more capitalization in Britain's transport system than was actually taking place, at least away from the coast. Losses of railway ships to enemy action were an obvious reason for reinvigorating the fleet, although direct damage to the railway system itself, with its enormous £179 million-worth of destruction and funding withheld because of emergency Trust Fund conditions, hardly seemed to spur a similar act of restitution. In the first ten years after the end of hostilities, more than twenty new vessels were commissioned by the pre-nationalisation companies before 1948, the paddle-steamer *Waverley* being the longest-lasting. In Scotland, seven new ships were ordered after Nationalisation, not including the famous paddler mentioned above, and this was in stark contrast to the almost total lack of new investment in Scotland's railways.

But organisational failings in 1947/8 could be held responsible for the UK's worst transport accident until the loss of PanAm 103 over Lockerbie in 1988 – and of course the latter was, strictly speaking, not an accident.

The loss of the ferry *Princess Victoria* with 133 lives took place in January 1953, but the tragedy had its roots in decisions taken at the birth of BR in 1948. This did not appear obvious when the news broke of the sinking of this comparatively new vehicle ferry on the Stranraer–Larne route on a stormy winter's day five years after Nationalisation.

The *Princess Victoria* was a post-war vehicle ferry fitted with rear vehicular doors. She had just cleared Stranraer with 170 people on board on 31st January when she ran into a severe storm. Her stern doors – which were not designed to seal the hull or superstructure – appear to have given way and she tragically foundered not far from the coast of Northern Ireland. 133 passengers and crew died. It appears that the captain fatally delayed giving the order to abandon ship, allowing a list to become so severe as to prevent the launching of lifeboats on one side, although his reluctance to commit passengers to the stormy water is perhaps understandable when he believed, wrongly, that help was near at hand.

A court of inquiry subsequently held in Northern Ireland was critical of the BTC for operating a vessel so clearly defective in design. There had been problems before with the *Victoria's* stern doors, but one incident had not even been reported to the marine authorities. Additionally, and fatally, the vessel had twice demonstrated an inability to drain her vehicle deck quickly, one of the previous incidents involving, of all things, quantities of spilt milk. The BTC appealed the court findings and the High Court of Northern Ireland, in a judgment handed down in November 1953, was more specific in assigning blame.

Unfortunately, it appeared that the Scottish Region Marine Superintendent, who controlled the vessel from 1948 until January 1952, was deemed to have failed to address the ship's design problems. The individual concerned, Captain Harry

Perry, had served the LNER as Marine Superintendent before moving up to the Regional post and had many years' experience in the operation of railway shipping. It might have been that, following Nationalisation, the post was simply too exacting, with responsibilities for marine services on both Scottish and Irish coasts. The 1948 remit documents assigned responsibility for docking arrangements at Larne to the Scottish Region and at Belfast to the LMR, but this division of staff and resources was hardly economical and Scottish soon gave up this onus.

Of course, moving the control of the Stranraer–Larne service to Euston in 1952 was hardly much of a solution to operational problems, particularly with the LMR not appointing a manager at Stranraer until *after* the disaster. The lack of local control was crucial here; after 1968, the Government established a company to run this ferry route, and no other, but this was nothing less than a policy blunder. The 'Short Sea Route', across the narrowest of seas, suffered more than any other from Government indecision.

Housing

Earlier, the lack of organisational commitment to, and media comment on, the future of railway- (and canal-) owned housing, was mentioned in passing and it is noticeable that, like shipping, this important area of transport administration did not receive the benefit of its own Executive. Nor did it attain departmental status in the BTC in either of the rail or canal Executives or feature in the remit instructions to the six BR Regions. The Commission did not discuss this subject – of fairly pressing importance to tens of thousands of transport employees – even once in its first four months of inception.

If it had a policy towards housing, the Commission can be said to have been in favour of reducing its housing provision. Not surprisingly, both politicians and civil servants tended to see housing as a responsibility for local government, but there was no concerted approach to the problem.

Dr. Bonavia believes that the old railway companies had achieved "extensive provision of houses for staff", but suggests that the Commission discouraged the RE from continuing the practice of loans at low rates of interest for house purchase. One long-term solution to the problem of nationalised housing would, of course, have been to do the opposite and encourage house purchase by staff. Alternatively, some arrangement could have been made with local authorities to transfer housing stock from the Commission – which would be freed of the rates burden – and this transfer would also provide tenants with an established range of local authority support services.

Midland Railway company houses on Midland Road, Derby, photographed in 1984 following their restoration.
(T.J. Edgington)

6

That first year – 1948

Newspaper readers in the 1940s were accustomed to Big News. Following so many years of war, and a complete change of government, nothing could really surprise the average British newspaper reader any more.

This might explain the comparatively low-key announcement of railway nationalisation on 1st January 1948. It made page four of *The Times*. Admittedly, this newspaper displayed only advertising on its front page, but its article on page four pointedly remarked on the lack of any public ceremony. The same newspaper published an imaginative, if somewhat negative, portrait of the transport revolution that was taking place:

"As the great expresses thunder through the night, as the arrival of a New Year is celebrated, a great chapter of British venture, enterprise, and pioneering achievement, which has left the world in its debt, will be closed."

Interestingly, a rumour had circulated at Westminster in the previous September that 'vesting day' might have to be postponed as market prices were high, so pushing up compensation, and that nationalisation would cause too much interference in railway organization. Perhaps the opponents of Nationalisation imagined that Labour would balk at public ownership of the rail system at the last moment! The rumour was potent enough for the Minister of Transport to confirm that the 1st January vesting would go ahead. And if it turned out to be a quiet transition from private to public ownership, this was in fact intentional.

As early as 11th November in the previous year, BTC commissioner John Benstead had circulated his colleagues, and the Railway Executive, with a memo which said that "it is impracticable to arrange formal general celebrations on Vesting Day", pointing out that 1st January was not a holiday and that normal services would have to be run. Adding that (surprisingly) there had been no trade union request for any festivities, he was prepared, however, to allow railway premises to be used for any locally-organised parties – providing these did not interfere with operational matters – and decreed that no objection should be made to any staff member wishing to attend one. This was a refreshingly humane gesture from one whom many railway staff might regard as a faceless 'mandarin'.

It is interesting that a BTC member should comment on the lack of a trade union request for a celebration of this great manifestation of socialism at work, because there was a considerable array of such activities, but they were clearly being conducted away from London's Broadway. Does this suggest that unions instinctively recognised a continuation of an 'us and them' relationship with the new transport managers? Or did the lack of a public holiday force the unions to conscientiously chose a weekend to celebrate? Certainly, the biggest rail union, the NUR, decreed that the first Sunday of 1948 would be 'Railway Sunday', with a rally for 2,000 railwaymen being held at the Coliseum Theatre in London's West End. From Week One, there seemed to be a gap between the People's Railway and those members of the People who operated it.

Another such celebration was organised in Newcastle on the third day of the new year, the local NUR branch hosting a party attended by the mayors of both Newcastle upon Tyne and Gateshead and a local MP. A BR official who attended described the railways as "long allied in service to the nation, and now united in national ownership. They will do their best to preserve the fine traditions they inherit, and in spite of the difficulty of the times, to provide a standard of service worthy of the rising national effort."

Such was the ideal of public ownership. Other events were held in Manchester and at least eleven other major centres. At one of them, Cardiff, future Prime Minister James Callaghan, then Parliamentary Secretary to the Ministry, suggested that there should be an annual 'Railway Day'.

The last LMS arrival at Euston station, just five minutes before the nationalisation of the railways would take effect, was an express from Blackpool headed by 'Jubilee' 4-6-0 No.5574 *India*. Seven minutes later, and two minutes into the era of the London Midland Region, unrebuilt 'Patriot' No.5508 took a Crewe departure out of the former LMS terminus. Over at Paddington, the last Great Western train to leave was the 11.50pm to Penzance, headed by No.5037 *Monmouth Castle*, followed fifteen minutes later by the first Western Region departure, a Birkenhead service headed by No. 5032 *Usk Castle*. The latter pulled out to a crescendo of exploding detonators – the only hint of celebration mentioned

*During the Locomotive Exchanges LMS 'Coronation' 4-6-2 No.46236 **City of Bradford** worked on the East Coast Main Line and is pictured leaving King's Cross with the 1.10pm Leeds express on 6th May 1948.*

in its records of the changeover by the authoritative *Railway Observer*. The magazine carried no reports from Southern or Eastern termini in London and no reports of celebrations elsewhere in the UK.

The national air of understatement was illustrated by a cartoon by 'Lee' in the *Newcastle Evening Chronicle* on 2nd January, with a station master shown advising an engine driver that "the new owners don't feel like going to work today, more like down the coast for a breath of fresh air". The humour lies entirely in the illogicality of the proposition – excursions were not permitted at this time, to save fuel – although Eastern Region reported an incident at King's Cross in the first week of 1948 when an inebriate attempted to order the crew of a newspaper train to take him to Yorkshire. This, though, was exceptional; the mantle of railway ownership sat lightly on the shoulders of the British electorate.

Meanwhile, Robert Lutyens, son of the eminent architect, wrote to *The Times* asking if, since the railways were now public property, their environs would no longer be desecrated by the appearance of commercial advertising hoardings. A lady correspondent who called herself 'Spinster' asked if porters would still expect to be tipped when the railway now belonged to them! *Punch* magazine illustrated a prosperous-looking businessman urging a mean-looking porter to light a fire in "our" waiting room, while novelist Evelyn Waugh found these newly-empowered porters to be "unusually insolent". The suggestion that railway staff were upstarts, with no right to regard the rail network as their own, seemed to drive pen and brush for many newspaper correspondents and cartoonists in that first month of 1948. And, unfortunately, in months to come.

Only eight days after the birth of British Railways, the new Regions received a memo from Robert Riddles – effectively Britain's new Chief Mechanical Engineer – on a subject which seemed to sum up the concept of a unified British railway.

Entitled 'Interchange of locomotives between regions', the document recorded that the Chairman (Riddles) of the BR Mechanical Engineers Committee had decreed that "it was desirable to obtain a preliminary comparison of the performance of the different standard locomotives in service". This should not be confused with the 'Standard' designation used for the '70000' classes, led by the Pacific *Britannia* which was introduced three years later. In fact the term 'Standard' referred to the classification used by the former companies – for example, the LMS had started to reduce its locomotive stock to seventeen classes, outside which there would be no new construction. This was a whopping reduction on the number of classes inherited by the LMS in 1923; the company history gave up listing them after 400!

The Mechanical Engineering Committee, one of eighteen in the Railway Executive, comprised an impressive list of names renowned from Britain's railways in the days of steam. Chairman Robert Riddles presided over Oliver Bulleid from the former Southern Railway, the GWR's F. W. Hawksworth, A. H. Peppercorn from the LNER, and H. G. Ivatt from the LMS. R. C. Bond and E. S. Cox completed the *dramatis personae* of this august collection of engineering luminaries.

Locomotives already in service, and mostly pre-war, were to be exchanged among the Regions for 'road testing', in that first summer of nationalisation, over routes on which their designers could never have imagined them operating. Riddles, formerly of the LMS, was in overall charge of what became known as the 'Locomotive Exchanges' – hardly an appropriate term for the comparative testing of a unitary body's equipment – with RE Deputy Chairman Sir William Slim being asked to handle the publicity. Yet documentary evidence suggests a locomotive design team headed by the same R. A. Riddles was already drawing up preparations for new British Railways designs, so the Exchanges seem, in retrospect, to have been quite unnecessary. Not only that, but more scientific testing could have been undertaken on Rugby testing plant, opening in the October of that year.

The 8th January memo is itself of some interest to transport historians in that it specifies that the former LNER express locomotive to be tested was the "latest 3-cylinder Pacific", in other words, one of the new A1s or A2/2s. Confirmed by the

Whatever the reasons for, or the results of, the Locomotive Exchanges, they certainly captivated enthusiasts by taking locomotives to far-flung 'foreign' routes! One of the most remarkable trials was of a Southern Railway 'West Country' Pacific on the Highland main line, where its performances were rather impressive. No. 34004 Yeovil *leaves Perth with a preliminary test run between Glasgow and Inverness on 5th July 1948.*

first Monthly Report of the BTC, these references contradict existing accounts of the 1948 Exchange trials; authors writing on this subject have always assumed that the streamlined A4 was requested as the LNER representative. However, the former company's authorities in the new Eastern Region were having none of this request for a new-fangled Thompson or Peppercorn locomotive and by April the *Railway Observer* announced that the A4 Pacific would be participating. The Eastern lines would be represented by Gresley's A4s – and nothing else!

The machinations necessary to do this are not mentioned in Cecil J. Allen's candid, indeed sometimes almost scathing, account of the 1948 Locomotive Exchanges, so the ER presumably relied on no-one having read the original memo too carefully!

Nevertheless, even the most uninformed train-spotter could have queried if a class of 34 streamlined locomotives could be regarded as 'standard' and whether it was likely to form the basis of a new class – after all, the former LMS 'Duchess' Pacifics were losing their streamlined casings altogether at this time. The lack of any such discussion in the technical press suggests that railway enthusiasts were happy just to enjoy the spectacle.

It is tempting for the historian to ignore the 1948 Locomotive Exchanges since they were hardly seminal and such analysis as took place retrospectively was confused, to say the least. The official report on these operations was published in the same week as Cecil J. Allen's first book on the subject, prompting that renowned journalist to hurry out a revised edition. In the latter, Mr. Allen took the official authors to task on a number of detailed points, prompting the reader to wonder why this unsurpassed analyst of locomotive performance – long an LNER staff member – had not been involved in the planning and execution of the trials.

Interestingly, 'CJA' chides himself in his second publication for being too enthusiastic about the work of Bulleid's SR Pacifics – a 'Merchant Navy' on the West Coast Main Line and a 'West Country' on the former Highland line. Although results from these engines were impressive, it certainly appears that their coal consumption was close to unacceptable, although Mr. Allen was highly critical of one test on the LMR where No.35017 *Belgian Marine* suffered so many signal checks as to make the test meaningless and its increased coal consumption on this run, compared with an earlier outing, was not explained in the official report. In Scotland, *Yeovil* had outperformed both a 'Black Five' and a B1 through the mountains, but had produced by far the worst coal consumption figures. At a time when Britain was desperately husbanding its fuel resources, such statistics resounded tellingly against these most modern of express steam locomotives.

Meanwhile, the darling of former LNER management, the A4s, gave a flawed performance in the trials, showing a tendency to run hot when under test; but the hill-climbing of the newly-renumbered 60033 *Seagull* on the Devon banks of the Western Region was an eye-opener and the streamliners could out-perform the GW 'Kings' – admittedly, an older design – home or away in economy of fuel consumption.

Nothing much resulted from these trials. If operational conditions were deemed worthy of including in the testing process – as opposed to the calibrations obtainable at Rugby – it would surely have been preferable to assess the selected locomotives on a single route – say Settle to Carlisle – and any subsequent transfers could have been made on the basis of demonstrated need. In particular, the idea of 'testing' a former LMS 'Duchess' Pacific and a 'Royal Scot' on the East Coast Main Line seems pointless when the former Great Northern main line was so lavishly equipped with Pacifics.

Mr. Allen found it impossible not to criticize the conduct of the trials in broad terms. He believed that the variations of driving and hand-firing introduced a welter of imponderables into the process of comparing locomotive performance, while some of the published returns omitted the difference between gross and tare loads – something an established recorder would regard as essential at a time when long-distance trains were usually full, with corridors often blocked by servicemen with their kitbags.

In this author's opinion, a more productive exercise would have been to attempt to even-up existing imbalances in motive power on different parts of the system. Within a few years, for example, Gerard Fiennes of the Eastern Region borrowed what he described as a 'Spam Can' (a SR Bulleid Pacific) which proved far superior to the former LNER 4-6-0s still employed on the Great Eastern. Similar trials of LNER Pacifics – too heavy for their own company's metals in East Anglia – could have been conducted on the Midland and West Coast Main Lines with a view to permanent transfers, not an exchange, of some 30 or so engines.

Many of the 'West Country' and 'Battle of Britain' Pacifics were to spend their working lives sauntering at the head of light semi-fast passenger trains west of Salisbury, while 'Black 5s' were regularly rostered to express duties on the West Coast Main Line as were B1s on the former Great Central and Great Eastern systems. Equally, Haymarket shed would daily supply Pacifics to haul five or six bogies on 35mph schedules from Edinburgh to Perth or via the Waverley Route to Carlisle while less powerful 'Black 5s' wrestled with excessive loads over Shap and Beattock.

One of the experimental liveries tried by BR was apple green on ex-LMS rebuilt 'Patriot' 4-6-0 No.45531 **Sir Frederick Harrison.**

If anything could be gleaned from the results of the 1948 Exchanges, it would be the inappropriateness of designing express passenger engines with restricted route availability. It is surely no coincidence that Riddles and his design team built their programme round a mixed traffic Pacific with the largest possible firebox within the loading gauge, while ensuring that the axle-weight would give the locomotive – the 'Britannia' class – the widest possible availability rating. In comparison with the solitary 8P Pacific designed, namely No.71000 *Duke of Gloucester,* there were to be 55 'Britannias'. Perhaps the Exchanges had taught the design team that producing the most powerful express engine was no substitute for introducing a lighter, go-(almost)-anywhere machine.

Scotland achieved the dubious distinction of being the scene of the first strike of 1948 on the nationalised railway system. Only two days into the new working regime, 300 blacksmiths were made idle at St. Rollox after boilermen took industrial action in a dispute over 'piecework rates'. More positively, however, the BTC Monthly Report recorded that, since the workers had theoretically taken control of Britain's rail system, absenteeism was greatly reduced.

BTC documents circulating in that first month of BR's existence noted that the unique problem of amalgamating LMS and LNER staff and working practices north of the Border was being addressed by Cameron's management team:

"The departmental officers appointed by the Executive have settled down to their new responsibilities and are energetically tackling the many problems which are arising, with a view to the integration of the former LMS and LNER Railways [*sic*] which constitute the Scottish Region, including a preliminary survey of the district organisation."

To say that the renumbering and 'rebranding' of BR locomotives in 1948 was complicated is to understate the case. A totem or crest for the new concern – what Tom Rolt later called a "mean little insignia" – was not immediately forthcoming, so 'BRITISH RAILWAYS' was the legend soon applied to tender and tank locomotives alike. In the case of some smaller tank locomotives, this necessitated the 'BRITISH' being transferred on above and in some cases, diagonal to, the 'RAILWAYS'. In the previous October, the Executive had informed the BTC that a crest would be positioned between the two words "on tank or tender", which would have compounded the problem on smaller locomotives, such as well tanks, had the crest been available immediately. As it was, 'Jinty' 0-6-0 tank locomotive No.47167 was seen in March with the legend 'BRITISHRAILWAYS' affixed with no gap between the words! The paint department at Derby Works avoided all this confusion by persisting with an 'LMS' transfer on all engines passing through Works for all except the heaviest overhauls and this went on into the autumn of that first year of BR.

So badly handled was this potentially important rebranding that when a former Southern Railway Class U1 Mogul was reportedly outshopped from Brighton in January with the legend 'B.R.S.' on its tender, no-one was particularly surprised. This report turned out to be inaccurate, but it was symptomatic of the lack of 'image' shown on the new BR that this particular branding seemed entirely possible.

The letter columns of the *Railway Gazette* devoted many column inches to the question of how the people's ownership should be displayed, one reader pointing out that, since there were no other railways to speak of in the UK, why "brand" the locomotives at all? (In fact, the number of non-vested railways was surprisingly large and this is dealt with in the Appendix). The BR totem, later nicknamed 'the flying sausage', and showing the words 'British Railways' within two oval shapes, was first published in February. It was the work of A. J. White, the RE Advertising Manager, and was intended for use on posters and stationery rather than rolling stock. Perhaps Mr. Rolt found this "mean" as well, although it stated its message simply and economically.

If any of this seems to represent criticism of John Brebner, BTC Public Relations Officer, then it should be said straight away that his appointment – endorsed by the Commission only six weeks before 'Vesting Day' – came so late that it must have been difficult for him to gather up the reins of an organisation running away from its elderly, and in more than one case inexperienced, Commissioners. In addition, Brebner had quite enough on his plate working in London Transport while making a difficult transfer over to the BTC, even if it only entailed a matter of moving to a higher floor in the building.

No.1 in the new British Railways locomotive list was *Hercules*. Far from representing the latest developments in contemporary motive power, this was an 0-4-0 saddle tank taken over from the GWR which in turn had acquired it from the derelict Ystalyfera Tin Works in Swansea when acquiring the site for carriage sidings. This 23-ton 'pug' was already nearly half a century old when it was nationalised, although

that was by no means exceptional. BR treated *Hercules* well, overhauling her by July, after which she sported a new coat of green paint, but carried a nameplate on one side only. But somehow, having this primitive, almost insignificant, shunting engine to numerically lead the national fleet of around 20,000 locomotives seemed to sum up the low-key approach to national ownership.

Locomotive numbers were a confusing area. The LMS had used four-figure numbers for its ex-Midland Railway and more recent 'standard' classes, so these were soon being prefixed with 'M'. The LNER had already begun the renumbering of its stock in 1946, starting with its Pacifics, all of which were to have 60000 added, but not before some engines passing through Doncaster Works received an 'E' prefix in front of their number. Most of that company's stock bore four-digit numbers, soon to be simply prefixed with a 6. The Southern had two themes to its numbering – a straight numerical sequence and a more recent hybrid numbering introduced by Bulleid for his Pacifics. But as if this was not complicated enough, some of the Pacifics were outshopped with an 'S' prefix before such numbers as 21C158, from Brighton, along with S21C158 from Eastleigh. The GWR theoretically operated a straightforward numbering scheme from 1 (*Hercules* again) onwards, although this was spoiled by different numbering sequences within individual classes. For example, the 'Castles' could be found scattered between 100 and the 7000s!

To complicate matters even more, War Department locomotives were finding their way on to BR tracks, by purchase through firstly the LNER, then through loan

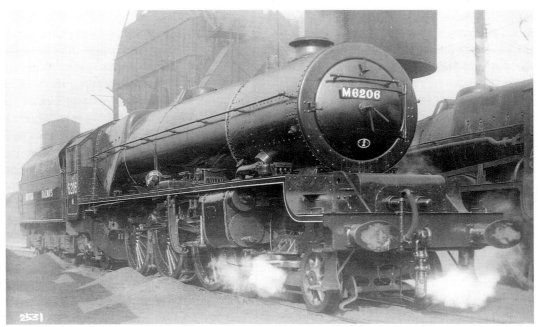

LMS engines began their nationalised ownership with the new owner's name in full and their numbers prefixed by 'M', as on 'Princess Royal' Pacific No.M6206 Princess Marie Louise *(in LMS post-war express black livery).*
(Barry C. Lane Collection)

A number of former LMS Pacifics received the LNWR-style lined black livery (which was to be adopted for mixed traffic classes) before the short-lived express blue was chosen. 'Princess Royal' Pacific No. 46212 Duchess of Kent is seen in action on the climb to Shap Summit. The steam drifting up from the tender shows that the coal is being sprayed with hot water to keep down the dust.

conditions, then purchase by the Executive, still bearing five-figure numbers starting with 7. This attracted criticism from the Railway Research Service which regarded these as numbers too far, pointing out that longer numbers were more difficult to communicate by telephone. By the time the WD classes were incorporated into BR numbering, matters were even worse, with the 'Austerities' relegated down to the 90000s!

The BTC did not concern itself with renumbering, allowing the Executive to get on with it. The Great Western was taken as the 'base' for a UK-wide numbering scheme; possibly it was felt that removing those brass cabside numberplates would be an unnecessary expense (although that had not stopped the company renumbering some of those engines converted to oil fuelling). Diesel and electric locomotives were to be numbered in the 10000 and 20000 ranges respectively, followed by Southern Region on 30000-39999. The LMR, with the largest stock, was granted 40000-59999, with the Eastern and North Eastern Regions following with 60000-69999, effectively denying both Regions an individual numerical identity. The Scottish Region was also ignored in this scheme, its operation of locomotives numbered with 4,5 and 6, betraying the Region's dual origin, something which Tom Cameron and his staff were supposed to be unifying. In practice, no-one north of the Border seemed too concerned.

Altogether, the former LNER Areas had no numerical distinction, except in their passenger stock. Here, the initial letter denoting the Regions was applied to stock in front of the running number and this policy was continued when diesel multiple units began national operation from 1954. It hardly facilitated public understanding of the new scheme that no announcement was made explaining it until BR was in its third month.

Liveries were just as complicated; despite a number of fanciful and unfulfilled schemes, the previous practice, of painting different types of locomotive according to the work they undertook, was continued. Neither Regional nor national identities were envisaged at this stage; indeed, the *Railway Observer* commented in its February 1948 issue that "at the time of going to press, no universal livery has yet been announced".

Unfortunately, it has to be said that the BTC did not noticeably assist in launching the corporate image of British Railways, although the national picture can only be described as confused. No wonder; when the Railway Executive put up a national liveries plan to the Commission on 31st December 1947 – perhaps a little late in the day – the reaction from the Commission was woolly and unhelpful. The Minutes for the BTC's second meeting of 1948, on 5th January, show that the Commission "reserved any conclusion [although?] in favour of a suitable shade of green for passenger steam locomotives [and] distinctive colouring for locomotives used on the principal express passenger trains, and for dining cars".

The last point was dropped in the following month; restaurant cars would be liveried in the same colour as other passenger carriages – although a separate livery would have been logical; management of restaurant cars were transferred to the Hotels Executive by the following July. Sir William Wood, former LMS President and now a Commission member, muddied the waters even more, expressing approval for LMS "Red" *or* LNER green *or* Caledonian blue, the last of these colours to be restricted to no more than 125 locomotives likely to haul the most prestigious of expresses. One livery suggestion apparently accepted by the BTC around this time – although not made by Wood – was 'golden ochre' for main line diesels! This must have been an exasperating time for railway managers!

In addition to a lack of inspirational leadership from the higher echelons of the railway industry, BTC and RE seemed to pay no heed to what the technical press was suggesting for a new British Railways livery. In August 1947 the *Railway Magazine* commissioned a painting of an LNER B1 in Post Office red, even checking with the Postmaster General that the shade was correct. This seemed to appear logical to many transport journalists and by the following May the *Railway Gazette* was deploring BR's failure to adopt this seemingly obvious choice of livery. After all, the magazine pointed out, the public associated this colour with Public Service.

Nevertheless, as if to convince the public that BR knew what it was doing with its new stock, a number of 'fashion parades' of liveries took place in the first six months of the year. In January an exhibition featuring former LMS, GWR, and SR locomotives was held at Kensington Olympia, with the scene being stolen, according to Dr. Bonavia, by a 4-6-0 in the old London & North Western Railway livery of lined black. A

Southern electric locomotive in light blue must have been worth seeing, too. Two more demonstrations were held, at Marylebone and Leith Central, where, in the latter case, a purplish shade of blue was seen on an A3 Pacific, with an A2/2 in LNER green and a (named) 'Black 5' in a colour which went unreported by the *Railway Observer*. Nationally, the picture was just as confused.

Within a single Region – and one of the 'second level' status – two painting and no fewer than three lettering styles were being applied at four Works undertaking even light repairs; all this in one of the smaller Regions. Meanwhile, Doncaster turned out a new A2 Pacific *Tudor Minstrel* with a builder's plate reading 'LNER 1948'!

As late as May, the technical press was carrying an announcement about liveries for both locomotives and carriages. The former would be blue, with red, cream and grey lining, for "the most powerful express locomotives", green with similar lining for "other" express engines and lined black for mixed traffic units. Electric locomotives counted as "most powerful", which in the case of steam seemed to cover both Classes 6 and 7P (later reclassified as 7 and 8P).

Incidentally, the "most powerful" class of express engines on the ECML comprised the new A2s, but the published accounts of the Leith display make it clear that this class was being officially treated as a "less powerful" express locomotive. This was confirmed in press announcements in April, placing these Pacifics in the same category as the former LMS 'Jubilee'. One assumes a clerical error at the RE; these engines had, on paper, a higher tractive effort than any other passenger-hauling unit on the former LNER system, except the solitary W1 4-6-4.

Carriages would be 'plum and spilt milk' for most express duties, but chocolate and cream for the Western. Suburban stock on every Region except the Southern which would retain existing colours, would have maroon livery with golden yellow/black/golden yellow lining. Fourteen routes would operate train sets made up in the new colours. These routes comprised both ECML and WCML, as well as Paddington to Penzance, Bristol and Swansea, Waterloo–Bournemouth, Victoria–Ramsgate and such cross-country routes as Liverpool Exchange–Newcastle, Leeds–Glasgow via Edinburgh and Glasgow–Aberdeen. The public was invited to send comments about these to 'Box A' at the Railway Executive, 222 Marylebone Road, London NW1! The *Railway Gazette* believed that such a public relations gesture would automatically trigger so many differing responses that BR would just proceed with its own intentions although, looking back, one can sense real indecision on this issue at both Marylebone and Broadway.

Incidentally, two years earlier, the Railway Research Service

The LNER-designed Peppercorn A1 Pacifics entered service after nationalisation and the naming of this class was one of the first cases to be considered by the RE's naming committee. No.60138, making a volcanic departure from York with the London-bound 'Scarborough Flyer', entered service in December 1948 and in 1950 was awarded the name Boswell, *one of thirteen A1s to perpetuate the LNER racehorse theme.*

was complimenting the Great Western on being the only 'grouped' company to continue painting its passenger stock in dual colours. "The popular appeal of this scheme of painting cannot be gainsaid," observed the Service in its *Monthly Bulletin* for December 1946 and the scheme's continuation, or readoption, in May 1948 was gratifying as a Regional addition to the 'plum and spilt milk' which was to become the BR standard elsewhere. Unfortunately, media reports predicting

the reintroduction of chocolate and cream livery were premature – by some eight years!

Naming of locomotives was a serious matter in steam days and with new locomotives emerging to pre-Nationalisation designs, and the 'Standard' classes already taking shape in the mind of Robert Riddles, the new British Railways took the usual organisational path to tackle a problem – and decided to set up a committee. This was established in September 1948 by Sir William Slim, Deputy Chairman of the Executive, just two months before he moved back to a more appropriate military posting. In retrospect, it seems unfortunate that numbering and livery decisions were not approached with the same gravity.

Chairing the naming committee was Derek Barrie, the Executive's PR officer, and he was joined by none other than E. S. Cox to represent the CME and George Dow to represent the Regions. Mr. Dow was a former press officer for the LNER and had authored a number of books published by that

company, although he is perhaps best remembered for his authoritative three-volume company history, *Great Central.*

One of the first classes whose naming had to be debated and confirmed was the former LNER Pacifics, the new A1s. Some 43 years later, Mr. Dow's son Andrew recorded in some detail what decisions this new committee took regarding the naming of these handsome machines. It was done with a formality characteristic of the times; the committee's first meeting, on 29th October, began by codifying the locomotive naming procedure. Mr. Dow quoted Derek Barrie's notes from the meeting, namely that:

naming must not be overdone.

names must be euphonious.

names must be such [that will] readily convey their meaning to those who see them.

names must not be ephemeral.

"class names must not be slavishly followed so as to include absurdities simply for the sake of keeping the series intact" [a nod at the LNER's inclusion of *Pretty Polly* in its A1/A3 'racehorse' naming, or *Bongo* among the B1s!].

The second of the new BR 'Britannia' class was named in honour of the Chairman of the British Transport Commission. No. 70001 Lord Hurcomb pounds up Brentwood bank with the down 'Norfolkman', the 10.00am Liverpool Street–Norwich, on 24th March 1951.
(Eric Bruton)

Ironically, despite all this, the 50 examples of Class A1 Pacifics were to bear names apparently selected by pepperpot – racehorses, characters from Sir Walter Scott novels, birds, major pre-grouping companies and CMEs. This was very much in the tradition of both LNER and LMS; the latter company's principal express locomotives contained names from royalty, the aristocracy (giving them their colloquial title of the 'Duchess' Class), British cities and the name of their designer. The Southern and Great Western Railways were more consistent – for example the 'Hall' class was actually named after halls, the 'Granges' after granges and the 'Kings' after kings. The Bulleid Pacifics of the 'West Country' class followed that particular naming theme to the point of geographical obscurity, but with unerring consistency. Sadly, the BR 'Britannias' were to follow the LMS/LNER record of inconsistent naming – encompassing famous figures from British history, former GWR classical names and Scottish firths, but not forgetting, at 70001, second only to *Britannia* herself, *Lord Hurcomb!*

'Rebranding' of Britain's railways was nevertheless important and necessary. With the monthly *Bradshaw* timetables perpetuating the names of the 'Big Four' in its January 1948 issue, it appears that the BTC or RE had not succeeded in building a façade to inform the travelling public about the new regime of railed transport. Not until February did *Bradshaw* employ Regional names where appropriate in its publication, but with the transport authorities proving so slow to establish a corporate identity for the People's Railways – John H. Brebner was only officially appointed in the last month of 1947 – who could blame a commercial publisher for being confused?

By the time the new year was three months old, the winter months posed a seasonal, or rather an unseasonal, problem for the BTC; winter weather had proved much milder than in the previous two years. In the previous winter, a Government directive had been issued during the six weeks of freezing conditions to divert as much goods traffic as possible away from rail to road, in order to conserve coal stocks consumed by the steam-powered railways and to free up mileage for coal traffic on rail. This proved to be disastrous – no such measures were required in the milder weather of winter 1947/8, but the Winter Transport Executive Committee continued its activities until March in the new, much milder, year. The effect on BR was by no means short-term; in 1950 one Region was to boast an approximate 22% increase in the mileage run of fitted and partly-fitted freights in the two years between the Februarys of 1948 and 1950, the Regional official conveniently forgetting that the initial figures were kept artificially low.

Nevertheless, to show any increase at all was meritorious, since many commercial rail users now found road vehicles to be well-suited to their needs, with petrol cheap, although rationed, compared with indigenous fuel sources. The railways had been dealt a serious blow by their new masters, although it should be mentioned that BR was competing for passenger traffic against motorists hamstrung by petrol rationing and a draconian restriction on car hire. Meanwhile, as discussed later, BR was fighting to bring its own fuel conversion programme to a halt.

The first two months of 1948 saw the symbolic restoration of headboards to the 'Royal Scot' express on the new LM and Scottish Regions, while in the following summer another pre-war tradition, running the 'Flying Scotsman' service non-stop between London King's Cross and Edinburgh Waverley, was resumed but on an unambitious schedule. While A4s headed the non-stop service over the Border in Berwickshire, the West Coast lines saw the introduction, almost from BR's first month, of diesel-electric power – and with no hint of golden ochre!

In the last month before Nationalisation, Derby Works had turned out, with English Electric traction equipment, the first of two 1,600hp diesels. Numbered 10000 and 10001, they were designed by H. G. Ivatt, who then received authority to construct two entirely new members of Stanier's 'Duchess' class to operate in comparison with the new form of motive power. The new Pacifics incorporated such innovations as roller bearings and such improved firebox arrangements as rocking grates, all designed to improve the engines' ability to undertake lengthy rosters with a reduced turnaround time. A 'photo-call' was held at Euston on 18th December, with No.10000 and 'Coronation' No.6256 standing on adjacent tracks. The diesel was actually a few days older than the Pacific, the latter having entered traffic, in black livery, only on the 12th.

If the LMS had intended an exhaustive comparison programme of testing – why else produce two updated examples of Stanier's pre-war steam design? – the nationalised railway management had no such intention, it seems. It was, in fact, in a Glasgow newspaper's correspondence columns that the matter received detailed consideration. A Mr. Menzies wrote to the *Glasgow Herald* strongly backing the Pacifics, pointing out that the diesels could only equal one of their steam rivals if coupled together. This meant their combined weight was 50% more than that of a 'Duchess' Pacific, while their length was twice as great, possibly necessitating a reduction in the number of coaches hauled where platform length was an issue. These very relevant points were echoed by Railway Executive chairman Sir Eustace Missenden in a paper he wrote two years later. But meanwhile Mr. Menzies had bestirred a formidable protagonist.

Cecil J. Allen was visiting Glasgow in that first week of 1948 on a speaking engagement undertaken with O. S. Nock to lecture to Scottish schoolchildren on the wonders of the modern railway system. (Did he mean British Railways?) Mr. Allen also wrote to the *Herald,* taking up cudgels on behalf of Nos.10000/1, pointing out that their greatest advantage was their guaranteed availability. Perhaps he was premature – the whole point of constructing an improved version of the 'Duchess' (BR Nos.46256/7) was to investigate whether technical improvements could increase steam locomotive mileage and the new BR administration does not appear to have prosecuted the comparisons as thoroughly as the LMS

Oil-burning GWR 'Hall' 4-6-0 No.3952 **Norcliffe Hall** *at Birmingham Snow Hill with the 7.05am from Paddington on 16th April 1948.* (T.J. Edgington)

had been preparing to.

Such mileage figures as did emerge were inconclusive and disappointing from the steam enthusiast's point of view. The two new Pacifics, with their modifications designed to lengthen annual mileages, ran approximately 5,080 miles a month (6256) and 4,070 (46257). In comparison, unmodified No.6240 accomplished 6,018 a month. No 'Duchess' achieved more than 90,000 miles annually, not even the last two, intended to reach the 100,000 mark. As a matter of interest, rival A4 No.60009 *Union of South Africa* ran a higher total mileage than any of its LMS rivals (1,850,000 approximately) at an average of 5,530 monthly. It was to enjoy nearly three years' more life than the 'Duchesses', but that fact merely reinforces the theory that the LMS Pacifics, with their limited water capacity tenders, were never able to deliver to their full potential.

One of the innovations featured on Nos.6256/7 was a rocking grate, designed to partially drop a steam locomotive's fire into the ashpan, thus removing unburnt fuel known as clinker. This process was key to an accelerated turnround at the depot and the Railway Executive set up a committee in 1949/50 to compare rocking grates with the older drop grate

as fitted to the pre-war 'Duchess' Pacifics and also the former LNER A4s.

Chaired by R.F. Harvey, the committee met four times in the comfort of the Great Northern Hotel at King's Cross before venturing out to examine operational conditions at Camden and King's Cross depots. It was forced to conclude that the efficiency of any firebox and ashpan arrangement was dependent on the method of ash disposal at the depot itself – in many cases there was simply a pit between the rails, sometimes filled with water, while underwater conveyor belts were available in a few depots. Whatever the method of disposal, the rocking grate was found to always offer some improvement in operation and it could save up to 75% of the time usually taken in this aspect of turning a locomotive around, if accompanied by a modern disposal method. The committee therefore recommended its adoption for all the forthcoming standard classes. The four 'wise men' on the committee also approved an intermediate setting for the grate, allowing for 'shaking' the fire during journeys.

Meanwhile, the two diesels are recorded as having notched up 50,000 miles in three months on the West Coast Main Line, creditable indeed when their availability figures could be affected by staff, inexperienced in diesel handling, being unable to remedy minor problems, the equivalent of which would not fail a steam locomotive.

On the other hand, construction costs, which would have favoured the Pacifics, do not appear to have been compared; not long afterwards, in January 1951, Missenden costed differing examples of steam and diesel motive power construction as follows:

Steam:	4-6-2 Express passenger loco	£17-18,000
	4-6-0 Mixed traffic loco	£14,000
	0-6-0 Tank loco	£5,500
Diesel	1,600hp Express loco	£70-80,000
	350hp Shunting loco	£20,000
Electric	1,600hp Express loco	£35-40,000

Steam locomotives would always have a lower first cost when the former companies' workshops were geared to their manufacture, but the figures given above look like underestimates – *Britannia* cost over £20,000 to build in 1951 and an order for the mixed traffic B1 was approved by the BTC in 1948 at £16,000 each. On the other hand, the cost of diesel was probably set too highly. The account for the two LMS main line diesels had come in at £66,000 the pair, of which £5,000 was regarded as recoverable, comprising the forging of reusable jigs. Missenden should have had good reason to remember this costing – as RE Chairman he was asked in May 1948 why there had been a four-fold increase in the cost of building these pioneering locomotives. Apparently the estimated £15,000 cost per pair had escalated to £66,000 "as the original cost was based on the assumption, since proved erroneous, that the work to be undertaken by the Railway Company would involve costs very similar to those incurred in building locomotive tenders. The estimate was prepared on a cost per ton basis accordingly".

The two LMS diesel-electrics Nos.10000 and 10001, newly turned out in BR green, at Crewe double-heading the 'Royal Scot' on 17th May 1957. (Barry C. Lane)

Steam, on the other hand, would benefit from considerable economies of scale, all the resulting economies being achieved entirely 'in house'. Missenden's doubling of diesel locomotive construction costs suggests a poor memory or a determination to build in an excess factor to justify his support for steam! (Incidentally, the document source makes it clear that the "tenders" referred to were not ordering submission documents but carried coal and water and were the basis for comparative costs for locomotives not requiring the usual frame and wheel arrangements. A more curious way to assess new traction costs can scarcely be imagined.) After all this, it appears that diesel cost around 50% more than steam at the production stage and not four times as much, as hinted by Missenden.

When operating together, from the second half of 1948 onwards, the two diesel units were perfectly capable of keeping the (admittedly very slow) schedule on the 'Royal Scot' between Euston and Glasgow; after all, they were almost equal to a later 'Deltic' in terms of power. They could even achieve the 'Royal Scot' journey non-stop – which a 'Duchess' could never do – on 1st June of the following year. The cabs of these pioneering diesels must have been an eye-opener for former LMS footplate crews. Locomotive engineer E. S. Cox records that No.10000 "rode like a charm from the first day".

Not surprisingly, they seemed able to inspire affection among those who built and tested them. In a letter to the author, Alan Robinson, a member of the Electrical Section of the CME's department at Derby, tells of a cab ride southwards on the 'Royal Scot' working. "We were checked all the way from Eden Valley Junction [just south of Penrith] to Crewe. All the same it was some ride!" Although a steam enthusiast, Mr. Robinson recalls how his department was determined to outshop at least one of the diesels before the LMS lost its identity on 1st January 1948. "They are the only diesels for which I have any affection," he says, although as a taxpayer he might have been less enamoured at the nationalised industry having to pick up the bill for a locomotive order which had been seriously underestimated by a commercial company.

The apparent consensus in 1948 in favour of renewing steam's grip on Britain's railways is worth considering at greater length. As we have seen, the former LMS had begun experimenting with diesel power for main line services, while the erstwhile LNER Board of Directors had decided, in July 1947, to invest in a fleet of 25 diesel-electric locomotives similar in power rating to LMS Nos.10000/1. The LNER's proposal was curious, even suspicious, considering that the company was in the middle of a renewed construction programme for no fewer than 80 Pacifics. The diesel plan could have been bluster, a gesture by this company – in the forefront of opposing Nationalisation – to project an image of an enterprising concern whose directors and shareholders

deserved maximum compensation. Only three months later, the BTC deferred approval for the building of an additional twenty Class A2 Pacifics for the LNER lines, suggesting that no desperate need for new power was discernible on the ECML. 40 B1s were approved for construction at the same time – this at a meeting on 9th October.

At around the same time, Robert Riddles, the former LMS locomotive engineer responsible for designing the fustian 'Austerity' 2-8-0s and 2-10-0s for the War Department, prevailed with his plans for a reinvigorated programme of steam traction on the new British Railways, whether using coal – or an alternative.

A plan to convert 1,229 steam locomotives from coal to oil firing in the late 1940s had to be abandoned before it reached three figures, with no less than £1.22 million (£27 million) already spent on storage depots. The Great Western was in the forefront of the experiment – in fact, had initiated it – with 37 converted engines out of 184 proposed and including five 'Castles'. Indeed, the GWR had begun the conversion scheme unilaterally in 1945 in co-operation with the Anglo-Iranian Oil Company and the North British Locomotive Company, centring this experiment on Severn Tunnel Junction depot. The first such conversion featured '28XX' 2-8-0 No.2872, commissioned on 27th October 1945 and operating out of Severn Tunnel Junction, one of seven GWR sheds with refuelling facilities planned.

This proved to be a case of 'What Swindon does today, the rest do tomorrow'. Early in 1946 the Ministry of Fuel and Power informed Minister of Transport Alf Barnes that it would require an annual saving of a million tons of coal on Britain's railways, one-third of the total required to be saved in nearly a thousand economy measures throughout the UK. The Minister duly passed this on to the Railway Executive.

On 30th July the CMEs of the 'Big Four' decided to expand the GWR programme nationally, adding 1,217 locomotive conversions to the twelve already carried out. The committee specified, however, that all special equipment had to be paid for by Government, while Government-appointed contractors working on converting rail depots must be under its control. A standing committee was set up, with one representative of each railway being joined by members of the Royal Engineers and the Equipment Section of the Ministry of Supply.

The Southern converted 31 engines out of a planned 110, these including a 'West Country' Pacific, and a higher proportion of passenger locomotives than on the other lines. These included 'King Arthurs', such as No.740 *Merlin* and even members of such veteran classes as L11 (eight), D15 (one) and T9 (thirteen). As Fratton was the only Southern MPD whose oil-fuelling facilities were completed, all of these engines must have operated in or from the Portsmouth area.

The Southern, in fact, heartily endorsed the new fuel, while the erstwhile Great Western and LMS (and their successor Regions) produced contradictory data on its effectiveness for express work and for freight.

The LMS had been planning the largest number of conversions, of some 485 engines working from 26 depots, but in the event converted only 24 locomotives. These represented a good cross-section of mainly freight engines – ten Stanier 8Fs, five 'Black Fives', four Fowler 4Fs and five 7F 0-8-0s. The sole LNER conversion was not even a company-designed locomotive, but a Riddles 'Austerity' 2-8-0, No.3152, suggesting that the four depot installations which approached completion on the LNER were a major waste of money and materials at a time of financial stringency. Making this investment even more of a waste was the transfer, in BR days from March to October 1948, of the sole LNER oil-fired representative to Old Oak Common on the Western Region, with a coal-fired sister locomotive being sent to the Eastern in exchange.

It was intended to assimilate oil-fuelling within existing motive power depots where possible, although that was not always feasible. At some rail centres there was some splitting of fuelling and maintenance, as at Durran Hill in Carlisle. This was no longer in use as an MPD and it can hardly have been administratively convenient to have an oil-fuelled locomotive visit two sites between duties. Strict procedures regarding spillage were put in place to ensure safety and the usual unkempt appearance of MPDs in the age of steam hardly lent itself to this.

To speed up the programme, and in particular to avoid the problem of delays in the supply of pumping equipment, a number of depots employed gravity as a propellant, positioning oil tank vehicles on a coal-loading bank and piping directly into the tender of a locomotive below. This was reported to be effective but slow and presumably hardly assisted in the efficient running of a steam MPD. As late as September 1947 the GWR announced that it was converting a number of water columns to feed oil direct to locomotive tenders, complete with a light at the end of fuel jib to aid night-time fuelling, but this logistical aspect of the programme really should have been thought out much earlier.

In a report to the BTC on 16th February 1948, Miles Beevor stated that a shortage of rail tank wagons was a limiting factor and that no more than 108 engines could be converted in the foreseeable circumstances. If the conversion programme was completed, Beevor anticipated that 4,000 such vehicles would be required, each carrying fourteen tons (3,200 gallons) of Pool Heavy Fuel Oil at 235 gallons to the ton, although use could be made of those vehicles previously carrying aviation fuel. Historian Alex Robertson, working from Fuel Ministry

figures, reports that 2,750 tankers would have been required, but Beevor may have been displaying the natural caution of a rail manager having to assess an unprecedented operational problem. No doubt for that reason, he reckoned that only one return trip could be completed between oil depot and MPD per week. This was despite a systematic arrangement of depots linked to convenient ports with suitable unloading facilities, as shown in this (unfortunately incomplete) list from the RE report (see bibliography).

Port	Depot or fuelling point
Avonmouth	Bath
Dingle (Liverpool)	Aintree, Lostock Hall, Newton Heath, Rose Grove
Jarrow (Newcastle)	Carlisle
Purfleet	Bletchley, Cricklewood, Northampton, Wellingborough, Willesden
Saltend (Hull)	Farnley Jct., Kirkby, Hasland, Leeds, Mirfield, Normanton, Nottingham, Staveley, Toton, Wakefield, Westhouses.
Swansea	Skewen (Llandarcy)
Stanlow (Ellesmere)	Crewe, Nuneaton, Shrewsbury

An archival copy of the report, examined by this author, carries an additional handwritten comment indicating concern over increased annual costs if the scheme continued, although no reason was specified – and it was almost certainly written by a BTC member, the accountant Sir Ian Bolton. When Beevor submitted his report to the BTC, there had already been a Ministry directive to abort the conversion plan in December 1947, although some depot installations continued until the following March.

With the technical press pointing the finger at Government for having imposed "this expensive experiment" in the first place, railway managers were not slow to suggest that the Government should compensate them for expenditure already committed. The *Locomotive Post* – edited by two locomotive engineers – suggested the cost of the scheme was £1.6 million (£32 million), although one Ministry estimate in November 1948 put the conversion cost as high as £3 million (£66 million).

The problem may have originated with the Ministerial statement of 8th April 1946, when Emanuel Shinwell gave a hostage to fortune by telling the House of Commons that factories converting to oil "can rest assured that we shall render every possible assistance to them if they do convert". From the frequency that the cost question recurs in both the

Ex-War Department 2-8-0 No.90659 clanks south along the the East Coast Main Line on 15th April 1950. It is on the up slow line near Marshmoor sidings, south of Hitchin, with a mixed freight terminating at Ferme Park yard. (Eric Bruton)

Railway Executive report and the transport press, it seems that gubernatorial underwriting of the conversion programme was by no means "rendered" at that time.

In January 1951 RE Chairman Sir Eustace Missenden specified the availability of coal as a major factor in renewing steam traction on BR – the first 'Britannia' Pacific emerged that year – but fuel availability was not the only doubt the Chairman entertained as to the future of diesel traction on main line work. Missenden believed that 1,600 horsepower was the most that could be generated within the profile of a single-unit locomotive and that twin-working would be undesirable where train length might be a problem – just as Glasgow's Mr. Menzies had believed.

The Chairman predicted that diesels might find their place on the system as shunting engines or in working secondary routes in support of electrified main-lines and (only possibly) operating railcar services. "It is most unlikely that diesel traction will sweep this country as it has done in the USA" – this was the opinion, expressed in an Institute of Transport

presidential address, of the operating head of Britain's railway networks just four years before the publication of the Modernisation Plan! Even as late as 1953, with Missenden retired, the Executive proposed a new construction programme for push-pull stock for steam-hauled branch services, in preference to diesel multiple units. This Riddles-inspired proposal "infuriated" BTC chiefs, according to Dr. Bonavia.

Meanwhile, the Western Region added another 343 steam shunting engines to its stock in the eight years up to 1956, despite the fact that even Riddles conceded that diesel shunters were superior in their high level of round-the-clock availability. Clearly, the low first cost of steam power was a factor the Railway Executive found too impressive to ignore in its traction policy.

Incidentally, the 'Austerity' freight locomotives designed by Riddles occupy a small but significant niche in post-war railway history. When hostilities ended, the LNER purchased 200 of these units, but when in November 1948 the Railway Executive decided to acquire a further 558 locomotives – currently on loan to BR but intended originally, Riddles is alleged to have said, to be dumped at sea after the war – the Executive benefitted from buying 'in bulk', acquiring these for a unit price of around £2,700 each. Nevertheless, this appears to have left BTC chiefs unimpressed and was seen as placing too high a reliance on improvised, non-standard equipment. So much so that an RE request for an extra 39 'Austerities', with 43 tenders, was costed in March 1949 at £200,000, making the unit cost nearly twice as expensive as the previous purchase – and that was before the individual reconditioning cost of £2,500 was taken into account. The records are unclear on this, but it would appear that this later order – and one Minute reference specifies "LMS-type 2-8-0s" (although that could mean Stanier 8Fs) – did not go ahead. BR was to operate 758 Riddles-designed 2-8-0s and 2-10-0s, purchased in the 1946 and 1948 transactions, and needless to say these most plebian of locomotives were still defying their watery destiny well into the 1960s.

The oil-firing experiment of 1946-8 has puzzled transport historians, although it seemed worth pursuing at the time. While oil had to be imported – at a time when the UK was importing far too many of its commodities already – this seemed less of a problem than it was to become within two decades, when the pricing of crude was beyond the control of the largest oil-consuming nations. In contrast, at the end of the Second World War much of the oil-producing Middle East was under direct Anglo-American control, while the Merchant Marine was large enough to guarantee low shipping costs at that time.

The cause of diesel – or any oil-fuelled form of locomotion – can hardly have been advanced by all this. Meanwhile, coal, while available locally, was subject to fluctuations in the labour market, which had seen conscripts – the 'Bevin Boys' – being pressed into service in the mines in the 1940s and newspapers reporting regularly on coal production, the way they do nowadays on house prices.

More seriously, absenteeism in the mines was twice as bad post-war as it was before 1939, with the worst figures being returned in February 1947 – 17.76% of the workforce not reporting – at a time when severe winter weather had struck and the nation's hearths had never needed coal so badly. Diaries published subsequently by Mass Observation show members of the public, who had conducted themselves with courage and dignity through the war years, becoming suicidal towards the end of the six weeks of snow and ice, at a time of limited coal supplies and power cuts.

So serious had been the coal shortage since the end of the War that the amount of steam locomotive mileage was having to be monitored and constrained. In 1947 the target mileage agreed for the following year for steam-hauled passenger duties was fixed at 3,107,360 – 6% up on 1947 but 4% down on the previous year's figure. Three expresses on the East Coast Main Line were stripped from the timetable in 1947 and even named trains were not immune, the GWR having to withdraw the 'Torbay Express' for a time.

Excursion trains were not permitted – a restriction touched on lightly in the front-page cartoon in the *Newcastle Evening Chronicle* on that first day of BR's existence – but the authorities began to reassess this rather harsh restriction as soon as Nationalisation was in place. On 22nd January 1948 Transport Minister Alf Barnes wrote to Hurcomb relaxing this ban, particularly for children's outings, but continuing it for sports events or for local holidays on days when factories were working "as we are anxious that this should not be construed as indicating a change for the better in our economic situation … rather it should be presented as a decision not to continue an emergency measure made necessary last year by the exceptional need to build up stocks of coal. I have agreed to consult the Chancellor of the Exchequer as to the form and appropriate time for such an announcement".

Ironically, this was almost exactly the anniversary of the 1947 winter beginning in deadly earnest, but bringing the Chancellor into a discussion on excursion trains indicates a rather different world from nowadays, when the Treasury no longer even pronounces on interest rates! BTC commissioners had decided on 9th December 1947 not to seek an increase in permitted mileage "unless it could be shown by the Railway Executive that no increase in coal consumption would be involved" – although this was the same month when it was decided to convert no more steam locomotives to oil-burning. By the following month the Commissioners were considering an approach to the Minister to allow special traffic in connection with the forthcoming Olympic Games in London. Within ten days of Barnes's letter (quoted above), BR management was disputing the continuing ban on sporting specials anyway, and with some success. Nevertheless, one Labour MP complained about midweek sporting specials arranged in connection with the National Hunt meeting at Doncaster in March and he did seem to have a point.

The railways lost no time in restoring sporting excursions on Saturdays, notching up badly-needed revenue from passenger stock which would otherwise probably have stood empty at weekends. As early as 28th February 1948 Southern Region had run four special trains to take Southampton fans to and from London for a match with Tottenham Hotspur. Each train was headed by a 'King Arthur' and one included two ex-Caledonian Railway twelve-wheel 'Grampian Corridor' coaches. On a wider perspective, by the beginning of May 441 specials had been run in connection with the FA Cup and Rugby League Finals alone, carrying nearly 240,000 people, with estimated receipts of £126,318. In the first of these Wembley matches, even the presence of Stanley Matthews was insufficient to stop Manchester United defeating Blackpool by four goals to two. In the Rugby League Challenge Cup Final,

The Lancaster–Morecambe–Heysham branch, previously electrified by the Midland Railway, was chosen by BR to test a 6,600V 50 cycles system. The trains were three-car sets converted from LNWR stock originally built in 1914 for the Willesden Junction–Earls Court service, one of which is seen at Lancaster Green Ayre station.

Wigan beat Bradford Northern 8-3. It seems incredible now, but almost 100% of the spectators at these two great events travelled to Wembley and back by train!

All told, 1,631 extra trains had been run in the four months since the end of January, carrying 938,111 passengers at an estimated gross of £336,397. This was despite the fact that Barnes's edict had hardly been comprehensive in its liberality and did appear to continue the ban on sports specials.

Incidentally, more than one historian has suggested that Britain's coal shortage after World War Two was the result of a personality problem, not one of resources or logistics. "Shiver with Shinwell" was the comment to be heard from Opposition politicians, a reference to Emanuel Shinwell, not regarded, then or retrospectively, as one of Labour's more efficient ministers. He seemed to believe that he had to convey optimistic estimates to the Cabinet, even when these were unjustified; not surprisingly, he soon lost his energy portfolio to an up-and-coming Hugh Gaitskell. When Shinwell was then appointed to be Secretary of State for War, the *Daily Express* commented that very soon Britain would have none of that either!

As we have already seen, Riddles believed that the steam locomotive had plenty of life left in it but acknowledged that, in the longer term, electricity would be the principal motive power of choice. This was reflected in the appointment to the Executive staff of C.M. Cock. After being championed by Riddles for the highest salary for any technical official employed by the Executive – and only £500 less than some of the Committee members, or even BT Commissioners – Cock undertook the chairmanship of a joint BR/LT committee on the provision of electric traction. This he was well-qualified to do, following his career on the Southern.

Unfortunately, the Cock committee failed to reach any long-term conclusions about what form electric traction should take on Britain's railways, except the possibility of using a comparatively low-powered 50 cycle system, which was soon tried out on the Lancaster–Morecambe–Heysham line. No recommendations were made about moving away from the 1,500V dc overhead system for all Regions (except the Southern) and this continued to be installed on the former Great Eastern lines and over the Pennines at Woodhead. Yet as early as 1956 BR decided on the 25kV ac system as standard, with its facility for using lighter catenary. Cock's lack of direction also led to an impossibly pessimistic estimate of the costs of electrifying Glasgow's suburban lines, effectively denying the least profitable Region on BR an electric train service until the 1960s.

A more immediate electrification problem was to be found on the Great Eastern lines out of London's Liverpool Street. Converting these to overhead 1,500V dc was a LNER project halted by the war, but its resumption after the conflict proved to be no easy matter and was the subject of a conference organised by the British Transport Commission, with civil servants and Railway Executive representatives present, on 3rd December 1947. Only two months previously, the *Railway Gazette* had reported that the completion date of the first coach for the Shenfield scheme "cannot yet be stated ... but deliveries are expected to begin next October [ie 1948]". The reality was somewhat different, however. At the BTC meeting, shortage of materials soon emerged as a crucial factor, with rolling stock contractors – the Birmingham RC&W and Metro-Cammell companies – requesting 'PML' status in order to accelerate their supplies of steel, enabling them to meet the Shenfield starting date in September 1949.

'PML' meant 'Prime Minister's List', a hand-picked schedule of priority projects. The civil servants present from the Ministries of Transport and Supply at the BTC's conference on the Shenfield scheme declined to recommend this to 10 Downing Street, but if the companies' request was a negotiating manoeuvre it worked admirably, with Birmingham and Metro-Cammell receiving an undertaking from the Ministry of Supply that their steel orders would be processed as quickly as possible. In that case, the contractors assured those present that the 184 Birmingham coaches and 92 Metro-Cammell vehicles "would be in the hands of the LNER (*sic*) by the end of June 1949". This 'clear the air' meeting certainly had a lasting effect; twenty miles of the Shenfield electrification scheme were opened on schedule on 26th September 1949 and by December had seen weekly journeys increase by 58%.

At the same meeting in 1947, rolling stock suppliers took the opportunity of complaining that they also lacked steel supplies to allow them to supply the 21-ton wagons ordered from them. Birmingham RC&W representatives pointed out that they had not received a supply of suitable steel in nine months, while it was reported that the Butterley Company had not delivered even one of 750 wagons ordered from it by the LNER earlier in the year, again because of a lack of steel supply. Gourvish produces figures to show that the Railway Executive itself never received more than 82% of its estimated requirements for steel rail and other products during 1947-49 – and Dr. Bonavia suggested that this was Government policy, driven by a belief in Whitehall that the railways "could live off their fat" meantime – so the private companies were little worse off. On this occasion, however, the civil servants promised that something would be done.

From the records, there appears to have been little input into this meeting at 55 Broadway by representatives of either BTC or RE. Clearly, the Ministry of Supply was the only authority which could decide priorities to assist industry, but the furnishing of a 'neutral ground' by the BTC may have had the desired effect of producing a positive outcome. Was the BTC a useless bystander in this matter, or metaphorically knocking heads together? Let us hope it was the latter!

Shenfield was not the only electrification scheme to defy the otherwise universal dearth of investment in rail infrastructure. As mentioned above, the electrification of the former Great Central line across the Pennines from Sheffield to Manchester via Woodhead was being proceeded with in 1948, at an estimated cost of £6.2 million. This contemporary estimate did not include the boring of a new Woodhead Tunnel, at a cost of £2.5 million. "Age and structural defects make replacement necessary" was the reason for the latter project and these were the words of the Chancellor of the Exchequer, in theory at least.

For in December 1947, after a year in which inflation accelerated at frightening speed and the Chancellor (Dalton) trying to deal with it had to resign over an inadvertent budget leak, the Treasury produced a Command Paper called Capital Investment in 1948. To the modern reader, this is very much a document of its time, mixing spending on defence and health service targets with a multiplicity of road, rail and ship renewals which would nowadays be dealt with by the private sector.

The Woodhead route and tunnel were joined on the 'Approved' list by Shenfield, the latter costed at no less than £17 million, although that expenditure included extensions at each end of the LT Central Line. Of Shenfield the document recorded that the modernisation "is badly needed for increased traffic which is now handled only with great difficulty", but there was no approval for a rebuilding of Euston at £4 million – that would have to await electrification in the 1960s – or for London Transport reconstruction at Notting Hill Gate at £600,000.

Recording that "the balance of need as between rolling-stock and track materials is particularly difficult to strike", the Treasury was prepared to sanction 125,000 tons of rails to be

The electrification at 1,500V dc of the Woodhead route between Manchester and Sheffield had been started by the LNER before the war. Work was resumed afterwards with the LNER, in its final months, having to decide on the construction of a new tunnel at Woodhead due to the poor condition of the originals. BR took the scheme forward to completion and this is the opening ceremony at Woodhead on 3rd June 1954.

ordered in the first six months of 1948 along with two million sleepers, these totals to be reviewed after July of that year. If anyone needed reminding that Britain's railways were now nationalised, the intervention of His Majesty's Treasury on the number of new sleepers to be provided for Britain's railways would be a useful reminder!

While locomotive trials were being carried out in various parts of the United Kingdom in 1948, mostly south of the Border, railway managers and footplate crews found themselves facing a trial of a very different kind in August of that first year of BR operations. It was created by freak weather conditions in south east Scotland, but it was to have repercussions throughout both Scotland and England, with floods closing the East Coast Main Line north of Berwick for three months. Michael Bonavia personally visited the area during this crisis, expressing amazement at the extent of the damage; in the following November the BTC approved remedial work costing £720,000 (£14.4 million), of which approximately one-sixth was for bridge replacement by McAlpine's.

All this resulted in the longest non-stop rail journeys ever undertaken in the UK, between London and Edinburgh, and

The 'Yorkshire Pullman' departs from King's Cross behind new A2 Pacific No. 60536 Trimbush *which entered service in May 1948 – complete with LNER builder's plate!*

done so entirely at the instigation of locomotive footplate crews from King's Cross and Haymarket depots who had to negotiate a diversionary route through Norham and Kelso. The interested reader is invited to consult the author's book *Rails Across the Border,* which has recently been updated with previously-unknown information about these journeys. The point to be noted about these footplate feats is that the non-stop journeys were not ordered or sanctioned by management, but improvised by crews who believed in doing the job, come what may.

Just to emphasise the national significance of the crisis, when Sir Eustace Missenden issued a press statement at the end of 1948 to sum up the first year of nationalised railways, it was the flooding problem in south east Scotland he marked as the most serious that the network had faced anywhere in the UK.

Pullman services were an ideological minefield for a Labour government bringing transport into public ownership and this came to a head in 1948. Luxury trains offering meals at the passenger's own seat had been operated by the LNE and Southern Railways before the war, in partnership with the Pullman Car Company. The latter owned 196 vehicles on UK metals in the summer of 1948 and its staff provided the attable service to passengers, with the railways undertaking the operational work. Pullman had a contract with the Southern running to 1962 and with the LNER for ten years from 1938, although the latter agreement had hardly been implemented before the onset of war and was dependent on new Pullman cars being supplied, an undertaking not fulfilled.

Nevertheless, the BTC was keen to see these services restored, as the two rail companies had found Pullman trains to be "popular and economic". However, when it was announced that services would resume in 1948, there were Labour protests in the House of Commons. The 'Devon Belle' had in fact been running four times a week during the summer months in 1947, proving so popular that its Saturday journeys in August were fully booked by the end of June. Fortunately, the rail authorities at all levels – Ministry, BTC, and Executive – could point out that excursions had by now also been restored for football supporters and Sunday school picnickers, so an ideological clash was avoided through a consistent policy towards non-essential, and luxury, travel.

The Pullman services running from the summer of 1948 were – on former LNER lines the 'Yorkshire Pullman' and 'Queen of Scots', and on Southern Region the 'Golden Arrow' and the Brighton, Bournemouth, Devon and Thanet 'Belles'. If the driver of the last-named Pullman service shared the dogmatic outrage of Labour MPs over the reintroduction of such *trains de luxe,* it was not evident from his expression as he was pictured at Victoria surrounded by five Kentish beauty queens posing in a publicity stunt before the departure of the first 'Thanet Belle' in May! In addition there were some Pullman operations in connection with 'Ocean Liner' specials between Waterloo and Southampton and on other occasional Kent Coast and Brighton line services.

In June 1948 Beevor was able to advise the Commissioners that "while present demand for seats on all Pullman services frequently exceeds capacity, experience has shown that these services are first to feel the results of any reduction in public spending power, but the burden of adjusting resources (including staff) falls on the Pullman Company in the first instance".

This statement by Beevor, that the Pullman company would feel any chill wind of recession before the railways did, was hardly a reassuring view of these operations, but more positively he gained the approval of Lord Inman, the newly-appointed head of the Hotels Executive, when Beevor minuted that Pullman trains were "a valuable pace-maker to the railways' own catering services soon to be taken over by the Hotels Executive".

With an enormous workforce, one would have thought that British Railways would be anxious to reach out to all sections of the network through the publication of a staff magazine. In fact, this did not happen for some time. In April 1948 J. H. Brebner, the BTC's newly-appointed Chief PR and Publicity Officer, set up a committee to examine how magazine coverage should be initiated to cover all six Regions. There was a strong moralistic streak in Brebner's pronouncement on this – "the magazine should be sold to the staff and not given away free of charge". In the meantime, the Regions muddled along with their own productions – for example, the *LNER Magazine* was converted at Nationalisation into the *British Railways Magazine (E., N.E. & Scottish Regions)* without any seeming 'makeover', although one suspects it did not enjoy high sales figures among former LMS employees north of the Border; they made do with the magazine *Carry On,* a phrase not then connected to low-grade comedy films. Not until January 1950 was publication of a BR magazine established, with Regional insets included in an overall BR master version which went on to achieve 116,000 monthly sales at three pence (1.5p) per issue.

On a wider front, Brebner argued successfully for dedicated PR posts in all six Regions, brushing aside a suggestion that no such appointment was necessary north of the Border, as the CRO of Scottish, Tom Cameron, was "persona grata" with newspaper editors there. This was hardly likely to wash with a media specialist like Brebner who was accustomed to organising press conferences for the likes of Winston Churchill and the PR chief commented "that [Cameron's] position may not be enjoyed by the COs of other Executives [and, presumably, Regions]". One hopes that Cameron received a copy of this unsolicited compliment!

The inaugural 'Thanet Belle' Pullman between Victoria and Ramsgate ran on 31st May 1948. Before departure the driver of 'Battle of Britain' Pacific No.S21C170 Manston seems to be enjoying his moment in the spotlight with five Kentish beauty queens including Miss Ramsgate, Miss Kent and Miss Broadstairs!

Accidents

Britain's nationalised railways did not get off to a good start in terms of safety. There were no fewer than twelve fatal accidents involving moving trains in 1948 and these were only those serious enough to be recorded in the authoritative *Railway Yearbook*.

One which was not occurred only five hours into the New Year. A goods train including petrol tanks was passing through Inver Tunnel, on the Highland main line north of Dunkeld, when a number of the vehicles became derailed. According to the somewhat lurid and difficult-to-decipher newspaper reports, two tank wagons were left suspended only by their couplings over a 60ft drop until "employees of the Petroleum Board" succeeded in draining off their loads. There were no casualties. How wagons derailed in a tunnel ended up hanging over a chasm was not clear from the reports.

Within two days there was an accident on the ECML at Killingworth, a derailed freight blocking both lines. However, the first accident involving a 'civilian' fatality occurred not long afterwards at London Bridge on the Southern Region. Three people were killed in what we would nowadays call a 'shunt' collision, where a train approaching the station failed to brake in time and propelled a stationary train over the buffers and into a newspaper kiosk. One of those killed was a passenger standing on the platform, and no fewer than 79 were injured, although thankfully not too seriously.

A4 No.60007 Sir Nigel Gresley *passes over the magnetic track inductor of the automatic warning system.*

The worst accident of the year took place at Winsford on the LMR in the early hours of 17th April. 24 died in the collision; on this occasion a train had been stopped in section on a two-track stretch of the WCML after a soldier had pulled the communication cord so that he could walk to his home nearby. His selfishness cost others their lives; while the train crew desperately tried, in darkness, to locate the carriage in which the brake had been activated, the local signalman allowed a second train into the section and a collision inevitably occurred. It is a comment on the lack of telecommunications on Britain's railways (to say nothing of track circuiting) that lineside managers only learned of the tragedy after some eighteen minutes had passed, while medical help did not reach the victims for nearly three times as long. In retrospect, it is difficult to imagine the accident happening if the line – only the West Coast route – had been completely track-circuited; tragically, the first express had stopped 650 yards short of a circuited section.

In May 1948 BTC commissioners considered the merits of ATC and track circuiting systems. For the uninitiated, the former is a form of cab signalling called Automatic Train

Control but also known at one time as Automatic Warning System, whereby a ramp between the rails confirmed signal readings to the driver by means of a bell ringing for 'all clear' or a horn sounding for a distant at caution. In the ATC mode, a partial brake application would be made automatically if the driver failed to respond to the audible warning.

Track circuiting was a guide for signalmen, showing line occupancy by the simple method of running a mild electrical current through the track, the resulting short-circuiting indicating, on a signal box console, that there was a train in section.

Unfortunately, in a memo written in May 1948, Hurcomb seemed to believe that the systems were competitive and he appeared to favour ATC. In fact, both could and should be part of a modern railway system. Hurcomb also complicated matters by deploring the continuing Government ban on radio experimentation, as he clearly believed that this had potential to improve rail safety, although he did not specify how. Certainly, as shown only too plainly at Winsford, radio could keep controllers informed and accelerate the delivery of assistance. However, in practice it had a comparatively minor role to play in rail safety in the immediate future, certainly compared with ATC and track circuiting, both of which should be considered essential to safe railway operation.

The tragedy about all this was that the BTC failed to insist on these two safety measures being adopted and suggesting – perfectly reasonably – that the Government should assist directly with the cost of installation. If the pre-nationalised GWR could plan to equip 2,280 miles of track with ATC in 1946 and the LMS installed 110 ATC ramps on the former London, Tilbury & Southend by the following year, the Commission should have been no less ambitious, particularly when the Railway Executive had publicized the low, indeed almost non-existent, level of investment over the previous years, to say nothing of bomb damage. The Commission's indolence in the matter produced a terrible harvest.

The Harrow Disaster of 1952, which caused 108 deaths, could almost certainly have been prevented by the implementation of ATC, as the authoritative *Railway Yearbook* was quick to point out. Indeed, in the Commission's first year, the Ministry's Chief Inspecting Officer, Sir Alan Mount, estimated that 285 lives would have been saved over the 35 years before 1947 if cab-signalling had been available on Britain's railways. Compounding this error of omission was the fact that the old North Eastern Railway had a (mechanical) cab signalling system in place in 1895, only to have it dismantled by subsequent owners, while track circuiting dated from the 1870s!

If 1948 was a bad year for accidents, curiously, and thankfully, not a single passenger was killed in the following year.

Profits

Every one of the six Regions ended the year 1948 in profit. The net figures were, in ascending order, as follows, and should be multiplied by twenty to give a modern reading:

Scottish	£200,000
Western	£500,000
Eastern	£800,000
London Midland	£2,300,000
North Eastern	£7,900,000
Southern	£12,300,000

It's no surprise that the Southern should show the best returns – it also showed the highest level of modernity in its motive power. Equally, the NER benefitted from electric traction in the Newcastle area, or appeared to, although in fact this Region maintained its profitability for four years after the system was replaced by DMUs. Indeed, the North Eastern remained profitable longer than any other Region, yet it was the first to be reorganized out of existence, being absorbed by the larger Eastern Region in 1967. Taken with the poor performance of the far-flung Scottish Region and, to a lesser extent, the London Midland Region, the success of the NER suggested that 'small' really was 'beautiful' in terms of railway administration in the days of public ownership.

While the London Midland creditably remained profitable until 1957, as did the Eastern – both of them outstripping the Western, which entered the red in 1954 – Scottish found that its geographical spread made it financially untenable. Only in 1948 and 1951 was no loss recorded north of the Border.

Yet Sir John Elliot, who was to succeed Missenden as RE Chairman in 1951, announced that the unification of LMS and LNER systems in Scotland had led to an annual saving of no less than £3 million per year up to 1953. Adjusted up to modern currency from values for 1950, this represents an annual saving akin to £50 million! It is presumably a misprint in both the printed version of his original speech (a presidential address to the Institute of Transport) and when reported by the technical press. In fact Scottish Region had hardly inherited a rich legacy – in 25 years neither the LMS nor LNER had built one marshalling yard between them in Scotland, or electrified a single mile of track.

As mentioned earlier, the Southern Railway and its Regional successor showed up well in any costing comparison with rival companies or Regions. This was because of its determination to electrify as many of its services as possible in south London and to the south coast. Labour historian P. S. Bagwell has cited this as almost the only important example of infrastructure investment in Britain's railways between 1920 and 1938, which totalled £125 million less than it should have, according to his calculations (and levelled up to modern values – £6.07 milliards – from those of 1938). Since he specifically excluded the Southern Railway from his criticism, the 'disinvestment' by the GWR, LMS and LNER assumes even greater proportions for each of these companies.

In 1952 the BTC analysed net revenue figures for passenger trains run on all six Regions during a single week (ending 11th October) in that year. From this review, it is interesting to compare the Southern and Scottish Regions in particular since the latter operated no electric trains at the time, and would not do so for another nine years, despite the availability of hydro-electricity.

Type of train	Scottish Revenue	Southern Revenue
Express	£26,348	£37,869
Semi-fast	£14,894	£82,755
Stopping	- £50,349	-£9,997
Suburban	- £8,850	£115,138

The final figure quoted – for Southern suburban services – was for electric trains only and helped the Region to a handsome £225,765 profit over its passenger services in their entirety. In contrast Scottish made an overall loss and it is possible that the 'express' element of the Regional figures included expresses to and from England, with much of that revenue originating south of the Border. A review of motive power modernisation some years later, in 1958, makes it clear that the Southern was by far the most modern Region, while Scottish was the most dependent on steam traction (see this author's *British Railways Region by Region (Scottish), 1948-73.*

Ironically, indeed disappointingly, while the North of Scotland Hydroelectric Board showed a positive willingness to work with Scottish Region in the 1950s in trying out new motive power forms – specifically, a battery car experiment first discussed in 1956 and implemented on the Ballater branch – the Hydro Board's minute books show that its members found the Scottish Regional board evasive and difficult to work with, thus eliminating any possibility of electrifying the lines in the Far North or in the West Highlands, using renewable energy.

Summarising 1948, it is pleasant to see that all six Regions began their working careers in profit and this was one of only two years in which this was to happen. With the monthly accounts being broken down into a Regional basis, it should have presented a powerful case for modernisation, with the Southern Region's good economic performance the proof of the pudding, but such a conclusion is absent from the contemporary technical press.

A quarter of a million miles were added to the summer timetables, compared with the previous year. Special trains were reactivated, carrying nearly a million picnickers and sports fans within three months. Punctuality overall was improved, although schedules were hardly demanding. It was pleasant to see so many named trains being restored (the 'Queen of Scots'), new ones introduced (the 'South Yorkshireman' and 'Thanet Belle') while the 'Flying Scotsman' was non-stop once again – and its operation through diversions caused by flood conditions was a credit to operating staff. Although the accident rate throughout BR was high, it was to improve radically.

If all this seems like progress at a snail's pace to the modern reader, consider that the present preoccupation with 'consumer choice' was a luxury 1940s society could ill afford. Rationing remained in place in the UK for many years after 1945 and, indeed, new consumer constraints – for example, on bread – were actually being introduced. Petrol rationing still impaired motoring and car hiring was restricted to a twenty-mile journey radius. While Government restrictions on fuel consumption had led to a reduction in rail services, this was equally true of road travel and it was unfortunate that BR was having to build itself up from such a low material base when it should have been attempting to recapture much more of a hamstrung leisure travel market.

Nevertheless, in the trying and difficult circumstances of 1948, the People's railways had got off, if not exactly to a flying start, at least to a hopeful one.

On 26th March 1949 most of those at the peak of the British transport hierarchy met at the Seymour Hall in Marylebone, on an occasion presided over by Sir Eustace Missenden, with John Benstead, Deputy Chairman of the BTC, looking on. Also present were General Russell, Lord Latham and Sir Reginald Hill, the chairmen of the Road Transport, London Transport and Docks & Inland Waterways Executives respectively. Representing the Regions were the CROs of London Midland, Eastern, Western and North Eastern, along with the Deputy CRO of the Southern. Also present were the President and General Secretary of ASLEF.

What was the subject of this colloquium of transport aristocracy? The answer is – boxing; the London Midland Region had just defeated the North Eastern Region by 25 points to 21 in the final of the BR Amateur Boxing Championships. Curiously, this evening illustrated perfectly the sense of community which existed among the elite of British transport, whether road, rail or water-borne. One cannot imagine anything similar happening nowadays when transport is little more than a commercial free-for-all.

7

Summing up

Historian Peter Hennessy has written an authoritative review of British history in the immediate post-war period entitled *Never Again*. Yet, in the book's 550 paperback pages, Professor Hennessy mentions the British Transport Commission only once, along with one mention each for the Railway Executive and the London Midland & Scottish Railway, the latter Britain's biggest commercial company. He describes transport nationalisation as "the most ambitious of the Attlee Government's public ownership projects", yet its "exciting" nature did not guarantee the subject more than a page in this otherwise comprehensive book. With the BTC commissioners described as "drab", the reader finds that the subject soon dries up (although the description of LMS President, Lord Stamp, as "outgoing" in 1947 causes some surprise as he had been dead for six years by then).

So, in summing up the story of the British Transport Commission, one can only describe it as a failure. While the politics of the day drifted inexorably to the right from 1951 onwards, rendering unfashionable the Commission's authoritarian character, it has to be said that the BTC could hardly be held up as a shining cynosure of Socialism at work anyway. Headed by a Civil Servant with no ideological animus and peopled by elderly men of conservative tendencies – whether conservative with a small or large 'c' – there was no sense of the Commission fighting to establish its place in the British way of life. This was partly due to a remittal error and partly to a personality problem.

The railway service was still expected – by press and public – to be run profitably, despite the fact that the 1947 Transport Act aimed at efficiency and integration, rather than measuring service against a fiscal yardstick. Indeed, the Act did not require transport to be run at a profit at all, merely "economically". Herein lay the challenge for Hurcomb and his colleagues. It might have been better if monthly traffic receipts had not been published from February 1948 – although the transport media was certainly demanding them – and some other means found for defining the railways' performance statistically, for example train mileage for passengers and ton-mileage for freight.

As it was, records of financial performance established the manner in which the railways would be evaluated and created a rod for railwaymen's backs. Not surprisingly, the closure of uneconomic lines proceeded as determinedly in public ownership as it had in private hands, reinforcing the profit imperative.

A 'socialised' (the Labour Prime Minister's term for a nationalised) industry should have been run on more socially-responsive lines. The joint committees begun in 1928 between railway and local authority officials should have been reinvigorated and formalized by legislation to create an awareness by railway managers of what kind of railway local people needed, and an understanding by democratically-elected authorities of what kind of railway they could expect within existing financial and logistical parameters. Apart from anything else, this would have removed the need for the largely ineffective TUCC system.

But all this would have required revised legislation and Sir Cyril Hurcomb was no legislator; as a career civil servant, he was adept at executing policies established by others. Although Lord Reith was mooted at the time as a possible Chairman of the BTC, he was probably never a serious option, with his reputation for a headstrong determination to do things his way. But more's the pity.

A one-time engineering apprentice at North British Locomotive Company, Reith had moulded broadcasting into a public service free of the commercial horrors found in the United States and had insisted on the highest technical standards. He could not be dictated to by any politician (except Churchill, who was out of power anyway), insisted on rewritten ministerial remits to allow for changing circumstances and had personally drafted legislation. Additionally, he had a gift for delegation – not a bad recommendation for the head of a major organisation. Reith had maintained an interest in transport matters after being transferred from the Transport ministry and had proposed what would have effectively been a British Transport Commission in a speech to the House of Lords in 1942. He would have been unlikely to have accepted that the Commission should be so small and so unrepresentative of

The 15in gauge Romney, Hythe & Dymchurch Railway escaped nationalisation, the RE concluding there would not be any advantage in its acquisition. Nevertheless, the railway had played a role in the Second World War when its position on the probable invasion coast led to its requisition by the Army. An armoured anti-aircraft train was operated, transport was provided for troops stationed in the Dungeness area, and men and materials were carried during the laying of 'PLUTO', the Pipe Line under the Ocean, between the Kent Coast and France. 4-6-2 No.8 **Hurricane** *is entering Dymchurch station.*

shipping – an area in which Reith had worked during the latter stages of the war. He would, if his broadcasting experience is anything to go by, have bombarded his Minister with demands for amending legislation and would have drafted it himself over a weekend. And he was no socialist. He would simply have taken the view – *did* take the view, as his 1942 Lords speech proved – that if the democratic will was for a People's railway system, then it should be set up properly.

Gourvish states that the "Nationalisation period got off on the wrong organization foot ... defective solutions were imposed from above" and this could be interpreted as a comment on the deployment of existing 'captains of industry' by a Government unsure of the mettle of the new highly-educated working class. Meanwhile, a Government White Paper issued in 1960 was to describe the BTC as "so large and so diverse that it is virtually impossible to run its activities as a single undertaking". Yet one of the contemporary criticisms of the Commission had been its omission of so many facets of transport (own-goods road carriers, inshore shipping, civil aviation) and of suitably-qualified commissioners, and these criticisms dated back to the *Economist* in 1947.

Despite having appointed an experienced and highly-esteemed financial controller in Reginald Wilson, the BTC showed a less than sure touch in its fiscal undertakings. There was a tendency to spend money without first establishing proper costings, as with the Morecambe hotel, a project tackled early in the Commission's existence. The spending commitments of the 'Big Four' were too often treated by the Commissioners as irrevocable and without fitting these into an overall long-term plan. But Wilson's task was a huge one, with

In 1951 the Talyllyn Railway became famous as the first railway to be saved and operated by volunteers. 0-4-2ST No.4 **Edward Thomas** *is seen at Abergynolwyn station. This locomotive was acquired from the Corris Railway which had been purchased by the GWR in 1931 and thus passed to British Railways in 1948. However, it was closed later that year due to flood damage. This little narrow gauge tank had thus actually been a BR engine before being sold to the Talyllyn in 1951!*

the BTC required by law to cover its costs, to say nothing of redeeming capital and pay dividends on British Transport Stock.

Meanwhile, the swelling of office staff at 55 Broadway in London allowed a freewheeling atmosphere to develop. Civil Servants would soon sense an organization without leadership or financial 'grip' and its working life would be limited as a result. There was no overall long-term plan, anyway. The

nearest that could be considered one was the Modernisation Plan of 1955, but its selective approach to recapitalization – of renewing and rebuilding some lines while doing nothing about those which were loss-making – was deeply flawed.

From Day One, the Commission's remit was muddled as to whether it was a direct operator or not; and it became both an operator in some areas of transport, particularly in shipping and canals, and a bystander in others. It failed to address the problem of under-investment in the railways, but permitted recapitalization of their shipping interests, an area in which the BTC Chairman had a professional interest. It paid no particular attention to rail safety issues and even less to the problem of rating burden or the social aspects of rail closures.

Both these last two points concerned policy formulation and if a British Transport Commission was unable to formulate policy, this prompts the question – what else was it there for? The question was still unanswered when it was wound up fifteen years later.

APPENDIX I

Omissions from 'Vesting' in 1948

Before the expiry of the '30-year rule' on the Government documents of the late 1940s, railway enthusiasts could only speculate as to why so many railways were not included in 'vesting' in a nationalised body after the passing of the 1947 Transport Act. Even now, the omissions policy is far from clear, particularly since the legislation permitted acquisition and subsequent sale, as happened with the Corris rolling stock and Morecambe's Midland Hotel.

The Act itself was not exactly clear; Section 13 was entitled 'Bodies whose undertakings are to vest in Commission' and it can only be described as labyrinthine in its complexity. Even a textbook of commentary relating to it, and published commercially for the use of legal practitioners, uses such terms as "obscure", "caution on the part of the legislature" and "this presumably applies to…" in attempting to clarify it. Documents subsequently issued by the Executive – listed below and detailing a number of rail concerns not vested – indicate that Broadway and Marylebone were keeping a wary eye on those railways remaining independent, with at least two reviews taking place in 1948, and a number of railways, particularly the Derwent Valley and Easingwold, having their futures reconsidered on an annual basis.

Tom Rolt is worth quoting on this – and was, earlier in this text – as he has recorded the care with which he "waded" through the Transport Bill and its attached list of railway and canal concerns intended to be incorporated "and found it almost all-embracing".

But "almost" is the operative word here, as lines as well known today as the Talyllyn, Festiniog, Romney, Hythe & Dymchurch, Glasgow Underground – all narrow gauge – were not included, but neither was a number of standard gauge railways, such as the Easingwold, North Sunderland, Derwent Valley and Liverpool Overhead. There were various reasons for that – municipal connections with the local authority were probably relevant in the case of Liverpool, Swansea and Glasgow – but Rolt posits an interesting theory about the omission of the first of all these, the Talyllyn Railway: "perhaps the architects of the Transport Bill were under the impression that the railway was already defunct, for did not the current edition of the Ordnance Survey mark Rhydyronen, Brynglas, Dolgoch, and Abergwynolwyn stations as closed?"

The same author suggested that such transport concerns as the Corris Railway and the long-lost Hereford & Gloucester Canal were included because they had been bought up at one time by a main line railway, in both these cases the Great Western. This explanation is true for some cases, but by no means all, and may support the theory that those concerns not nationalised were those not under Railway Executive control during the recent war. As far as the Talyllyn was concerned, the Executive's survey of October 1948 concluded that "it is very doubtful whether this railway could be made into a paying proposition, and its acquisition is not recommended. The track is in very poor condition."

Ironic comments indeed on a line which proved to be the pioneer of the British railway preservation movement and whose track was passed as suitable for passenger traffic by a Ministry inspector four years after this date, and with little improvement by that time!

By 1948 those railways which had been omitted from the 1923 Grouping but were now nationalised numbered four: the East Kent Railway, the Kent & East Sussex Railway, the Cheshire Lines Committee and the Forth Bridge Railway. However, they were outnumbered by those neither Grouped in 1923 nor nationalised in 1948, listed as follows, with comments from an Executive communication to the BTC in October 1948, summarising (in some cases, surely to nobody's satisfaction) why the railway concerned had not been taken, and should not be taken, under the Commission's control. They are listed here in alphabetical order.

Standard gauge

Barrington Light Railway. A 1¾-mile private line which left the ER Hitchin–Cambridge branch at Foxton, but was described in this 1948 survey as "an elongated siding". Since the cement works it served had just switched to road transport, the Light Railway seemed unlikely to survive and acquisition by the BTC was not recommended. Interestingly, it lasted in operation until 2005, the last standard gauge quarry line to do so.

Corringham Light. Although situated in Essex, this private line, 2¾ miles long and effectively running services for its own staff using one engine and a couple of carriages, connected with the new ER near Thames Haven. Verdict: "Ownership of line should remain unchanged".

Derwent Valley. Running for 20 miles south east from Layerthorpe station, York, this concern owned seven vehicles but hired motive power from the North Eastern Region. By the time this report was drawn up in October 1948, the BTC had already decided to preserve the line's independence, even although it was making a loss.

Easingwold. Already well-known to the administrators at the Ministry, the RE, the former LNER and its successor in this area, the NE Region, this 2½-mile line from Alne owned one carriage and an unserviceable locomotive, having to hire engine power from the Region. A loss-maker, the BTC had already agreed to review the line's future on a 12-month basis, but in the meantime decided on 26th October 1948 that no further assistance be extended to the Easingwold.

Liverpool Overhead. This unique 6½-mile line resembled US-style elevated systems in connecting the docks run by the Mersey Docks and Harbour Board and offered a transport service to the dock employees. Unlike nearly all the other railways considered in this October 1948 survey of "unvested" concerns, the Overhead made a profit – the modern equivalent of half a million pounds in 1947. The National Union of Railwaymen made representations to the Ministry around this time that the system be nationalised and specifically asked for it to be incorporated into the LMR. The BTC asked for more information on this line on 30th November 1948, but it was never to be taken into BR's hands.

Manchester Ship Canal Railways. A surprising inclusion in this list, considering that the Port of London Railways were not included. Comprising no fewer than 180 miles of single track, the system was shown as generating some £10 million in gross receipts, with expenditure not much less than that. The Executive's description does not mention that some passenger services were operated within the system and this, as with Liverpool, seemed to mark it out as a private concern which should remain that way. The Canal itself was not nationalised, as the local authority held so many of the shares anyway.

North Sunderland. Running from Chathill on the East Coast Main Line to the Northumberland coast at Seahouses, this six-mile line incurred expenses at nearly twice the level of gross receipts. Like the Easingwold Railway, it had to hire a locomotive from NER in 1948 and again, like the railway at Alne, the BTC was advised to review the future of the North Sunderland in 12 months' time. In the meantime, the BTC decided on 26th October 1948 that this line, along with the Easingwold, should receive no further assistance.

Ravenglass & Eskdale. Rather better known as a narrow gauge railway, the 'Ratty' – which is thankfully still with us – used to operate standard gauge trains over one-third of its length, using gauntleted track. Interestingly, the Executive regarded this as an industrial concern – "it is worked primarily to serve roadstone quarries and there would be no advantage in the line being acquired."

Stocksbridge Railway. A two-mile long industrial line in the Barnsley area, and with its own locomotives, this was a surprising nomination for possible vesting. It was described as "in effect a private siding, and its acquisition is not recommended".

Swansea & Mumbles. An electrically-operated tramway did not detain the mandarins long – it handled only passengers over its five-mile length but its future was threatened by the planning policies of the local authority. The Executive advised the BTC to steer well clear of potential local complications and this attractive and interesting line was doomed whoever ran it.

Trafford Park Light Railway. Another surprising inclusion in the list for reconsideration, this was a railway no fewer than 49 miles in length, forming an annexe to the MSC (see above). Its accounts showed a working loss but it was clearly an industrial/docklands line and the survey produced the "recommendation that the ownership remains unchanged".

Narrow gauge

Ashover Light Railway. This was an interesting 2ft gauge line connecting with the LMR between Ambergate and Clay Cross, carrying freight only over its eight miles. Part of it was planned for conversion to standard gauge "in which event LMR will gain additional traffic without expenditure by Railway Executive … it is not recommended that the line should be acquired".

Festiniog Railway. Any enthusiast who has read J. I. C. Boyd's account of the Festiniog's years as a 'sleeping giant' of narrow gauge railways between 1939 and 1955 will not be surprised to learn that London-based administrators failed to grasp the complicated situation in which this railway was to be found. Noting that the fourteen-mile line was open only for 650 yards in the Blaenau Festiniog area for slate traffic only, the Executive opined that "no advantage is to be gained by acquisition of railway or that portion of line at present worked by Quarry owners". Boyd painted a picture of a line which was firmly closed when the local rating officer made enquiries, while a wagon miraculously made its way along the track once a year to ensure the company's rights-of-way, ensuring immunity from scrap merchants or negatively-minded council planning officials. Presumably, the line was firmly 'closed' when this 1948 survey took place!

Romney Hythe & Dymchurch. The 'Premier Line' of Britain's miniature railways, apparently charmed the Executive's members. Needing no introduction to present-day readers, the RH&D had made a small profit in 1946, its first year of post-war operation and "It is not felt that there would be any advantage in the acquisition of the line. In fact it is suggested that such a step would probably destroy the essentially individualistic character of the enterprise which owes its attraction largely to its unique status."

However, this verged on the misleading; there was no acknowledgment of the railway's use by the military during the recent war, indicating its value in more than just 'entertainment' terms. Unfortunately, the requisition had been conducted with heavy-handedness bordering on vandalism.

Snailbeach District Railway. A mineral railway hauling stone some 3½ miles over 28-inch gauge track, this little line failed to impress the Executive as it was now delivering its cargoes to road instead of the Western Region at Pontesbury (although this should not have mattered, as road freight was being nationalised anyway). In 1947 it made an operational profit of exactly £2, but "miscellaneous expenditure" (paper clips, milk for the crews' tea?) sent the line tumbling to a net loss of £11 annually. "Railway should not be acquired" was the verdict.

Despite the thoroughness of the authorities, there were still unexplained omissions. The following are shown in the 1950-51 *Railway Year book* and even this failed to list some industrial and dock railways, such as the railway systems of the National Coal Board and some of the major ports, but did include Felixstowe Dock & Railway, Fishguard & Rosslare Railways & Harbours (including broad gauge lines in Ireland), Mersey Docks and Harbour Board, Port of London, Royal Arsenal and – not forgetting narrow gauge – Brighton Electric, Glasgow Underground and Snowdon Mountain. The Isle of Man systems were specifically excluded from the Transport Act, as were Irish railways.

In the year following the Transport Act becoming law, its less than watertight clauses were exposed to a critical examination. In September 1948 the *Railway Gazette* pointed out that the BTC had "no railway monopoly in Great Britain". It went on: "Not only were some of the smaller railways, including the Liverpool Overhead and Glasgow Underground, omitted from Nationalisation, but also it is still possible in theory for a new private railway enterprise to be promoted."

This was written around the same time that the Executive listing "unvested" railways was drawn up and it is significant that the latter omits the Glasgow Underground in dismissing Scotland as having no railways worthy of inclusion. Perhaps it is no coincidence that the Railway Executive's only Scottish representative was a shipyard owner!

It is tempting to conclude that the Transport Bill was poorly drafted, a victim of a degree of overwork to which civil servants were probably being subjected at the time. On the other hand, the casual way in which the BTC was prepared to sanction the sale of hotels suggests a less than totally inclusive attitude to transport concerns.

APPENDIX II

The birth of the Preservation Movement

It is no coincidence that the birth of what became the heritage movement in Britain took place at the time when railways and canals came under what many perceived as the thrall of nationalisation. It is surely impossible to see the post-war preservation movement, including the later heritage industry, as having anything other than a political motivation.

Britain's preoccupation with its heritage is a fact of present-day life. Every town and city has its museums, its heritage trails, its working preserved railways or canals, reopened 'real ale' breweries or cinemas. Up to 30 million people are believed to have travelled on steam-powered railways in one recent year. 3,000 miles of canals are given over, almost exclusively, to leisure use, by more than 60,000 boats. Once the exclusive preoccupation of hobbyist vicars or right-wing political reactionaries, railway and canal preservation has provided the impetus for the modern heritage industry. It has changed our landscape and the way in which we take our constantly increasing vacations.

While there had been preservation activities before World War Two – the rescuing of the *Cutty Sark* by Captain and Mrs. Dowman from Portuguese shipbreakers was a famous case in point – Tom Rolt and his friends seemed determined to preserve by reprivatising.

Tom Rolt – perhaps better known to readers as L.T.C. Rolt – is not a name well-known today. Yet he deserves to be regarded as one of the major influences on Britain in the second half of the twentieth century, along with such political figures as Churchill, Wilson and Thatcher. His legacy is the one of the fastest-growing industries of Britain today – Heritage.

It is difficult for us to grasp nowadays how people like Tom Rolt, who had never really given much thought to politics, felt suddenly finding themselves faced with a Labour government ascending to power in 1945 with a huge majority of 146 seats. Labour had held power before, or – to put it another way – had formed two previous governments, but had been hamstrung with slender majorities or forced to accept coalition partners unprepared to share socialist dogma, or any kind of legislative programme based on one.

In 1945, to people like Rolt, there seemed a long tunnel of socialism to be threaded through, with no possibility of light at the other end for ten years or more. As matters turned out, Labour held power for only six years and, unlike nowadays, saw its majority whittled away by by-elections. Compared with the present time, by-elections were a regular feature of political life, not least because MPs tended to be older than they are today, were predominantly male, all of whom, it seemed, smoked excessively, leading to lower life expectancy and the prospect of up to a dozen by-elections a year.

But this political vista was dismal enough to cause a reaction among the better-educated members of society, those who would regard themselves as members of 'the establishment'. To those thus disenfranchised, Labour's nationalisation plans were a red rag to a bull. Steel, coal, railways, canals, all were to be nationalised, with a National Health Service to be loaded on to the backs of the unwilling medical profession. Voters lived then in interesting times, but they were a little too interesting for those of conservative mien, if not party membership.

In his book *Railway Adventure*, Rolt leaves the reader in no doubt that Labour's nationalisation programme was a major spur to him and his colleagues in their preservation efforts; any reader doubting the political motives of the early preservationists at Towyn need only read this book. In *Railway Adventure* Rolt comments on the "political dogma then prevailing which was going to rescue road, rail and canal transport from the thrall of 'private enterprise' and dedicate them to the especial service of humble British servants like myself".

Although this book was given a 'rave' review by the magazine *Trains Illustrated,* the reviewer nevertheless complained about Rolt's repeated and wearying diatribes against nationalisation in the text. John Betjeman put it rather more succinctly in his foreword to Rolt's book when he wrote "We 'own' British Railways, but we are allowed no say in them. We really do own the Talyllyn Railway."

ARCHIVES (NAS)

BR/BTC/1/1-12   Minutes and meeting papers of the British Transport Commission, August 1947–August 1948. (Includes six regional Instructions).

BR/BTC/5/1 The coal:oil conversion scheme on British Railways, 1945-48. Railway Executive, 1949.

BR/RSR/5/45 Minute of a meeting of the BR Mechanical Engineers' Committee, 8th January 1948. ('Interchange of locomotives between [among] the regions').

BOOKS (Transport titles)

Allen, C.J. *New light on the Locomotive Exchanges.* Ian Allan, 1948.

Bonavia, M.R. *The Birth of British Rail.* Allen & Unwin, 1979.

Bonavia, M.R. *British Rail; the first 25 years.* David & Charles, 1981.

Bonavia, M.R. *The nationalisation of British transport: an early history of the British Transport Commission, 1948-53.* Macmillan, 1987.

Boughey, J. *Hadfield's British Canals.* Sutton, 1994.

Carter, Oliver. *An Illustrated History of British Railway Hotels 1838-1983.* Silver Link, 1990.

Clegg, W.P. and Styring, J.S. *British Nationalised Shipping, 1947-1968.* David & Charles, 1969.

Communist Party of Great Britain. *Full Steam Ahead.* 1948.

Foster, C.D. *The Transport Problem.* Croom Helm, 1975.

Glaister, S. and Mulley, C. *Public control of the British bus industry.* Gower, 1983.

Gourvish, T.R. *British Railways 1948-73: a business history.* C.U.P., 1986.

Hurcomb, C.H. *The organisation of British transport.* BTC, 1948.

Morrison, H. *Socialisation and transport: the organisation of socialised industries with particular reference to the London Passenger Transport Bill.* Constable,1933.

Murphy, B. *ASLEF 1880-1980: a hundred years of the Locoman's Trade Union.* ASLEF, 1980.

Railway Correspondence and Travel Society. *Locomotives of the Great Western Railway. Pt. 8,* 1960.

Rolt, L.T.C. *Railway Adventure.* Constable, 1953.

Sixsmith, I. *The Book of the Coronation Pacifics.* Irwell, 1998.

Smith, M. *Britain's Light Railways.* Ian Allan, 1994.

Thomas, D. St J. *The rural transport problem.* Routledge, 1963.

BOOKS (Non-transport titles)

Barry, E.E. *Nationalisation in British politics: the historical background.* Cape, 1965.

Garfield, S. (Ed.) *Our Hidden Lives: the remarkable diaries of post-war Britain.* Ebury, 2004. [Based on Mass Observation data].

McIntyre, I. *The expense of glory: a life of John Reith.* HarperCollins, 1993.

Pearce, R. *Attlee's Labour Governments 1945-51.* Routledge, 1994.

Robertson, A.J. *The Bleak Midwinter 1947.* Manchester University Press, 1987.

Rolt, L.T.C. *Landscape with figures.* Alan Sutton, 1992.

ARTICLES

Dow, A. 'How the Peppercorn A1s were named', *Steam Days,* (26), October 1991, pp17-21.

Elliot, J. 'An account of stewardship'. Presidential address, 5th October 1953. *Journal of the Institute of Transport,* 25, (7) 1953, pp243-52.

Missenden, E. 'Some thoughts on railway motive power'. *Journal of the Institute of Transport,* 23, (8) 1951, pp230-7.

Thanks to Richard Lacey, Alan Robinson and to the staffs of the National Archives of Scotland, National Library of Scotland, Edinburgh City and Newcastle City Libraries. I am particularly indebted to Martin Smith for supplying information on those railways not 'vesting' in 1948 and to Joan Bakewell for permission to quote from her *Guardian* article on the Attlee government. Thanks also to Michael Blakemore and Barry C. Lane for their work on the production of this book.

FINALISTA

FINAL 2009

FINAL 2009

COPA
—BNP PA

THE YEAR
IN TENNIS 2009

DAVIS CUP®
by BNP PARIBAS

ITF
International Tennis Federation

Text by Mark Hodgkinson

The International Tennis Federation

Universe

First published in the United States of America in 2010 by
UNIVERSE PUBLISHING
A Division of Rizzoli International Publications, Inc.
300 Park Avenue South
New York, NY 10010
www.rizzoliusa.com

© 2010 by the International Tennis Federation

2010 2011 2012 / 10 9 8 7 6 5 4 3 2 1

Designed by Domino 4 Limited, Weybridge, United Kingdom
Printed in Italy

ISBN: 978-0-7893-2067-4

CONTENTS

President's Message

Year on year, Davis Cup by BNP Paribas generates new narratives, yet the 2009 season ended with a poignant familiarity. Eight decades of Davis Cup history saw Spain lift its fourth title in the very same stadium where it won its first. Nine years down the line, it was heartwarming to see that the joy on their faces remains as great today as it was when the nation lifted Dwight Davis's 109-year-old silver trophy for the first time in 2000.

As the modern-day guardian of the Davis Cup, we at the ITF can firmly say that Spain is an exemplary tennis nation and its team ethic an asset to this competition. Rafael Nadal, David Ferrer, Fernando Verdasco, Feliciano Lopez, and captain Albert Costa led Spain to victory over the Czech Republic, reminding us of the importance and satisfaction that this unique competition brings to the sport of tennis.

The victory was not just another title for Spain, it was also a huge part of a personal journey for both Albert Costa and Rafael Nadal. A young Costa had won the Davis Cup as a player at the Palau Sant Jordi in 2000 under the guidance of Javier Duarte, and this year became the first man since Duarte to win the Davis Cup in his first year of captaincy. Many people had doubted Nadal's resilience this year, but his outstanding talent and conduct throughout the final proved that he remains one of the sport's greatest ambassadors. I look forward to watching his development as a Davis Cup player and his healthy return to the tour next year.

It was very special to see so many familiar faces supporting Spain in Barcelona: Manuel Santana, Juan Gisbert, Jose Arilla, Manuel Orantes, Andres Gimeno, Fernando Luna, Juan Avendano, Carlos Costa, and Julian Alonso, to name but a few. And it was gratifying to see Crown Prince Felipe personally congratulate the players on the court after their victory. I would like to thank all the players, past and present, for their on-court and off-court dedication to Davis Cup.

Of course a competition is nothing without an opponent, and the Czech team was responsible for some of the most riveting Davis Cup moments this year. I was fortunate enough to witness their fearless victory over Croatia in the semifinals that led them to their first final in almost three decades. Their fans have been just as committed as the team's stalwarts, Tomas Berdych and Radek Stepanek. It was a pleasure to see them in the final, and even though the result was not in their favor, the smiles on their faces regardless spoke volumes.

The 2009 Davis Cup final was the perfect platform to announce the results of our long research project into the economic and commercial impact of the competition, and we were pleased with the outcome. In 2008 Davis Cup had an economic impact of $184 million worldwide, which will provide a substantial long-term legacy for the development of tennis in the cities and nations where it is staged. The continuous international appeal of Davis Cup stretched to more than half a million spectators this year, and 122 nations competed. Next year four continents will be represented in the sixteen-nation elite World Group alone, and I would like to make a particular mention of India and Ecuador, who have made a spectacular return to the World Group through their efforts this year.

As I leave you to reminisce on the chapters of this year's Davis Cup, chronicled eloquently by Mark Hodgkinson, I would like to thank the many photographers whose hard work has not only provided this book with some of the most stunning images in tennis, but also captured the spirit of this special competition.

Congratulations to Spain for its remarkable achievement and also to the National Associations that have been involved throughout the year in staging the eighty-three ties. I look forward to the stories that next year's season will unfold.

Francesco Ricci Bitti
ITF President

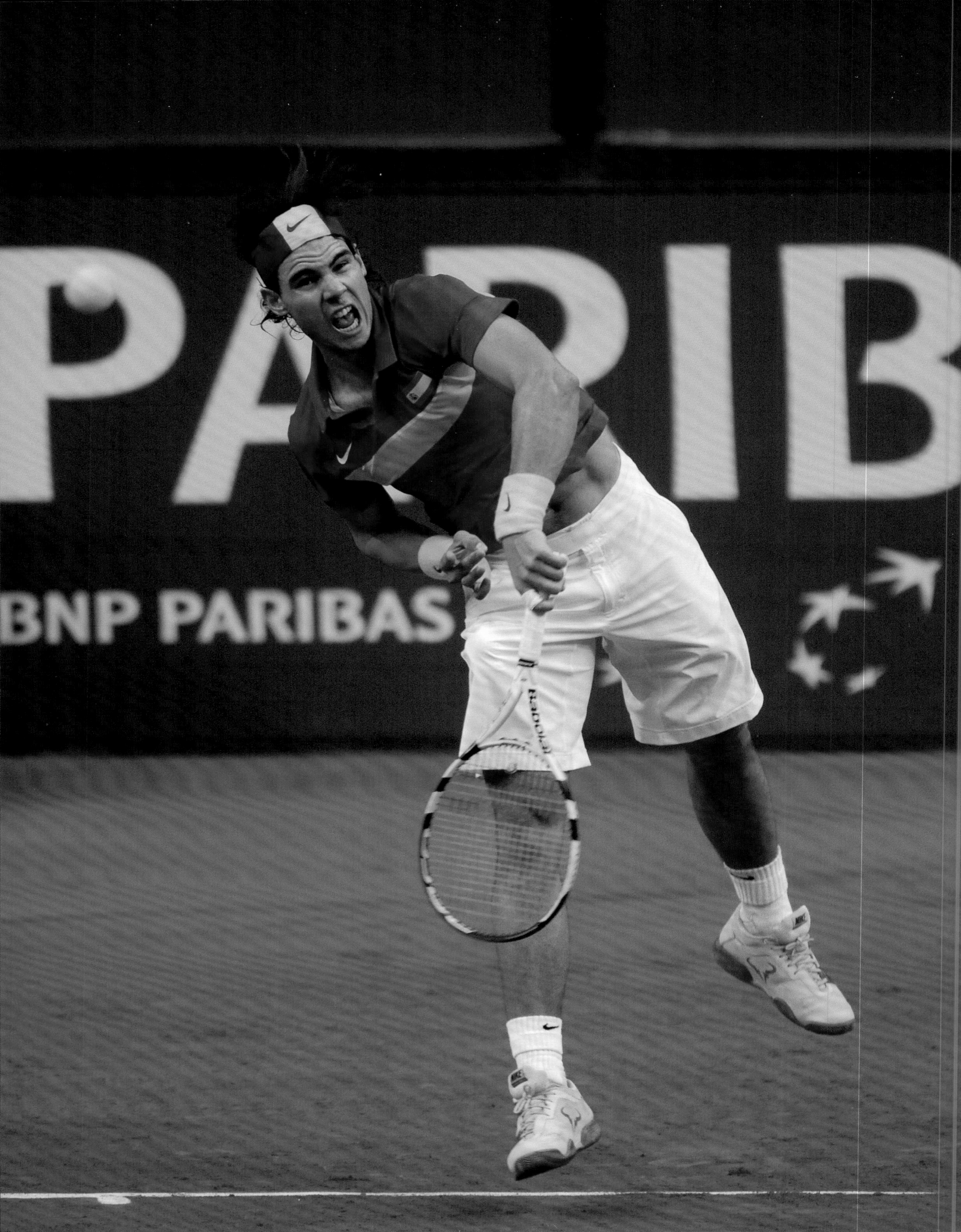
PARIB
BNP PARIBAS

BNP PARIBAS | The bank for a changing world

The love affair continues

According to the main criteria, the BNP Paribas group today ranks among the top ten banks in the world. BNP Paribas places its abilities and skills at the service of its clients in all of the countries in which it operates. It also places them at the service of its sports sponsorship. BNP Paribas has supported tennis since 1973, demonstrating its capacity to adapt through a policy based on a warm and dynamic partnership. The relationship between BNP Paribas and tennis is mutually beneficial. It has been developed with care and loyalty to the sport in order to attain a worldwide reputation that reflects the qualities of the group's work in the field of banking.

Sports sponsorship at the service of the brand

The BNP Paribas brand is a major asset for the company in its contact with people across all areas of its activity. In it they see a human quality, as it conveys emotional values and, above all, acts as a familiar landmark in an increasingly globalized environment. The BNP Paribas brand system is a means of reconciling a strong international image with a local relationship. BNP Paribas has now become a powerful, innovative, warm, and cohesive international brand. Tennis sponsorship is one of the springboards used to spread its influence.

Tennis sponsorship at the service of the international deployment of the brand

BNP Paribas has gradually developed its partnership mechanism to accompany all aspects of the tennis boom: professional, family, educational, and social. From the year 2000 on, the emphasis has been placed on developing tennis partnerships on an international basis in order to support the growth of the group's banking activities throughout the world. Thus sports sponsorship became the chosen means of supporting the development of the reputation of the BNP Paribas brand in countries where the group is established. This strategic choice initially took the form of Davis Cup sponsorship, which started in 2001. Step by step the structure was reinforced with support provided for the Monte Carlo Masters, the Internazionali BNL d'Italia in Rome, and most recently the BNP Paribas Open in Indian Wells.

In the same way, the Group's values and social commitments are reflected in the further development of its sponsorship program, which includes:

- Sponsorship of women's sport through Fed Cup by BNP Paribas, the Bank of the West Classic tournament in California (WTA Tour), and the Strasbourg Women's International Tennis tournament
- Support for the underprivileged youth through the "Fête le Mur" charity (created by Yannick Noah)
- Diversity through the Invacare World Team Cup and NEC Tour wheelchair events

Our commitment is one of the longest in the history of the sport, just like the relationship the bank aims to develop every day with its clients, based on trust and reciprocity.

We are proud to be the title partner of Davis Cup and hope you will enjoy reliving the great moments of 2009 in this yearbook. We would like to congratulate all the teams who took part in the competition and in particular the Spanish team for its tremendous back-to-back victory. See you in 2010!

7 Pébereau

Michel Pébereau
Chairman, BNP Paribas

Foreword

There is no question that for me it is an honor to represent my country. I have been fortunate to play for Spain at the Olympic Games and in Davis Cup and I also remember very well how I felt when I was part of the Spanish team that won the Junior Davis Cup in 2002.

While the crowds have become much bigger and my experience much wider, there is no better feeling than to share this kind of victory with your friends, with your team. I love the competition and I love team sports. We all know that tennis is an individual sport, and to play the Davis Cup allows us to play with that team spirit I miss on the regular tour.

Last year, when I was not able to play in the final in Argentina, I watched every point and I felt enormous pride because, even though I wasn't there, I was very much a part of the winning Spanish team, together with Feli, Fer, and Ferru over there in Argentina and Tommy and Nicolas who had also got the team to the final. This year, we were a team of six under new captain Albert Costa and we needed every member of our team to secure victory.

My first personal experience with Davis Cup was at the Palau Sant Jordi in 2000. At age fourteen, I was lucky enough to carry the flag behind Spain's first winning team. It was a big moment for Spain and for me personally because I understood the importance of this competition. I saw the Davis Cup trophy in person with the names of all the greatest players carved in its base. I saw the happiness of Juan Carlos Ferrero, Alex Corretja, Albert Costa, and Juan Balcells, who won the Davis Cup for the first time.

Four years later, I played for the first time against Czech Republic in Brno in the opening round. I lost that first match but happily I redeemed myself by winning against Radek Stepanek to put Spain on the road to the final. Ten months later, our team found itself playing the final against the United States before the largest crowd ever to watch a tennis match: 27,200 every day. It was amazing. And when Carlos Moya defeated Andy Roddick to make Spain the champion again, I cannot explain how I felt, just happiness and pride in my team and country.

This year, 2009, has been a difficult one for me. After a very good start, much of my season was affected by injury. While I am now healthy again, I can think of no better way to finish this year than to share a win like this with my team and captain: David, Feliciano, Fernando, Juan Carlos, Tommy, my captain Albert, and all the other people who make Davis Cup in Spain so special.

My congratulations also to the Czech team, who played well all year for their country. I know that they are disappointed but they should feel proud of their achievements.

I would also like to thank our fans in Spain who support the team so enthusiastically. They make everything special for us and I know we are all grateful to them. Their support is among the best I have ever felt on a tennis court, and you feel you are playing for them, for the whole country.

Davis Cup is a unique competition, founded to build friendships among nations. I feel that, on a personal level, it has also helped me to build friendships with both my team and my opponents and to give something back to my country, Spain.

Rafael Nadal

Spain, the ultimate team

Which moment in Catalonia best illustrated the togetherness and happy disposition of Spain's Davis Cup team? Was it the episode with a car on a Barcelona backstreet? Or was it at the Palau Sant Jordi, when the team's celebrations after winning the Davis Cup for the fourth time in a decade included giving bumps to Juan Carlos Ferrero, as a show of respect and thanks to a former world No. 1 who had not been selected in the four-man team for the final?

A couple of days before the final began on top of the Montjuic Hill, the Spanish team was being driven to dinner at a restaurant in the city when their vehicle had its route down a narrow backstreet blocked by a broken-down car. The two elderly gentlemen pushing the car were not making much progress, so the Spanish players all hopped out and volunteered to push the old banger down the road. The two old men stood there in astonishment as Rafael Nadal, Fernando Verdasco, David Ferrer, and Feliciano Lopez provided them with some emergency roadside assistance. Nadal and company did not consider calling for help from the team's security muscle; they got on with the job, shifted the car out of the way, and still made their dinner reservation.

On the second day of the tie, after Verdasco and Lopez won the doubles rubber against Czech Republic's Radek Stepanek and Tomas Berdych to give Spain an insurmountable 3–0 lead, the players gave bumps to their captain, Albert Costa, and to Ferrero. Though Ferrero did not feature at the "Palace of St. George," Spain would not have made it to the final if it had not been for Ferrero's contribution earlier in the season, when, playing in his first tie in four years, he won a decisive fifth rubber against Germany's Andreas Beck at the quarterfinal in Marbella. Ferrero had been thrilled when the crowd recognized his efforts by chanting his name during the final, but he was most touched by being flung high into the air by his friends, colleagues, and coaches.

In Barcelona, it was clear that the Spanish players saw each other as friends as well as teammates, and that Costa did not have to spend any of his time in Spain's second city massaging egos. Ferrero may not have been on the team, but he still came to Barcelona to watch. "We are all very good friends, and that counts for a lot," Nadal said. "And we always make ourselves available because we love representing Spain."

This was the year when Spain confirmed its status as the superpower of men's team tennis, when it became the first nation since Sweden in 1998 to win successive trophies.

Spain has an extraordinarily strong group of players to pick from. The week of the final, Spain had nine players inside the world's top 50. Just consider who did not play in Barcelona. Ferrero, the 2003 French Open champion, used to be regarded as the King of Clay and was at the top of the rankings. He was also the one who scored the point that gave Spain its first Davis Cup title, also at Palau Sant Jordi, when he beat Australia's Lleyton Hewitt. But he did not make the team for the final. Another top 25 player, Tommy Robredo, also did not make the team. Like Ferrero, though, Robredo was in Barcelona to support his countrymen. Another indication of Spain's strength in numbers came at Thursday's draw ceremony, when Costa disclosed that, though world No. 9 Verdasco had recovered from his injury, he would be rested from the opening singles rubbers. How many other countries have so much talent at their disposal that a top 10 player could be kept back for the doubles?

"It's not easy for me to choose who should play," said Costa. "We have so many good players, and they all deserve to be there."

Spain had Nadal only for the first round and the final. Nadal, who began the season as the world No. 1 and ended the year as the No. 2, missed the quarterfinal and semifinal ties through injury, but his country had not always needed him. Over the course of the year, six different players carried Spain to the final: Ferrer, Nadal, Verdasco, Robredo, Lopez, and

Ferrero. "I don't know exactly the secret," said Ferrer after Spain added to the titles it won in 2000, 2004, and 2008, proving that the team can win outside Olympic years. "But we are very good friends and we are fighters."

For much of the twentieth century, the grand slam nations of Great Britain, the United States, Australia, and France dominated the Davis Cup. In the twenty-first century, Spain has been the leading nation. At the turn of the millennium, Spain had yet to win the trophy, but after finally winning its first by beating Australia in the 2000 final in Barcelona, things happened quickly, and the team has since added three more. There were strong links between the 2000 and the 2009 titles. In 2000 Costa won the trophy as a player, and nine years later, he did so as a captain. Ferrero won the decisive point against Australia, and received bumps in 2009. And Nadal, who played such terrific tennis in 2009, carried the flag for Spain in 2000 during the opening ceremonies.

Yes, Spain had the good fortune to play all four ties at home in 2009—a first-round tie against Serbia in Benidorm, the quarterfinal against Germany in Marbella, the semifinal against Israel in Murcia, and then the final against the Czech Republic in Barcelona. Spain's victory in Barcelona extended its winning run to eighteen ties at home, matching the United States for the competition's record, and also took its undefeated spell on clay to twenty ties. Spain's last defeat on "la tierra batida,"—and also its last defeat at home—was when it lost a World Group first round tie to Brazil in Lerida in 1999. But before anyone suggests that Spain's domination of the Davis Cup has only been possible because of the kindness shown by Lady Luck, they should be reminded of how the Spanish won the trophy in 2008, with a victory in front of a vocal Argentine crowd, on an indoor hard court in Mar del Plata, and at a time when Nadal was unavailable because of a knee injury. Few had predicted that Spain would defeat an Argentine team that included David Nalbandian and Juan Martin del Potro.

If Spain's victory in Barcelona did not shock tennis, there were a few surprise results in the 2009 World Group, with Israel reaching the semifinals for the first time, and the Czech Republic reaching its first final since Ivan Lendl's Czechoslovakia was the champion in 1980. In 2009 Stepanek led the Czech effort. And though Stepanek lost both his matches in Barcelona, with defeat in a singles and a doubles rubber, and Spain became the first country in twelve years to win all five rubbers at a Davis Cup final, he was rightly proud of his efforts over the course of the year. To reach the final, Stepanek's Czech Republic beat France, the 2008 runner-up Argentina, and then Croatia. In Croatia, Stepanek won an astonishing six-hour singles match against Ivo Karlovic, despite his opponent serving a world-record seventy-eight aces. It did not feel at all strange that the Czechs were celebrating after winning just two sets all weekend. This was Stepanek's year as much as anyone's. Both sets of players congratulated one another for what they had accomplished in 2009.

"To win the Davis Cup four times in a decade just says everything," said Stepanek after Spain had sealed the tie. "In Spain, they have a huge amount of players and tennis centers, and there's always someone coming up. The toughness and the team is so strong that you could even build a second team almost as strong."

Though Spain will begin the defense of its title with a first-round tie at home to Roger Federer's Switzerland, perhaps the team can win a third successive title. "There are no limits to what this team can achieve," said Costa. "They're young, there's a great atmosphere in the camp, and they are committed. If they maintain their motivation there could be many more Davis Cups on the way." Motivation is unlikely to be a problem. Verdasco is already hoping to win more. "The goal now is just to keep on winning Davis Cups," Verdasco said. "The more the better." ●

First Round 6–8 March

Spain defeated Serbia 4–1   BENIDORM, SPAIN—OUTDOOR CLAY

Czech Republic defeated France 3–2   OSTRAVA, CZECH REPUBLIC—INDOOR CARPET

USA defeated Switzerland 4–1   BIRMINGHAM ALABAMA, USA—INDOOR HARD

Croatia defeated Chile 5–0   POREC, CROATIA—INDOOR HARD

Russia defeated Romania 4–1   SIBIU, ROMANIA—INDOOR CARPET

Germany defeated Austria 3–2   GARMISCH-PARTENKIRCHEN, GERMANY—INDOOR HARD

Israel defeated Sweden 3–2   MALMO, SWEDEN—INDOOR CARPET

Argentina defeated Netherlands 5–0   BUENOS AIRES, ARGENTINA—OUTDOOR CLAY

Introduction

The truism that a new season of Davis Cup competition brings with it the possibility of a fresh start could not have been better illustrated than by the return to Argentina's team for Lucas Arnold Ker, the doubles player who, having survived testicular cancer and the apparent end of his marriage, was selected to represent his country for the first time in five years.

In fact, Arnold Ker's selection was one of four changes to Argentina's team sheet; there was not one player in the line-up for the first round tie who had featured in the 2008 final. The previous November, the South Americans had turned up in Mar del Plata to play Spain for the trophy, with the apparent belief that they were destined to win. In 2009 the hope was that everything would be different. The new-look team was not entirely out of choice, because of pull-outs, but there was a new captain on the bench, plus a determination that Argentine tennis "politics" would not intrude on the court.

That was in Buenos Aires for a tie against the Netherlands, but several thousands of miles to the east, in the Spanish coastal resort of Benidorm, the Spanish team was about to begin the defense of the Davis Cup with the best player back on court. In 2008 they had done it without Rafael Nadal in the final, but for the start of their 2009 campaign, the Mallorcan was eager to demonstrate his value to the team. He was going to have to do it against Novak Djokovic's Serbia in a highly anticipated tie between the world No. 1 and the world No. 3.

What was deeply unfortunate about the opening weekend was that much of the buildup did not focus on the players, but on the news that Sweden's tie against Israel was going to be contested in front of row after row of empty seats. The politicians in Malmo had made the controversial decision for the tie to be played in an empty stadium, as they were concerned about the anti-Israel protests that were planned in the city so soon after the conflict in Gaza. By the Sunday evening, that decision looked all the more unfortunate. Surely this would not be the only tie decided by the fifth set of the fifth rubber?

Spain v Serbia

Spain's defense of the Davis Cup title started in a theme park near Benidorm, the resort on the Costa Blanca. A temporary clay court had been built on a car park in the Parque Tematico Terra Mitica, which literally translates into English as the "Theme Park of the Mythical Land." As soon as the Spanish Tennis Federation decided that the team, who had lifted the "La Ensaladera" in 2008, were going to open up their 2009 season by playing Serbia in a mythical theme park, it only reinforced the feeling that it was going to be a memorable Davis Cup weekend.

So it proved, as a couple of newsworthy things happened up in the limestone hills above Benidorm. The first was when high winds damaged the temporary stadium, delaying the start of the tie by a day, and the second was the quality of tennis that Rafael Nadal produced. Call that Hurricane Rafa.

The popular view of Benidorm is of a holiday destination where the sun shines almost every day, and yet a few dollops of SPF 30 would not have protected you from the weather—hard hats were

Pictured clockwise from top left:

Janko Tipsarevic (SRB);

Victory for Spain;

Feliciano Lopez (ESP)

needed. On Thursday afternoon and evening, the Costa Blanca was hit by high winds, with some gusts measuring 55mph. The winds ripped off the gangway that had been attached to a yacht moored in Benidorm and also caused considerable damage to the temporary stadium that had been put together from scratch, and with a scaffolding base. The worst damage was to the upper tiers. Many of the seats were whipped off by the wind and smashed into bits after landing on the ground.

Once the site had been inspected by engineers, it was decided that it would be unsafe to start the tie on Friday. The fine weather on Friday afternoon—the sun was out and the winds had dropped to a gentle breeze—allowed the engineers to make the necessary repairs, and it was agreed that the tie could start on Saturday, some twenty-three hours later than planned.

What made the delay all the more frustrating for the Spanish tennis public was that they were keen to watch Nadal back on court for his country again. Although Spain had beaten Argentina in Mar del Plata in the 2008 final, they had done so without an injured Nadal, whose only direct involvement was sending text messages of encouragement to those on the bench before Fernando Verdasco handed Spain the winning point. Nadal had helped his country into that final. Spain also had a new captain, Albert Costa, who had replaced Emilio Sanchez, but the main focus was naturally the return of Rafa.

Nadal is arguably the greatest player of all time on clay, so it made perfect sense to put down a clay court to play Serbia. There was little doubt that, of all the eight first-round ties, the one that promised the most exciting tennis was Spain against Serbia, as it would involve two of the world's top three players: world No. 1 Nadal and third-ranked Novak Djokovic. Nadal, the reigning champion at Roland Garros and the undisputed King of Clay, would be making his first appearance on the beaten earth for six months, since Spain beat the United States in the 2008 semifinals of the Davis Cup. Djokovic, meanwhile, had not played on the surface for nine months, when he lost to Nadal in the semifinals of 2008 Roland Garros.

If Serbia were to beat Spain, then Djokovic was probably going to have to start things off by beating David Ferrer in the opening rubber. That didn't happen. In fact, Djokovic didn't even win a set, losing 6–3 6–3 7–6(4) to Ferrer, and afterward he suggested that sliding around a clay court had made it feel as though he was "on foreign territory." Like someone riding a rollercoaster, Djokovic had his senses scrambled at the theme park.

Of course, it did not take much time for Nadal to get back into the clay court swing and pulverize Janko Tipsarevic, losing just three games as he beat his unfortunate opponent 6–1 6–0 6–2. Perhaps Nadal's brilliance was due in part to pent-up energy, having had to wait an extra day before he was swinging away

Pictured above from left:

Viktor Troicki (SRB), left,

and Nenad Zimonjic (SRB);

Novak Djokovic (SRB)

Pictured below:

Packed stands in Benidorm

Pictured opposite from top:

Spanish captain Albert Costa

and Rafael Nadal (ESP);

Spanish supporters

for his country again. Tipsarevic simply had no response to Nadal's energy. To think that there had been some concerns about Nadal's health before the tie; he had limped around on one leg when he lost the Rotterdam final to Andy Murray the month before, and had then decided to drop the event in Dubai from his schedule. Put Nadal back on a clay court, back on the granules, and suddenly he is at his potent best again.

Afterward, Tipsarevic grumbled about the quality of the surface, complaining that it had been more like "a beach" than a clay court, but his comment was irrelevant. They could have played this on the finest clay court known to man, and Nadal, in that sort of form, would still have won in straight sets.

Still, the tie was not all over inside a day, as Viktor Troicki and Nenad Zimonjic won a point in the doubles on Saturday, with a 7–6(5) 6–4 7–6(7) victory over Feliciano Lopez and Tommy Robredo, who was back in the team in the absence of an injured Verdasco. Djokovic had originally been down to play in the doubles but opted against playing two matches in a day, knowing that he was going to have to face Nadal the next morning.

The rest did not do Djokovic that much good. Nadal soon ended any doubt as to which nation would go through to the quarterfinals, as he was in such command over Djokovic that he beat him 6–4 6–4 6–1. A weekend in Benidorm had brought contrasting experiences for the world No. 1 and the world No. 3:

Nadal had dropped only twelve games over his six sets. Djokovic had lost all six sets he played.

In the dead rubber, Ferrer beat Troicki 6–0 6–3, but this weekend, once the weather had had its say, belonged to Nadal. Anyone who lives on the Costa Blanca must have grown used to the sight of European men staggering around in the middle of the afternoon, but that is usually because of San Miguel or sangria. Over this weekend, the mid-afternoon staggering and stumbling was all because of a tennis player. The Serbians were intoxicated by the power and the class of Rafael Nadal. ●

Czech Republic v France

Before the French team began its first-round tie against the Czech Republic, captain Guy Forget played a dangerous game when he suggested that his modern generation was the best unit since the "Four Musketeers". Henri Cochet, Rene Lacoste, Jean Borotra and Jacques Brugnon ruled the competition from 1927 until 1933, in what was the golden era of French tennis.

Forget assembled the young quartet of Gilles Simon, Jo-Wilfried Tsonga, Gael Monfils, and Richard Gasquet in Ostrava, the first time the foursome had been selected together, and at the time, each was either a top 10 player or a former top 10 player. "Apart from perhaps the Musketeers, we've never had such a strong French team on paper in our history," said Forget. And he was not alone in talking up the Fab Four, as prior to the 2008 Paris Masters, the French sports newspaper L'Equipe had reached for the dressing-up box, putting the four in 1920s-style clothes, and describing them as the "New Musketeers."

Sadly for Forget, and everyone on the French tennis scene, the tie was not played "on paper"; it was played on an indoor carpet court in the Czech city of Ostrava at the CEZ Arena, birthplace of Ivan Lendl. The champagne bottles were pushed to the back of French fridges as the victory celebrations were instead enjoyed by the Czechs, with Radek Stepanek getting down on the court to gyrate and perform his signature "worm dance."

There were some unfortunate statistics that could not be avoided post-defeat. Having reached the quarterfinals or beyond for the previous eight years, France saw that sequence come to an end in Ostrava and had yet to win a tie on Czech soil since the Musketeers did so in Prague in 1926.

In the end, one of the four modern-day Musketeers did not even make it on court. Monfils arrived in Ostrava from Acapulco in Mexico, where he had reached the final of a clay court tournament, so he was going to have to deal with the long journey, a different time zone, and a different surface if he was going to make his first appearance in the Davis Cup. Forget decided against playing Monfils, instead opting for Simon and Tsonga as his singles players and Gasquet and Michael Llodra, who also traveled, as his doubles team.

For all the talk of a new golden age of French tennis, there was no disguising the fact that Simon did not have much by way of experience in the Davis Cup. In fact, his match against Tomas Berdych both opened the tie and opened his career in the team competition. This was another of those occasions that showed that the emotional and mental demands of playing for your country are very different from the workaday pressures of competing for yourself on the solo tour.

Simon appeared nervous in the opening stages and lost the first set, and although he later leveled the rubber at a set apiece, he was beaten in four sets,

with Berdych winning 7–6(3) 4–6 7–6(3) 6–3 to put his country ahead. Simon had earlier suggested that "playing the Davis Cup is like playing any other big match." Not quite, Gilles.

And Tsonga was not exactly a grizzly old veteran of the competition either, as before this tie he had only made one previous appearance in the Davis Cup, when he beat Romania's Andrei Pavel during the first round tie in 2008. But his second match in the competition went well for the Frenchman, who beat Stepanek in straight sets, 7–5 6–2 7–6(1). "It was good to win for the team and for Gilles Simon," said Tsonga. "I know what it's like to play a first Davis Cup match and I wanted to give him a second chance." By that, Tsonga meant that he had ensured that the tie would still be alive in Sunday's fourth rubber, when Simon would be due for another go at Davis Cup tennis.

Pictured above from top:
Gilles Simon (FRA); Czech fans;
Michael Llodra and Richard Gasquet
(FRA) with captain Guy Forget
Pictured opposite from top:
Radek Stepanek (CZE) and
captain Jaroslav Navratil;
The French cheer on their teammates

Stepanek combined with Berdych in Saturday's doubles rubber for a 6–3 1–6 6–4 6–2 victory against Gasquet and Llodra, which meant that the next day, Simon was going to have to beat Stepanek if the New Musketeers were to stay in the tie. Unfortunately for Simon, there were times against Stepanek when he appeared to be more nervous than he had been against Berdych. Again, the 7,500 Czech supporters got into Simon's head, just where Forget did not want them to be. Stepanek put the pressure on the Frenchman: "He needed to win, so I needed to give him even more pressure with my game. So I was changing the rhythm, coming to the net, hitting big returns, making him feel I'm not scared to do anything."

Stepanek managed to frighten Simon into defeat, and when he finished off his 7–6(2) 6–3 7–6(0) win to give the Czech team an unassailable 3–1 lead, his trademark worm dance was a certainty. He was then joined on court by his teammates, who were given a standing ovation.

It was a weekend to remember for Simon, and for all the wrong reasons. "You should never forget a weekend like the one I just had," said Simon. "You need to ask yourself the right questions in order to be ready for a similar situation in the future." In the fifth dead rubber, Tsonga beat Jan Hernych 6–2 6–7(5) 7–6(0), but by then it was all too late for French ambitions in the 2009 World Group. "It's an amazing feeling to steal three points from the French team," said Stepanek. "They have such a talented team." Yes, they are talented, but it was too early for Forget and others to have likened them to the original Musketeers. ●

Pictured from top:

Flags adorn the stadium in Birmingham;

Tomas Berdych (CZE);

Andy Roddick (USA)

Pictured opposite from top:

Gilles Simon (FRA);

Radek Stepanek (CZE)

USA v Switzerland

To borrow from the lexicon of American high school movies, Andy Roddick has always seemed like so much more of a jock than a nerd. And yet there are some occasions when Roddick just cannot control his inner-nerd. When Roddick turned up in Birmingham, Alabama, his main goal was to ensure that the United States defeated Switzerland to reach the quarterfinals, but he also knew that he would have the opportunity at the tie to move into second place

on the list of America's most successful players of all time.

On arrival, Roddick had twenty-nine Davis Cup victories, his win on the first day of the tie put him level with Andre Agassi at thirty, and another success on the third day gave the United States a place in the quarterfinals and took him to thirty-one, second place on the all-time list. Only John McEnroe, with forty-one wins, is ahead of the Nerd from Nebraska.

Not that anyone needed to tell Roddick any of that; he already knew. "I'm kind of a nerd about the history of our sport," said Roddick. "That was kind of in the back of my mind."

Roddick is a former world No. 1 and a former grand slam champion, having won the US Open in 2003, but in years to come he is just as likely to be remembered for what he did for the Davis Cup team as what he achieved during his solo career. Roddick's end-of-career highlights reel is going to contain plenty of moments from the Davis Cup, particularly when the United States won the trophy in 2007.

Surpassing Agassi on the list was hugely significant for Roddick, who had grown up watching Mr. Las Vegas play in the competition. "There are probably a few moments in your career when you can sit back and be a little impressed. It's great to get mentioned with Andre, he was always the guy that everyone leaned on to come through. To kind of surpass him now is extremely surreal, but it's definitely one of those fun moments."

Of course, Roddick was helped by the fact that Roger Federer could not make it to Alabama, largely in part to his hapless 2–16 career head-to-head record against the Swiss. Federer had previously committed to being there but was unable to make it because of a sore back. So without the world No. 2, Switzerland's two singles players were Stanislas Wawrinka and Marco Chiudinelli.

The only rubber that Switzerland won at the Birmingham-Jefferson Convention Complex Arena was the first of the tie, with Wawrinka beating James Blake 3–6 6–4 6–3 7–6(3). Then Roddick leveled the tie with a 6–1 6–3 7–6(5) victory over Chiudinelli, helped by the might of his serve and his forehand, but also the noise of the crowd.

Roddick felt that the spectators could unnerve the Swiss. "I thought the crowd could be important. I even said to our guys in the locker room before the match that it was their job on the bench to get everyone enthused and not to be scared of making eye contact with people and getting them pumped up. Marco plays a lot of tennis but maybe not in that sort of atmosphere. In Davis Cup, the crowd is there to be utilized, and I thought that was maybe a factor," said Roddick. With the power of his racket-arm, and the decibels from the stands, he was suddenly level with Agassi on thirty wins, which was definitely "a wow moment."

A couple of days before the tie began, the home team had had a "wow moment" after the official dinner when, on the way back to the hotel and still feeling hungry, they asked the driver to pull in at a waffle house. Their waitress, who was wearing a nametag introducing her as "The Old Goat," entertained the players and captain Patrick McEnroe by rapping at the table. The performance was filmed, and there was talk of the players uploading the footage on to YouTube, the video-sharing website.

The players weren't so shabby in front of the cameras either, and the Bryan brothers, Mike and Bob, gave another racket-swinging, chest-bumping display of their control on a doubles court, when the identical twins beat Wawrinka and Yves Allegro 6–3 6–4 3–6 7–6(2) on the Saturday. The United States has never had a more successful doubles team, as this took the Bryans' record to fifteen wins from seventeen appearances together.

Their victory also set up Roddick to finish off the tie—a position in which Roddick is at his most reliable. When he went onto the hard court, it was the eleventh time in his Davis Cup career that he had been given the opportunity to clinch a tie for his country. And when he walked off the court, he had beaten Wawrinka 6–4 6–4 6–2.

That statistic is arguably more impressive than moving into second place on the American list of most career wins in the competition. "I think I've simplified the way I look at it. Regardless of what the score is, my job is to come in and try to get a point," said Roddick. "But when you pass someone like Andre Agassi on an all-time list, especially in Davis Cup, it's humbling." ●

Croatia v Chile

When the Chilean team arrived in Croatia, it was with the knowledge that their country had not won a tie in Europe since 1967. It almost goes without saying that no one on the Chilean team had been born then, so to hear about how the nation's last success on a European court had been when their predecessors had beaten the Greeks in Greece forty-two years earlier, well, that must have sounded like ancient history.

Even so, the Croatians at home on a fast surface were going to be tricky opponents, and that prospect became even more complex with the unfortunate news that Fernando Gonzalez, a former Australian Open finalist and Chile's highest-ranked player by some distance, could not play because of injury. Despite this, the South Americans traveled to Croatia trying to believe that anything was possible in Europe.

But the Chilean optimism—or should that be wishful thinking—came to nothing, as they were soundly beaten at the Zatika Sports Hall, a new facility in the old town. In fact, the tie could hardly have been more one-sided; but for one dropped set, the Croatians would have achieved a whitewash.

On the opening day, Croatia won the two singles rubbers without anything so traumatic as losing a set, although it did get a little chancy when one of the sets went to a tiebreak. The day after, Croatia dropped

a set in the doubles but still won another three sets to achieve an unassailable 3–0 lead. The dead singles rubbers went the same way as the live ones, with Croatia winning both in straight sets.

So Chile did not even come close to achieving a win in Europe, with the tie instead bringing what must have been Croatia's easiest-ever success in the World Group, which handed the 2005 champion a place in the quarterfinals for the first time in three years. The Croatians, gentlemen that they are, would not admit that it had been easy, with captain Goran Prpic saying that "sometimes it's hard to win relatively easily something you should, or must win, on paper. The result may have looked easy, but it was not always like that on the court," he said.

Marin Cilic and Mario Ancic, the Croatian giants, were simply too strong, too powerful, and too classy for the Chileans. Cilic stands at six feet, six inches in his socks, Ancic is only an inch shorter, and for one of the dead rubbers, Croatia was able to call upon Ivo Karlovic, who is six feet, ten inches and somehow looks even taller.

However, it was not just a height advantage that Croatia had over Chile. Cilic also turned up in the Roman town on a strong run of form—although it was only early March, he had already won two titles on the tour, in Chennai and Zagreb. Ancic's season had not

Pictured above:

Chilean captain Hans Gildemeister

Pictured below from left:

Paul Capdeville (CHI);

Mario Ancic (CRO) signs autographs

Pictured opposite from top:

Nicolas Massu (CHI); Marin Cilic (CRO),

left, and Mario Ancic (CRO)

been too ropey either: he had been Cilic's opponent in the Zagreb final, and he had reached the semifinals in Rotterdam, losing to Britain's Andy Murray. After all the problems that Ancic has had with his health in recent times—he had glandular fever—anyone connected with Croatian tennis must be pleased whenever he is able to take to the court.

The Chilean players had not had anything like those sort of results. In fact, Nicolas Massu, a former Olympic gold medalist at the 2004 Athens Games and once ranked in the top 10, came into the tie without a match to his name all season. Massu had lost in the first round of the qualifying competition for the tournament in Auckland, in the first round of the main draw of the Australian Open, and then in events in Vina del Mar, Costa Do Sauipe, and Buenos Aires. Thousands of air miles, and no wins to show for it.

As for Paul Capdeville, he came into the tie having lost in the opening round of his two preceding tournaments in Costa Do Sauipe and Delray Beach. The opening day of the tie would see him play his first live rubber in the competition, and although he had made nine previous appearances in the competition, he was the King of the Dead Rubbers. Gonzalez's injury meant that Capdeville was finally going live.

One of the attractions of the Davis Cup has always been that form on the solo rankings tour does not always mean that a player will turn in a good performance for his country. The Davis Cup can energize a player, but it can unnerve him too. That was what Hans Gildemeister, the Chilean captain, was hoping for. "Many things can happen in the Davis Cup—history has shown that everything is possible. Now, with Gonzalez out of the tie, Croatia is a slight favorite," said Gildemeister. He should have held the "slight."

Massu, hoping to get his season going by the seaside, never looked as though he was going to beat Ancic, the Croatian winning 6–3 6–3 7–6(4). The quality of Ancic's serve was such that he dropped only five points on his delivery in the first two sets, adding later that he "played extremely well, almost without a fault."

Next, Cilic recorded his first victory in a live singles rubber when he lost just four games against Capdeville, taking just over an hour and a half to beat

him 6–1 6–2 6–1. Cilic had lost his first three live singles against Argentina's David Nalbandian, to Murray when they played Britain, and opposite Italy's Andreas Seppi. This time, he recorded the easiest win, in terms of games lost, by a Croatian in the World Group. In fact, the main inconvenience for Cilic at the indoor hall was not Capdeville, but the fact that he had a nosebleed. "It was not very pleasant," Cilic said. "But it was not a great problem. I managed to keep it under control. It started in the morning and continued during the match, but it was not a big deal."

The same four players who had featured in Friday's singles matches were involved in the doubles rubber on the Saturday, with Ancic and Cilic registering a 6–3 6–3 3–6 6–4 victory over Massu and Capdeville. Croatia was the first nation into the quarterfinals, but for the Chileans, there was to be no repeat of what happened in 1967, a victory on European soil. ●

Pictured above from top:
Croatia wins the doubles;
Nicolas Massu (CHI)
Pictured opposite:
Mario Ancic (CRO)

Romania v Russia

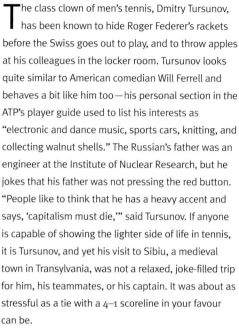

The class clown of men's tennis, Dmitry Tursunov, has been known to hide Roger Federer's rackets before the Swiss goes out to play, and to throw apples at his colleagues in the locker room. Tursunov looks quite similar to American comedian Will Ferrell and behaves a bit like him too—his personal section in the ATP's player guide used to list his interests as "electronic and dance music, sports cars, knitting, and collecting walnut shells." The Russian's father was an engineer at the Institute of Nuclear Research, but he jokes that his father was not pressing the red button. "People like to think that he has a heavy accent and says, 'capitalism must die,'" said Tursunov. If anyone is capable of showing the lighter side of life in tennis, it is Tursunov, and yet his visit to Sibiu, a medieval town in Transylvania, was not a relaxed, joke-filled trip for him, his teammates, or his captain. It was about as stressful as a tie with a 4–1 scoreline in your favour can be.

Tursunov had his game face on. He was involved in two extremely tense matches over the weekend. Both involved a comeback from two sets down, and both astounded the Russian bench, the Romanian bench, and everyone else inside the Sala Transilvania. Tursunov lost one of them and won the other. After two matches like that he would have needed a long lie down, to rest his nerves as well as his body.

Although Russia went into the tie as the No. 1 nation in the Davis Cup rankings and was therefore expected to beat Romania, the visitors were not helped by the absence of their leading player and someone noted for his consistency of shot. Nikolay Davydenko was unavailable because of a foot injury, the same problem that had prevented him from playing in the Australian Open. With Mr. Consistency missing, captain Shamil Tarpischev used three players for the live rubbers who could all be a little on the unpredictable side.

Marat Safin is a former world No. 1, but last year he was still up there as the best on the planet when it came to erratic tennis; he is capable of going from brilliant to terrible in the time it takes to say, "racket abuse, warning, Mr. Safin." Youzhny can be unpredictable on a court, too. He famously came from two sets down against France's Paul-Henri Mathieu in the fifth rubber of the 2002 Davis Cup final, and in 2008, he was must-see viewing on YouTube when he cracked a racket against his own head at the tournament in Miami, causing blood to run down his face. And Tursunov is not exactly Mr. Ordinary either—he has likened his powerful, erratic game to being the trigger-happy owner of a machine gun. When the bullets go in, there is not much that his opponent can do about it, but when the bullets fly out, they can look

like terrible misses. Whatever happens, he just carries on pulling the trigger.

Whatever Russia was expected to do, Tarpischev had an unpredictable set of players out there on the court. This was quite a tie for the Russians, but also for the Romanians, who had a new captain in Andrei Pavel.

Tursunov was not involved on the opening day, still unaware of what was to come. It was Safin who appeared first for the Russians, and the former US Open and Australian Open champion gave his country the first point with a 7–6(5) 6–4 6–4 victory over Victor Crivoi. Youzhny collected the second singles rubber when he won 6–4 6–2 6–4, with Victor Hanescu unable to play at the level that had been expected of him by the home crowd. So on the Friday night, the Russians with their 2–0 lead looked extremely well placed to advance into the quarterfinals.

But then the match changed. Suddenly, Copil and Tecau found confidence and composure. The encouragement of the crowd had helped Copil to play his way into the match. The Romanians won a couple of tiebreaks to level the rubber, and then in the decider it was Copil who served out the match, even closing out the contest, which had lasted more than four hours, with an ace. The Copil who finished the rubber was unrecognizable from the Copil who started it. "I must admit that I was very, very nervous before the match," said Copil after their 4–6 6–7(2) 7–6(4) 7–6(5) 6–4 victory. "But gradually I was able to overcome my nerves, and in the end I felt very confident." Tecau thought that match had been "just unbelievable." It was all extremely unfortunate for Tarpischev, who turned sixty-one on the day of Romania's comeback from two sets down.

Pictured below from left:

Horia Tecau (ROU), left, and Marius Copil (ROU);

Dmitry Tursunov (RUS)

And they appeared to be in even better shape the next day, with Safin and Tursunov taking a two-set lead against Marius Copil and Horia Tecau, who had a combined doubles ranking of 733. Copil, an eighteen-year-old rookie, was extremely nervous as he played for his country for the first time. On the other side of the net, Safin and Tursunov were an established, experienced pairing, and almost everyone at the tennis in Transylvania must have thought that Russia was just one more set away from an unassailable 3–0 lead, winning the three rubbers without dropping a set.

The momentum of the tie had turned Romania's way, that was for sure, and it was Hanescu who started well in the first of the reverse singles rubbers on the Sunday. He was two sets up against Tursunov, who had been brought in as a substitute for Safin. Tursunov, although famed for his risk-taking, attacking game, was being too timid with his shots. The man who sometimes goes for too much wasn't going for enough, he was being too passive, too diffident, and Hanescu, who was playing considerably better than he had on Friday, was in control. Perhaps Tursunov was still

Pictured above from left:

Victor Crivoi (ROU);

Mikhail Youzhny (RUS)

Pictured right:

Romanian fans

affected by what had happened on the doubles court, as he had now lost five sets in succession. Still, Tursunov showed that what Romania had done to him on Saturday, he could do back to them on Sunday.

With Romania threatening to take the tie to a decisive fifth rubber, Tursunov believed that he had been thinking too much. Tursunov was agitated with the crowd, asking them not to move around during the points. Tarpischev paced up and down between points. The Romanians were getting inside the Russians' heads. Hanescu went a break up in the third set.

The way forward for Tursunov was to "stop thinking so much," to swing through his shots more.

With Hanescu beginning to suffer physically because of a cold, and with Tursunov smashing some big forehands at him, the tie had its second turnaround in two days. Tursunov, no longer inhibited with his stroke play, won 4–6 5–7 6–3 6–4 6–2, and Russia had a 3–1 lead that took them into the quarterfinals.

But it had not been that comfortable for the Russians, and for Tursunov in particular. Comebacks from two sets down don't happen that often, so for him to have played two matches in two days that featured turnarounds of that magnitude was quite extraordinary. "I was making far too many errors in the first two sets against Hanescu," Tursunov said. "But after falling two sets behind I was able to calm myself down and as a result started playing much better. In the fifth set I saw he was tired so I tried to put more pressure on him and it worked."

Tarpischev's team was through. The captain said, "A lot of people kept calling us big favorites against this Romanian team but I knew it wouldn't be easy. Even after we won both singles rubbers on Friday I said the tie is not over just yet. I guess some of our guys just didn't listen. Of course, I would have liked to have finished it on Saturday so I wouldn't have to sweat it out on the bench on Sunday. But I'll take it. In the end, Tursunov proved me right." ●

Pictured clockwise from top left:

Jurgen Melzer (AUT);

Christopher Kas (GER);

Philipp Kohlschreiber (GER)

Pictured opposite:

Nicolas Kiefer (GER)

Germany v Austria

A Bavarian town on the German-Austrian border, Garmisch-Partenkirchen is best known for its snow and mountains. Having hosted the 1936 Winter Olympics, it is now a popular ski resort. In early March, you are more likely to hear visitors to Garmisch talking about black runs, bindings, and goggles misting up than to catch conversations about string tensions, first-serve percentages, and cross-court forehands. But it was there, in the ski resort, that the German Tennis Federation took the first-round tie against Austria, the first meeting with their neighbors for fifteen years. It was also there that Germany's Nicolas Kiefer, making his return from a two-month absence caused by a freak injury to his ankle, finished off the tie.

With the tie played on the border, it was easy for Austrian fans to travel to the tennis, and there were a fair number of them inside the Olympia Eissportzentrum over the three days. Even so, this all-Teutonic rivalry remained frustratingly one-sided for the Austrian supporters, as Germany extended its unbeaten record to five victories from five ties against Austria, having also won in 1932, 1937, 1971, and 1994.

And while Germany advanced to the quarterfinals to play Spain for the second year in succession,

Austria had the familiar feeling of losing in the first round. This was the sixth season in a row that they had lost their opener in the elite World Group, meaning that their next appointment would be in September's play-offs, to keep their status at the top table. "We're used to it by now," Jurgen Melzer said after Austria was again unable to progress on a World Group drawsheet.

It was Kiefer, the former world No. 4, who took center stage in the ski resort, giving Germany an unassailable 3–1 lead when he achieved a straight-sets victory over Melzer on the third and final day. What made it all the more satisfying for Kiefer was that he had had an extremely unfortunate start to the 2009 season. During an appearance at the Hopman Cup exhibition in Perth, he suddenly collapsed into a crumpled heap after sustaining a double ligament rupture to his ankle and then left the court in a wheelchair. The injury prevented Kiefer from competing at the opening grand slam of the season, the Australian Open, and he did not play any tennis on the tour in January and February.

So when Kiefer turned up in the mountains he had no form to go on. Even so, the Austrian captain, Gilbert Schaller, was a little surprised that Kiefer was not chosen for the opening day's singles rubbers. German captain Patrick Kuhnen instead put forward Rainer Schuettler and Philipp Kohlschreiber as his two nominations.

Schuettler, a surprise semifinalist at the 2008 Wimbledon Championships, had not appeared in the Davis Cup since playing a dead rubber in the first-round defeat to France in 2006. Koubek sounded pleased when he learned that he would open the tie against Schuettler, ranked 224 places above him, suggesting that his opponent "doesn't have a strong serve and won't kill me from the baseline." The Austrian's pre-match confidence proved worthwhile as he came through to win 6–4 7–5 5–7 6–2 and put his country a point up. Schuettler took a while to get going, and by the time he did, it was too late: "I overslept in the first two sets. The start was terrible. This is bitter." An emotional Koubek collapsed onto the court in delight.

It later seemed as though Austria was on the way to finishing the day 2–0 up, with Melzer winning the first two sets against Kohlschreiber and having his chances in the third set too. But Kohlschreiber came back to win 6–7(4) 4–6 6–4 6–3 6–3 after almost four hours of tennis, leaving him "exhausted but happy" and the countries level after day one. "That's Davis Cup," Kohlschreiber said, having recovered from two sets down for the first time in his career. "It's all about fighting, fighting, fighting."

In the doubles rubber, Kiefer played his first competitive tennis of the season, partnering Kohlschreiber to a 6–3 7–6(6) 3–6 6–4 victory over Julian Knowle and Alexander Peya. Kiefer was pleased for the team and pleased for himself for coming through the match. Despite what had happened to his ankle in Australia, Kiefer moved well around the court in Bavaria. "It was a very good win for me and for the team," said Kiefer. Having played no proper tennis all year until that doubles win, Kiefer was then asked to play two matches in two days, replacing Schuettler in the first of the reverse singles rubbers. Kiefer achieved a 7–6(3) 6–4 6–4 victory over Melzer, maintaining his perfect 8–0 record against the Austrian and ensuring that Germany also maintained a perfect record against Austria.

It was as if Kiefer had never been away; his comeback weekend could hardly have been better. "That was overwhelming, one of the best weekends of my career," said Kiefer. "Because of the ankle injury at the start of the season, I didn't know where I was with my tennis until this weekend. I'm happy that I could

help my team. I love playing for my team, I love playing for my country, and I felt great out there. I left my heart on the court. I am already looking forward to playing for Germany again in the future." Koubek won his second rubber of the tie, beating Christopher Kas 6–2 6–3 in the redundant fifth rubber, but the weekend already belonged to Kiefer, and to Germany. ●

Sweden v Israel

In 1975, when Sweden played Chile in front of an empty arena in Bastad due to security concerns over demonstrations, a Swedish singer-songwriter, Mikael Wiehe, was outside making his feelings perfectly clear about Pinochet's dictatorship with his song "Stop the Game." Wiehe and others did not manage to have the tie stopped, but it was closed to the public. Thirty-four years later, Sweden hosted Israel in Malmo, and Wiehe again reached for his guitar, and for the second time in 109 years of the competition, the public was barred from a Davis Cup tie.

Of course, Wiehe was not the only one who felt strongly about the Israeli Davis Cup team visiting Malmo so soon after the conflict in Gaza. Malmo, the third largest city in Sweden, has a large Muslim population, and it was suggested before the tie that around ten thousand people would turn out for anti-Israel protests. That led the local council to make the contentious decision to ban spectators from the venue, as they argued that they could not guarantee the safety of the Israeli players, captain, and traveling delegation.

The International Tennis Federation strongly disagreed with the decision made by the politicians in Malmo, as did the Israeli players. It meant that the two images that defined the tie were sadly not, say, of a forehand winner being struck down the line or of a team clearing a bench in celebration; instead, it was rows and rows of empty seats at the Baltic Hall and ugly demonstrations outside on the middle day of the tie. Unfortunately, only a few people came away from Malmo discussing how Israel had beaten Sweden 3–2 after winning the decisive fifth set of the decisive fifth rubber—the only tie of the weekend that went the distance.

Andy Ram, Israel's doubles player, was quoted as telling a Swedish newspaper that the decision to play the tie in a near-empty stadium was "idiotic." The tie came soon after a female Israeli player, Shahar Peer, was denied entry into the United Arab Emirates to play a tournament in Dubai; there had been some doubt over whether Ram would be allowed to compete in the men's event in Dubai, but in the end he was. "Sweden's actions are way more degrading than Dubai's," Ram was quoted as saying. "Dubai is

an Arab state that we don't have any ties to. That they, right after a war, find it hard to accept an Israeli, I can understand. But with Sweden we have normal ties."

Around one thousand police officers set up a security cordon around the stadium in Malmo, with only about four hundred accredited officials, guests, and media allowed to pass through to watch the three days of tennis and try to create some atmosphere in the Baltic Hall. But, despite their efforts, it was never going to be the same as having a proper crowd. Mats Wilander, Sweden's captain, said that it would be tricky for his players to compete without the vocal support of their home fans.

Both of Wilander's singles nominations went into the opening day without any form to speak of. Thomas Johansson, the former Australian Open champion, was making his first competitive appearance of the season after coming back from Achilles surgery, and Andreas Vinciguerra, who is from Malmo, had not played professionally since 2006 because of problems with his knees. So the Swedes had no home crowd and no clear idea of how they would fare on the match court.

Johansson was "totally exhausted" after beating Israel's Harel Levy 6–7(3) 6–4 7–5 4–6 8–6 on the carpeted surface. "I emptied myself completely today," said Johansson. "I've got the world's biggest ice pack on my foot right now. Maybe I'll need an ice bath to be able to walk tomorrow." The second rubber also went to five sets, with Dudi Sela coming from

Pictured above from top:
Harel Levy (ISR);
A protestor outside the stadium
Pictured opposite from top:
Setting up camp at the Baltic Hall;
Harel Levy (ISR), left, and captain Eyal Ran

two sets to one down to put Israel level after a 4–6 6–3 3–6 6–3 11–9 victory over Vinciguerra. Levy said it had been odd playing in a near-empty stadium: "It didn't feel like a Davis Cup match in the World Group, more like a Challenger tournament. It's sad. I think it has affected Sweden more than Israel; hopefully it will never happen again."

On Friday, there had been some protests outside the arena, but nothing too alarming. However, as expected, the second day brought confrontations between the riot police and masked protestors, several hundred of whom had reportedly joined a peaceful pro-Palestinian demonstration of around six thousand people. But none of the masked protestors managed to force their way into the Baltic Hall, where the Swedish combination of Simon Aspelin and Robert Lindstedt were on their way to a 6–4 1–6 7–6(4) 6–4 defeat of Ram and Amir Hadad.

For the second time in the tie, Sela made a comeback from two sets to one down, winning the first of the reverse singles rubbers when he beat Johansson 3–6 6–1 4–6 6–4 6–2. The tie would therefore go down to a fifth rubber, and it was Levy who took his country into the quarterfinals after his 6–4 4–6 6–4 3–6 8–6 win over Vinciguerra. When the two countries played each other in the first round of the 2008 World Group, Levy lost to Jonas Bjorkman in the fifth rubber in Tel Aviv, so there was added satisfaction for Levy in Malmo when he won the match and the tie for Israel. "That was amazing. My best day ever," said Levy. "It was so close, a point here and there. I feel sorry for Vinciguerra, and maybe Sweden lost the tie because they didn't have the normal advantage of a home crowd."

Vinciguerra was understandably distraught, saying afterward that he did not want to see any tennis rackets or tennis balls for several days, "maybe ever again." Still, when the initial disappointment had faded, perhaps Vinciguerra came around to the conclusion that he produced an impressive level of tennis over the weekend. Despite losing his two singles rubbers, on both occasions he took an experienced opponent to a fifth set and then troubled him in the decider.

All four of the singles rubbers had gone to five sets and could not have been any tighter. Plus, with the doubles rubber going to four sets, twenty-four of the maximum twenty-five sets had been played. If there was one tie over the weekend that deserved a live audience, it was this one.

The ITF's Davis Cup committee, after a meeting in Amsterdam later that month, announced that Malmo had been banned for five years from hosting a Davis Cup tie. It was also decided that Sweden "will suffer an automatic loss of choice of ground for the next tie if a similar situation occurs in the future." In addition, all host city contracts entered into by the Swedish Tennis

Pictured below, clockwise from top:
Sweden wins the doubles;
Andreas Vinciguerra (SWE);
Dudi Sela (ISR)

Association must include a provision guaranteeing that the tie will be open to the public. Unfortunately, for all the entertaining tennis that was played by the Swedish and Israeli players, and despite Israel's captain Eyal Ran suggesting that "tennis was the winner," the weekend in Malmo is likely to be remembered for what happened outside the tramlines. ●

Pictured clockwise from top left:

Champagne celebrations;

The Argentinean team; Dutch fans

Argentina v Netherlands

On a Saturday afternoon in Buenos Aires, at the Estadio Parque Roca, the celebrations that followed Argentina's success in the doubles rubber were understandably emotional. Lucas Arnold Ker and Martin Vassallo Arguello's straight-sets victory over Jesse Huta Galung and Rogier Wassen ensured that Argentina had won the tie in two days, but that was not even the half of it. Arnold Ker, a doubles specialist in his mid-thirties, was representing his country for the first time in five years—in the interim, his wife had left him, he had survived testicular cancer, his wife had given the marriage a second try, his mother had died, and he had made it back into the Davis Cup team. He had also felt moved to change his name.

If you go back to 2004, life was pretty good for Lucas Arnold (as he was then known). That year, Arnold was in the Davis Cup team that reached the quarterfinals, although they managed to go no further on the draw sheet after losing to Belarus in Minsk. However, in 2005, Arnold's wife, Yannina, told him that the marriage was over: "My wife said: 'Enough. I can't take any more. Goodbye.'" Lucas and Yannina had a young son, Ignacio.

Arnold was already at a low point in his life when, in 2006, he was diagnosed with cancer. "Everything was quite good in my life until the end of 2004," he recalled. "But then in 2005 I broke up with my wife.

My wife and I had been together for ten years. The next year I was diagnosed with testicular cancer and I felt so lonely. I underwent surgery. Then the doctors told me that the cancer was also in my stomach and lungs. I had to go through chemotherapy. Those were probably the six most difficult months of my life."

In Argentina, testicular cancer is not openly discussed. "There is no awareness of this disease in Argentina," he said. "When I had a tomography taken before the operation, I was ashamed to say why I was there. The girl who took it calmed me down, told me I could not imagine how many men go through the same things. But it is a macho society and people don't talk about it. I went to psychologists and didn't talk. I read Lance Armstrong's book and it helped me a lot, his account of how he handled chemotherapy, which was similar to what I was going through, and how he always thought he was going to survive. I was very bad. I had a terrible depression, like a death inside."

One happy development was that Yannina got back in touch. "I got back with my wife, and she and my son helped me a lot over this problem, as did my mother, my father, my sister, and her children." The testicle was removed, and Arnold successfully fended off the cancer. He started to regain his fitness and strength, and soon it became clear that he had a chance to play professional tennis again.

Sadly, as Arnold made his recovery, his mother, Lindsay Ker, passed away. As a tribute to his mother, who had given him so much encouragement when he had been ill, he added her surname to his. And then Arnold Ker was back on the team, selected to play against the Netherlands on a clay court on the outskirts of Buenos Aires, the city where he was born. "It just makes me happy to be a part of the team again," said the thirty-four-year-old. "The Davis Cup motivates me like no other event. I always thought about being back in the team when I was fighting the cancer. And now I dream about winning the Davis Cup."

Given what had happened in the life of Lucas Arnold Ker, it seemed trivial to point to all the differences between the team that played and lost the 2008 final to Spain, and the team that met the Dutch. All four of the players who were picked for the final against Spain in Mar del Plata—Juan Martin del Potro, David Nalbandian, Jose Acasuso, and Agustin Calleri— were missing from the tie at Estadio Parque Roca. There were various reasons for this: Del Potro, for one, did not want to play on clay in the middle of a run of

hard-court tournaments, and Nalbandian was unwell. This time, Argentina's four players were Juan Ignacio Chela, Juan Monaco, Arnold Ker, and Vassallo Arguello. Argentina also had a new captain in Tito Vazquez, as Alberto Mancini had retired from the role after the defeat to the Spanish, suggesting that "everything had become political."

"It's a chance to experiment," Vasquez said of the absence of the country's leading players. "But we still have a chance to win. I'm tired of hearing about Del Potro, about Nalbandian, about a crisis." Naturally, it was the new beginning for Arnold Ker that had the greatest resonance. In September 2008 Arnold Ker took his son, Ignacio, to the Estadio Parque Roca to watch Argentina beat Russia to reach the final. Six months later, Ignacio was back at the stadium, and for the first time, the six-year-old watched his father representing his country.

When Chela opened the tie against Huta Galung, it was the Argentine's first Davis Cup rubber since 2006. Chela, who had missed a great chunk of the 2008 season because of injury, needed five sets to beat the Dutchman, picking up the first point of the weekend with a 6–2 2–6 6–2 6–7 6–2 victory. All of Monaco's previous experience in the competition had been in dead rubbers, and he had been in some discomfort during the build-up to the tie because of shin splints. Even so, his first "live" tennis in the Davis Cup brought him a straight-sets victory over Thiemo de Bakker, with Monaco winning 6–1 6–2 7–6, although shin splints appeared to bother him more and more as the match continued.

Everything was set up nicely for the return of Arnold Ker, who, along with twenty-nine-year-old rookie Vassallo Arguello, made sure of the home win when they beat Huta Galung and Wassen 6–4 7–5 6–3. The only sets that Argentina dropped all weekend came in Chela's opening match, as Vassallo Arguello beat Matwe Middelkoop 6–2 6–4 in the first of the dead rubbers, and Chela then defeated de Bakker 7–5 6–2 in the second.

Some in Buenos Aires had said this was Argentina's B team for the tie, that the Netherlands was not the strongest nation they could have drawn in the first round of the World Group, and it was a long way from being a sell-out. But none of that mattered to Lucas Arnold Ker, the thirty-something with the new name in a new-look team. He had played tennis for his country again. "I'm very happy to be a part of the competition again. I missed being focused on the competition, being part of my team, to have dinner with them, to be together on the court, and to have the support of the crowd. That is the most beautiful feeling." ●

Pictured from top:

Thiemo de Bakker (NED) and captain

Jan Siemerink; Juan Monaco (ARG)

Pictured opposite:

Lucas Arnold Ker (ARG), left,

and Martin Vassallo Arguello (ARG)

The Longwood Cricket Club, Boston, MA, USA

The name Longwood means different things to different people. For anyone who has studied French history, it is reminiscent of Longwood House, Napoleon Bonaparte's home while exiled in Saint Helena. For anyone who knows their tennis history, it means Longwood Cricket Club, a place where the first Davis Cup tie was played in 1900.

Founded on the outskirts of Boston in 1877, a year later the first grass tennis courts were added at the club, and in 1882 the first tournament was played. Richard Sears, who would win a record seven US Open titles in the 1880s, was a member and the club, despite its name, would become best known for tennis.

Dwight Davis, a senior student at nearby Harvard University, was from a wealthy St. Louis family and spent a considerable amount of money on a silver punchbowl. In 1900 he invited a British team to Longwood for what was originally called the International Lawn Tennis Challenge but would soon became known as the Davis Cup. The United States, captained by Davis, beat the British Isles.

There were many reasons why Britain, after an eight-day voyage across the Atlantic Ocean, could not cope with their American opponents when they played the first Davis Cup rubbers in August 1900. The British were without their most talented two players, Laurie and Reginald Doherty, plus they had gone on a trip to Niagara Falls and arrived at Longwood just the day before. They could not work out the new "American twist" serve, plus they struggled with the different balls, the weather, and even the length of the grass. Still, the British, having traveled all that way, had the enjoyment of a post-match dinner of clams and filets of sea bass cooked in white wine.

It was not until after the match that the British revealed their true feelings about the first Davis Cup tie, with one player later complaining that, "the ground was abominable," "the grass was long," "the net was a disgrace to civilized lawn tennis, held up by guy ropes which were continually sagging," and "the balls were awful, soft and mothery-looking."

Davis went on to become the secretary of war under President Calvin Coolidge and the governor-general of the Philippines, but his greatest contribution was to tennis's international team competition. The competition grew and grew, and by 1999, the centenary year, some 129 nations had teams in the Davis Cup, and it seemed appropriate that America should play a tie back at the Longwood Cricket Club, the fifteenth Davis Cup tie held there but the first in forty years. When tickets for the tie went on sale for the quarterfinal against Australia, they sold out in just over an hour, showing that East Coast tennis fans enjoy a bit of nostalgia.

Even though the club had moved a little farther from downtown Boston and the tie was played on a hard court rather than traditional grass, the weekend was an opportunity for everyone in tennis to think back to what had come before. There was even a Harvard connection. The United States had played an all-Harvard team in 1900, and in 1999 the American hitting partner for the week was James Blake, who had studied at the university. John Howard, the Australian prime minister, was there at Longwood, as was former president George Bush, whose uncle, Joseph Wear, had been a Davis Cup captain. The American old boys were there in great numbers, as there were fifty-one former American Davis Cup players and captains in the stands.

"I have a feeling a lot of ghosts of the past will be there looking down on us," said John Newcombe, the Australian captain. "This is where it all began in 1900. There were a bunch of guys battling it out in 1900. And here we are now with another bunch of guys battling it out. I think people will begin to understand the history of this now."

If there was history at Longwood that weekend; there was also a bit of edge, as the Australians had been unhappy about how the International Tennis Federation had agreed with the United States Tennis Federation that the tie should be played at Longwood. It was Australia's turn to host a tie against the United States. Another subplot was that Pete Sampras had only committed himself to playing doubles against Australia, since he had missed the first-round tie against Britain, and "felt uncomfortable with jumping on the bandwagon." So Todd Martin and Jim Courier were nominated as the singles players. The Australian team, which contained Lleyton Hewitt and Pat Rafter, won 4–1. ●

COMETH THE HOUR, COMETH THE MAN

Davis Cup matches are a hotbed of emotion—the intensity of playing for your country can impassion a competitor like nothing else.

Quarterfinals 10–12 July

Israel defeated Russia 4–1   TEL AVIV, ISRAEL – INDOOR HARD

Croatia defeated USA 3–2   POREC, CROATIA – INDOOR CLAY

Czech Republic defeated Argentina 3–2   OSTRAVA, CZECH REPUBLIC – INDOOR CARPET

Spain defeated Germany 3–2   MARBELLA, SPAIN – OUTDOOR CLAY

Introduction

A touch of complacency can be dangerous for a Davis Cup player. Would Marat Safin end up regretting the observation he made during the buildup to Russia's tie in Tel Aviv, when he had said that Israel had been lucky to get to the quarterfinals? Safin's comment went against the norms of Davis Cup: players generally talk up the strengths of the opposition.

Safin was not indulging in a bit of pre-tie trash-talking; he was just speaking openly and honestly by suggesting that perhaps Israel had been fortunate to have played a relatively weak Swedish team in the first round in Malmo. For the neutral, there could be little doubt which of the teams was favored to win the quarterfinal on the Mediterranean coast, on an indoor court in Tel Aviv. Russia had twice been Davis Cup champions, in 2002 and 2005, and although Safin was coming to the end of his career, he had once held the world No. 1 ranking and won a couple of grand slams. It was to be Israel's second appearance in the quarterfinals, and their first since 1987, when they had lost away to India on a grass court, so they were attempting to reach the semifinals for the first time. None of the Israeli players could be considered household names. But fame and a team's past record do not win many ties, and if Russia failed to reach the semifinals, it would be the last Davis Cup appearance for Safin in his retirement year.

Israel v Russia

Israeli Prime Minister Benjamin Netanyahu was on the line. "We are on the map again," was Netanyahu's message to the captain and the members of Israel's victorious Davis Cup team. "You have made our country proud, you have filled our hearts with pride and joy." To the great surprise of the tennis world, Israel had reached the semifinals of the Davis Cup for the first time in the country's history. Before the tie, it appeared as though Israel had little chance, but on an indoor hard court in Tel Aviv something remarkable happened, with Israel not just beating Russia, the leading nation in the Davis Cup rankings, but beating the supposed tennis superpower with a day to spare.

In Ostrava, Ivan Lendl's hometown in the Czech Republic, people were speaking of nothing else but Radek Stepanek's knee. If you listened to the Czech team, Stepanek's knee was causing him such discomfort that there was a chance he would only appear in the doubles rubber, and maybe not at all. If you listened to the Argentine team, Stepanek's knee was not as bad as he was making out, and they were expecting to see the player in the singles as well as the doubles. The state of Stepanek's knee could decide the tie, and bad knee or no bad knee, the Czech team needed him on court if they were to reach the semifinals for the first time since 1996.

The United States arrived in the seaside town of Porec hoping for a first victory against Croatia after defeats in their previous two meetings, but they would have to do it without Andy Roddick, who was forced into withdrawing from the quarterfinal because his body was fatigued after his five-set defeat to Roger Federer in the Wimbledon final the previous week.

For some time, defending champion Spain had accepted that Rafael Nadal would be missing because of the tendonitis in both knees, but after David Ferrer withdrew a few days before the tie against Germany in Marbella came an unexpected recall for Juan Carlos Ferrero, a former world No. 1 and the 2003 French Open champion. The weekend would bring Ferrero's first appearance in the Davis Cup in four years.

Pictured above,

clockwise from top left:

Andy Ram (ISR);

Igor Andreev (RUS) and

captain Shamil Tarpischev;

Marat Safin (RUS), left,

and Igor Kunitsyn (RUS)

Before the phone call from the prime minister there were tears. Andy Ram, who is usually the ebullient one of the Israeli Davis Cup team, lost control on the court. For the first time in his career, Ram disclosed he had "absolutely nothing to say." The emotion was such that he admitted he had cried "like a little boy." Soon the Israeli captain, Eyal Ran, was likening his doubles pair of Ram and Jonathan Erlich to a couple of F-16 fighter jets.

When Russia's Marat Safin remarked before the tie that, "with all due respect, Israel is lucky to get to the quarterfinals," he was not intending to antagonize the opposition. Safin had plainly not been alone in his belief that Russia had the ability to reach the Davis Cup semifinals for the umpteenth occasion in their history. Russia has been the Davis Cup champions twice, in 2002 and 2006, and was facing Israel as the No. 1 Davis Cup nation. Israel, meanwhile, was only making its second appearance in the quarterfinals of the competition, and the first since the 1987 season, when the team lost heavily on an Indian grass court. When Ran started as captain in 2005, his players had needed to win a relegation play-off tie against Zimbabwe to avoid dropping into Group II of the Europe/Africa zone, so what hope did they have against Russia, who had twice won the trophy?

Still, if Israel lacked world-class singles players and a record of brilliance in the competition, what they did have was a sense of togetherness, a strong team ethic. All four team members contributed against Russia, with Harel Levy and Dudi Sela winning their singles rubbers. "What a team," Ram said. "I think that as a team, we are the number one team in the world, the most united in the world. I know all the squads, all the players in the world, and I can say with certainty that we are the most solid team. The captain, the doctor, the players, everyone—we are all supportive of each other and love each other. We are all friends, we all grew up together since the age of fourteen, we know each other so well, and the families too, so I don't think there has been any other team like it. There is such friendship, and it's great to experience. The reason we are in the semifinals is because of the motivation, because we are a united team. Everybody pushes everybody, and it's a really nice feeling. If you look at it, many would say that we're not a semifinal team, but we have got there because we work together."

Since that victory against Zimbabwe in 2005, captain Ran said Israel had "slowly put together a team that has galvanized into a homogenous unit that rises to the occasion and plays above itself." What was even more remarkable about the tie was that Israel won comfortably, as they required just two days at Tel Aviv's Nokia Stadium to defeat Russia and become the first country that weekend to reach the semifinals. Spain, the 2008 champions, needed a third day to complete their victory and play Israel in the semifinals of the 2009 competition.

Israel's progress over previous years contrasted with Russia's record. For Russia, an unfortunate pattern of results continued with this defeat. Every year since it had become the Davis Cup champion for the second time in history by defeating Argentina in the 2006 Moscow final, Russia had gone out a round earlier than the year before. In 2007 Russia was the beaten finalist, losing away to the United States, and in 2008 they had only gone as far as the semifinals, losing away to Argentina. And now this, the top-ranked tennis nation falling in the quarterfinals to a country that had never previously appeared in the semifinals of the World Group. After the weekend's results, Russia fell from the top of the Davis Cup rankings, which are calculated over a four-year rolling period. Russia found itself in third place, behind Spain and the United States.

It was the first time since the 1980s that Israel did not play a home tie at the open-air Canada Stadium in Ramat Hasharon, but the decision was made to break that unbroken sequence of twenty-two ties and play indoors in the middle of summer, as Tel Aviv's Nokia Arena could seat more than double the number of spectators. The home stadium for the Maccabi Tel Aviv basketball club had eleven thousand seats. For the first time in the season, Israel would experience competing in front of a crowd, since their opening-round victory had come in the Swedish city of Malmo, where the local councillors had controversially banned spectators. The noise from the Tel Aviv crowd would help the home players to compete above their natural levels, to produce the unexpected.

Shamil Tarpischev, the Russian captain, was without Nikolay Davydenko, his highest-ranked player, and Dmitry Tursunov was also missing from the squad, but neutrals were still predicting that the visiting team would end the first day with a 2–0 lead. Russia won a total of two sets all day. Though he was ranked outside the world's top 200 at the time of the tie, and he was on the wrong side of age thirty, Levy struck the ball beautifully from the baseline to take the opening rubber with a 6–4 6–2 4–6 6–2 defeat of Igor Andreev. The Russian was astonished by the quality of Levy's tennis. The perfect day for the home team continued when Sela beat Mikhail Youzhny, an opponent who famously won the fifth rubber in a Davis Cup final,

coming from two sets down to beat France's Paul-Henri Mathieu in the 2002 title match. Sela, after dropping the first set, dominated the second and third sets, and was narrowly the better player in the fourth set. His 3–6 6–1 6–0 7–5 victory meant that the home team was just one more point away from the semifinals.

Ram and Erlich, the 2008 Australian Open doubles champions, did not always play their best tennis against Safin and Igor Kunitsyn. It was the first time in over a year that Erlich, who had been out for several months recuperating from an elbow injury, had partnered Ram. After gathering the first two sets, the Israelis could have won the match in straight sets, but Ram dropped his serve. The Russians won the third and fourth sets to take the match into a decider, but the home pairing regrouped for the fifth set, taking the match 6–3 6–4 6–7(3) 4–6 6–4.

The frustrated, self-deprecating Safin, a former US Open and Australian Open singles champion, blamed himself, saying that, "Israel should thank me—I am responsible for this defeat," but it was not the time to remark on it being the Muscovite's last appearance for his country before his retirement at the end of the season. The day was all about what Netanyahu would call "Israeli joy and pride." "Everybody has dreams," said Erlich. "but there are some that you don't even allow yourself, and beating Russia was one of those. But we did it." ●

Pictured above from top:
Andy Ram (ISR), left,
and Jonathan Erlich (ISR);
Harel Levy (ISR)

Pictured above from left:

Mike Bryan (USA), left, and Bob Bryan
(USA) show support for James Blake (USA)

Pictured below:

Sportska Dvorana Zatika;

The Croatian team at the draw

Croatia v USA

The moment that shaped Andy Roddick's summer came during the fourth set of the five-set Wimbledon final against Roger Federer, when the American slipped on the grass and ended up in a crumpled heap. Roddick yelped and stayed down on the lawn for a while. If it had not been for the damage to Roddick's right hip, would he have gone on to win Wimbledon's Challenge Cup for the first time? Perhaps.

The next day, Roddick announced that he was withdrawing from the United States Davis Cup team's quarterfinal against Croatia in Porec. With the tie starting just five days after the Wimbledon final, and to be played on clay, the American didn't feel his body would cope with a long weekend in the Croatian seaside town. So, for the first time in eighteen ties, the U.S. team would be without Roddick, a player who had won more singles rubbers in the competition than any other American, apart from John McEnroe.

Captain Patrick McEnroe understood that Roddick could not play in Eastern Europe because of his fatigued, injured body. "Andy has been a stalwart for this team the past nine years, and his dedication to the Davis Cup, and to his teammates,

is unquestioned," said McEnroe. "Andy had a great run at Wimbledon. He battled for more than four hours in the final, and he had fought hard to reach the final. Understandably, Andy's body is not up to the rigors of playing in the Davis Cup after such a short turnaround."

Looking to fill the Roddick-shaped hole in his plans, McEnroe asked Mardy Fish, who had entered that week's grass court tournament at Rhode Island, to instead compete on clay on the other side of the Atlantic. Fish accepted, joining James Blake and the twins Bob and Mike Bryan in Eastern Europe, but, to the neutrals, it appeared as though the fate of the Davis Cup quarterfinal had already turned during that ominous moment when Roddick lost his footing on the Wimbledon grass.

Croatia was without Mario Ancic, who was suffering from a recurrence of the mononucleosis virus. But Croatia has never relied on Ancic like the United States has relied on Roddick. And what about history? Anyone who had glanced through the record books before the tie would have seen that history was against the United States, one of the superpowers of the competition who has won the Davis Cup a record thirty-two times. The Americans had lost their two previous Davis Cup encounters against Croatia, in Zagreb in 2003 and in Carson, California, in 2005.

The opening day of the third American-Croat encounter brought eight hours and one minute of clay-court tennis, and it was nearly 1 a.m. when play finished at the Sportska Dvorana "Zatika". The long-running opening day didn't go the Americans' way. Both matches saw the American player go two sets to one up, only for his Croatian opponent to come back to register a five-set win. In Roddick's absence, James Blake was the leading singles player for the Americans, and he did not find life at all easy during the opening rubber against Ivo Karlovic, which was understandable, given that the Croatian hit forty-seven aces, equaling the record for the Davis Cup. Only once in the match did Blake break Karlovic's serve. But the American's main gripe was with some of the Croatian spectators, who had apparently repeatedly distracted him during his service motion and then applauded his mistakes.

After three hours and thirty-eight minutes, Karlovic won a match in five sets for the first time in his career, with a 6–7(5) 4–6 6–3 7–6(3) 7–5 victory, and Blake was soon claiming that the crowd had been "pretty hostile." "To boo our fans is something I find unacceptable, to yell out when I'm serving, to clap when I miss a first serve and things like that on a pretty consistent basis, that all seemed pretty hostile to me," said Blake. It was not an opinion that Blake's captain shared, with McEnroe suggesting that noise from the crowd was just part of the experience of playing an away tie. In the opening stages, the crowd had also appeared to work against Karlovic. "I was a bit nervous at the start, playing before a home crowd," said Karlovic. "But I became more relaxed as the match went on, and I managed to turn it around, and it was surely one of the biggest matches of my career."

Even though he received treatment during the third set for a rib strain, Fish found himself leading by two sets to one in the second rubber against Marin Cilic, a twenty-year-old who was standing in for Ancic as the home team's first-singles nomination. Fish, though, was unable to close out the victory. Cilic came back into the match, and although he dropped his serve when he served for the rubber at 5–3 in the fifth set, he took the match on a break. Cilic's 4–6 6–3 6–7(3) 6–1 8–6 victory took four hours and twenty-three minutes. It had been one of the longest days in the history of the competition. "Two great matches and two tough losses," was McEnroe's assessment. The United States was two rubbers down by 1 a.m. on Saturday—an American Davis Cup team had not won a tie from 0–2 down since 1934.

Still, it did not take long on Saturday for the Americans to win the doubles rubber, as the Bryan twins required just over an hour to defeat Roko Karanusic and Lovro Zovko 6–3 6–1 6–3. Karlovic was given the day off, with the Croatian captain Goran Prpic deciding to rest the player ahead of the reverse singles on Sunday. As it happened, Karlovic was not needed again on the clay court.

Cilic's superb tennis against Blake gave him a 6–3 6–3 4–6 6–2 victory on Sunday and Croatia an unassailable 3–1 lead in the tie. "I think this is one of the greatest ties I've played so far," said Cilic, who wore a red and white checkered shirt. "I was a little

tired from the five sets on Friday so I played a lot of the match on adrenaline, and the crowd was carrying me throughout the match. I felt good on court. I think I've gained a lot of experience, everyone supported me, and it felt really good to play at home."

Cilic, who also contributed a couple of points in the opening round against Chile, impressed Blake. "Marin played some great tennis over the weekend," said Blake. "He took care of business against Mardy and he played a very solid match today. I felt I gave him a few too many chances, I played a little too passively, didn't take as many risks as I normally do, and he took advantage of that. Any time I left the ball a little short or in his strike zone, he took care of it, and that's why he is as good as he is right now."

For the third time in three meetings, the United States had lost to Croatia. One of the reasons for the American defeat was Roddick's tumble on the Wimbledon grass. Another was the brilliance of Cilic. In 2005 Ivan Ljubicic effectively defeated the United States on his own at that tie in California, and later that year the small, young nation won the trophy for the first time. That year, Cilic was just a junior. In Porec, Ljubicic was back for Davis Cup, but only to provide commentary for Croatian television and to sit on the team bench. This time it was Cilic, the young man in the checkered shirt, who "took care of business." ●

Pictured above from top:
Captains Goran Prpic (CRO), left,
and Patrick McEnroe (USA);
Mardy Fish (USA); Ivo Karlovic (CRO)
Pictured opposite:
Marin Cilic (CRO) seals
Croatia's place in the semifinals

Czech Republic v Argentina

Here was one occasion when Radek Stepanek did not mark a significant victory by immediately performing "the Worm", the break-dancing routine he learned when drinking schnapps a few years ago at an Austrian ski resort. Perhaps that had something to do with the fact that the buildup to the tie, and then the tie itself, had been dominated by news of Stepanek's knee, an injury that kept him off court on day one. On day three of the quarterfinal, Stepanek's knee held up, and when he defeated Argentina's Juan Monaco in the decisive fifth rubber, he was soon sitting on the court while turning an imaginary steering wheel. When it comes to consistently weird and wonderful celebrations, no one on the tour gets close to Stepanek.

Of course, funny celebrations are worthless if you do not have the game to win tennis matches for yourself or for your country, and on that Sunday in Ostrava, Stepanek produced one of his best Davis Cup performances. This was certainly a victory worth celebrating, whether by doing the Worm or pretending to drive a school bus, or whatever else Stepanek thought he was doing while seated on the fast indoor carpet court, as the Czech Republic's defeat of Argentina, the runners-up the previous year, put the Eastern European nation into the semifinals of the Davis Cup for the first time since 1996.

But before Argentina had to watch Stepanek's wheel-turning, there had been some differences of opinion between the two teams about the player's knee, with the South Americans appearing to doubt whether Stepanek really was in as much discomfort as he said he was.

Less than a fortnight before the tie began in Ivan Lendl's hometown, Stepanek was complaining of pain in his knee after his fourth-round five-set defeat to Lleyton Hewitt at Wimbledon. And at the draw ceremony, Stepanek was only nominated to play doubles with Tomas Berdych, who with Ivo Minar was chosen to play singles. "Radek has been having knee problems the whole week," said the Czech captain, Jaroslav Navratil. "We decided that he would not play on Friday, because there is too much burden on him." Even so, the Argentina camp felt as though those nominations would almost certainly change over the weekend, as they suspected that Stepanek would end up having some involvement in Sunday's singles rubbers. Tito Vazquez, the Argentine captain, had his theories about Stepanek's knee. "They've probably decided to save Stepanek against our best player—not to expose him against Juan Martin del Potro—and save him for the next two matches, the doubles, and maybe the last day, that's what I think," said Vazquez. "We're still not 100 percent sure.

Pictured below from left:
Radek Stepanek (CZE), left,
and Tomas Berdych (CZE);
The Argentine team consoles
Juan Monaco (ARG)

Pictured above from left:

Ivo Minar (CZE);

Czech victory celebration

We've prepared ourselves to play Stepanek, so in our minds we're ready just in case, if something happens and he plays."

Unfortunately for Argentina, there was no doubt whether they would be without David Nalbandian, as it had been known for some time that the former Wimbledon finalist would not be involved because of an operation on his hip. Even so, Argentina's team did include del Potro, a top 10 player with the game to do well on a quick indoor court.

Stepanek's knee was not the only thought that went through Vazquez's head before the tie, as he also suggested that playing the tie on such a speedy indoor carpet—a surface that players rarely see on the tour—was not fair. "I think it's quite unfair, as there aren't too many tournaments around the world on that surface, and I think the ITF should take note of it. Ties should be played on surfaces which are used at grand slams or at a number of tournaments," said Vazquez. "It has been a very strong sacrifice for us to be able to get into good shape for this surface. We went with the whole team, which is around fourteen people, to Paris

to train on a similar court just to be able to have some type of chance." Despite Vazquez's concerns, it was one of his players, del Potro, who looked the most comfortable on the surface, as he did not drop a set in winning two singles rubbers. And, as it turned out, he became the only Argentine to contribute any points over the course of the weekend.

With Stepanek not playing in the opening day's singles rubbers, the home team was reliant on Berdych winning his singles rubber. Berdych did defeat Monaco, but only after coming back from two sets to one down for his 6–4 2–6 2–6 6–3 6–2 victory. Next, Minar made his second career appearance in Davis Cup, his first having come two years earlier with a four-set defeat against American Andy Roddick. On this occasion he did not win a set and gathered just seven games with a 6–1 6–3 6–3 defeat to del Potro.

Stepanek's first performance of the weekend came in the doubles rubber, and the veteran and Berdych registered a 6–1 6–4 6–3 victory over Leonardo Mayer, a Davis Cup rookie, and Jose Acasuso. Stepanek's knee had made it through a doubles match, but he was

required to play again, after del Potro's comfortable 6–4 6–4 6–4 win over Berdych meant that the tie would be decided by a fifth rubber. For Stepanek, playing singles would plainly be a greater physical effort than partnering Berdych to a doubles win.

According to Stepanek, it was only by deceiving himself about the pain that he was able to beat Monaco. He did a good job of self-deception then. The man with the suspect knee had not dropped a set all weekend. "It was the biggest effort I have ever done in the Davis Cup," said Stepanek after he wrapped up the tie with a 7–6(5) 6–3 6–2 victory. "After the doubles I was 90 percent sure that I wasn't going to play singles, but I was assured by the doctors that it wasn't going to damage my knee. I had to lie to myself that it didn't hurt." But Vazquez, who had always suspected that Stepanek would play in a fifth rubber, suggested that the Czech's knee had not been as serious as the player had made out. "We knew that Stepanek was going to be in good shape, and it proved that he was not injured at all. You cannot run a lot when you are injured, and he had the game that

allowed him to bother a player like Monaco." But nothing, not even the scepticism on the Argentine bench, could alter Stepanek's mood. "It is unbelievable," he said. "I did not have the energy to spare and tried to collect one point after another." After two ties in the 2009 World Group, Stepanek had now won four of his five matches.

Given the Czech Republic's draw, it had been a real effort to make the semifinals for the first time in thirteen years. The team had beaten a couple of strong tennis nations in France and Argentina to make it into the last four. The last time the Czechs had won the Davis Cup trophy had been in 1980, during the Iron Curtain days when the Czechs were still part of Czechoslovakia and Lendl was starting to establish himself on the international scene. For all the excitement that was generated by Stepanek's victory over Monaco, the Czech team also spoke of being far from satisfied, that they wanted to go much deeper into the competition. Soon, preparations began for the semifinal with Croatia. "We're excited to be in the semifinals, but we're not satisfied yet," said Stepanek. "We want to go further and play in the final." ●

Spain v Germany

What was the link between a committee room at the All England Club and a bullring on Spain's Costa del Sol? The committee wouldn't have known at the time that their decision to award Juan Carlos Ferrero a wild card into the Wimbledon Championships would end up having an impact on events in the Plaza de Toros in Marbella. This was the summer when Ferrero took the unexpected opportunities that came his way, the summer when he reminded the Spanish tennis public that the talent that once brought him the 2003 French Open title, a place in the US Open final that year, and the world No. 1 ranking for a couple of months that season wasn't all gone. There was still some tennis life left in the twenty-nine-year-old.

A lot has happened since the 2003 season. Ferrero had to deal with chicken pox and a number of injuries, including some serious damage after an unfortunate tumble on the practice court. And then came Rafael Nadal, the Majorcan whose brilliance on a tennis court has eclipsed Ferrero's achievements. But with Nadal missing from both Wimbledon and Spain's Davis Cup quarterfinal tie against Germany because of the pain in his knees, it was Ferrero who took center stage.

In the spring, Ferrero found himself outside the world's top 100 and outside the cutoff for Wimbledon. He had not featured in the Davis Cup since the 2005 season. But despite all that, Ferrero ended up having a summer back under the arc lights. First, he reached the Wimbledon quarterfinals, his run on the grass ending with defeat to Andy Murray. The following week, David Ferrer withdrew from the Spanish team because of injury and Ferrero was asked to represent the defending champions. Ferrero's results at the All England Club helped his case.

A couple of Ferrero's career highlights had been in Davis Cup—he had been part of the winning teams in 2000 and 2004—but he had had no involvement whatsoever when his countrymen won the 2008 competition. With the emergence of the likes of Nadal, Fernando Verdasco, and Ferrer, and because of his own health problems, Ferrero had not competed for four years.

But just as Ferrero had not wasted the gift of a wild card into Wimbledon, he also made the most of his opportunity in Marbella. Ferrero wasn't involved in the opening day's two singles rubbers, or in the doubles rubber on Saturday afternoon. But when it really mattered, he played some fine tennis on the third day, in the rubber that decided which country would go through to play Israel in the semifinals. With the countries level at two rubbers apiece, home captain Albert Costa opted to play Ferrero instead of Tommy Robredo in the fifth and final rubber.

It was to be Ferrero's first appearance in the Davis Cup since a World Group play-off away to Italy in 2005, when he had won the tie by beating Daniele Bracciali in the fifth rubber. The form he had built up on London's grass courts had survived the journey south to a clay court on the Spanish coast, in a converted bullring that seated some eleven thousand spectators. It soon became clear that Ferrero had too much all-around ability, and too much experience, for his opponent, Andreas Beck, whose first appearance in the Davis Cup had come just two days earlier.

Not long after Ferrero had won 6–4 6–4 6–4, he was carried around the bullring on the shoulders of teammate Feliciano Lopez. Ferrero also seemed to believe that the only adjective worth using was "amazing." "To come back and play the last rubber, I felt amazing on the court," said Ferrero. "This competition is amazing, and to play for your country is very special. There are no words to properly explain how I feel right now, but I'm pretty happy about it. I hadn't played in the Davis Cup for a long time, and this tie was very special for me."

Pictured above, clockwise from top left:
Philipp Kohlschreiber (GER);
Fernando Verdasco (ESP), left,
and Feliciano Lopez (ESP);
Plaza de Toros de Puerto Banus, Marbella

Pictured opposite from top:
A hero moment for
Juan Carlos Ferrero (ESP);
Mischa Zverev (GER), left,
and Nicolas Kiefer (GER)

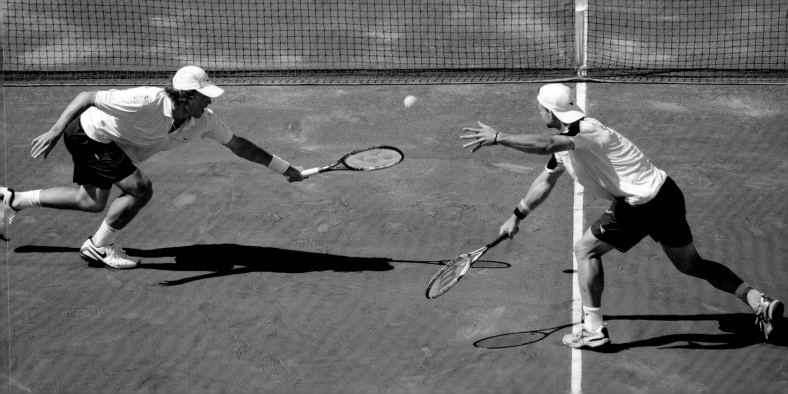

Pictured above from left:

The German team stays focused;

Fernando Verdasco (ESP)

Pictured opposite:

A lap of honor for Juan Carlos Ferrero (ESP)

Before Ferrero had his close-up on the Sunday, there was also a return to the Davis Cup for Verdasco, who had missed the first-round victory over Serbia. Verdasco appeared in the opening rubber for his first appearance in the competition since his defeat of Argentina's Jose Acasuso in the 2008 final, which gave Spain the winning point. When Verdasco won the opening set in twenty-one minutes against Beck, dropping just six points against the debutant, it appeared as though he was going to have a very comfortable and pleasant afternoon. But in the end, Verdasco had to come back from two sets to one down for a 6–0 3–6 6–7(4) 6–2 6–1 victory. Anyone who had been snoozing on the upper deck of a nearby yacht would have been woken up by the noise from the stands when Verdasco won the first rubber of the weekend. Nerves had affected Beck's tennis. "It was a good experience for me, my first Davis Cup in a huge atmosphere, but sure I'm disappointed," said Beck. "I was very nervous in the beginning, and the emotions were very high, but then I relaxed on the court. In the fourth and fifth sets, Fernando served better, and his experience helped him through."

Phillip Kohlschreiber, Germany's first singles nomination, had lost his previous four career meetings with Robredo, three of which had been on clay. But, as the German wanted to remind everyone, he is "not a stupid player," and he had finally worked out how to beat Robredo. It helped Kohlschreiber that Robredo made so many mistakes. "I never missed a forehand in the whole match, and that was the key," said Kohlschreiber, who won 6–3 6–4 6–4. "If I lose to a player I try to figure out what to do the next time. Sometimes it takes more than four times to do that."

On the Saturday of the tie, Germany used another rookie, with debutant Mischa Zverev partnering Nicolas Kiefer in the doubles rubber. The Spanish pairing of Verdasco and Feliciano Lopez targeted Zverev on the way to a 6–3 7–6(1) 6–7(6) 6–3 victory.

But for the second time in the tie, Kohlschreiber put Germany level. Kohlschreiber had had the Saturday off and had only played three sets before his singles rubber against Verdasco on Sunday. Verdasco, though, had played nine sets across Friday and Saturday. "It's going to be hard if I play three matches but I am ready for this and it's not a problem," Verdasco had said at the pre-tie draw ceremony, but there were times against Kohlschreiber when he lacked energy. After almost four hours of tennis, Kohlschreiber won in five sets, 6–4 6–2 1–6 2–6 8–6. "My legs were not working like I wanted and it was so tough to play," said Verdasco. "It is unfortunate that I lost 8–6 in the fifth set but I was proud that I was able to give more than 100 percent of myself." Kohlschreiber was soon speaking of what "a pleasure" it was playing for Germany, but than came Ferrero, beating Beck in the fifth rubber.

If the Spanish tennis public had almost forgotten what it was like to see Ferrero playing for his country in the Davis Cup, the sight of Spanish players celebrating after a home tie was familiar enough. By beating Germany, Spain had won the last sixteen ties it had played in Spain. The weekend's results also took Spain back to the top of the Davis Cup rankings. With Fererro's appearance in a Wimbledon quarterfinal, and then a decisive win that put Spain into the Davis Cup semifinals, his summer had been unexpectedly busy. ●

Nimes Arena, Nimes, France

About the only time you should be allowed to describe tennis as "gladiatorial," which has become the emptiest of clichés, is when the French Davis Cup team is playing at the Roman amphitheater in Nimes. In the same arena where gladiators used to fight for their lives and for the entertainment of the crowd, French tennis players and their opponents have competed for the rather less significant prizes of winning points, games, sets, and rubbers in the Davis Cup.

There is a reason why the amphitheater at Nimes, which was built in the first century AD, is so well preserved, yet has been so well used. The Visigoths put a wall around the amphitheater and turned it into a castle, and in years to come the viscounts of Nimes made it a fortified palace, with the outside walls converted into ramparts. It would later become the home to hundreds of people, a slum dwelling where they lived in shanties between the seats, the arches, and the vomitoriums. In the early nineteenth century, when a team of restorers moved in, there was twenty feet of rubbish on top of the original sandy floor of the gladiators' ring. In the second half of that century, the amphitheater was adapted to be used as a bullring, and to this day there are annual bullfighting ferias there.

In modern times, the amphitheater in the southern French city has also been used for concerts, from opera to the heavy metal band Metallica, plus theater and Davis Cup tennis. For all the tennis history of the Longwood Cricket Club, home of the first Davis Cup tie in the summer of 1900, it seems a bit modern-day when compared with the Nimes Arena. The facilities have been modernized at the amphitheater, which has a maximum capacity of more than 16,000, with the structure enclosing an elliptical central space that is 133 meters long and 101 meters wide. In the late 1980s a heating system and retractable cover were built to protect against inclement weather.

Though Spain's Davis Cup team has become known for playing some of its home ties at bullrings, France was effectively doing so in the early 1990s—the amphitheater was not built for what Ernest Hemingway called "death in the afternoon," but that is what most people in France now associate the place with. The Davis Cup first came to Nimes in 1991 for France's quarterfinal against Australia, and the tennis lived up to the backdrop, as a young Fabrice Santoro, who was playing in his first tie, scored the decisive fifth rubber for his country by beating Wally Masur on the open-air clay court. That was plainly a time when tennis players could

have been seen as gladiatorial, even if Masur did not have to wait for a thumbs-up from the crowd before knowing he would return to the locker room in one piece.

France went on to win the Davis Cup that year, though the semifinal and final, which were both home ties, were played at indoor venues elsewhere in the country. Yet the idea of playing tennis where thousands of gladiators, and bulls, had met their ends had proved to be a popular one with both the locals and the French Tennis Federation, and it was not long before the Davis Cup returned.

The second time that France appeared in the amphitheater, for the 1992 quarterfinal against Switzerland, the tennis was under cover, turning the open-air arena into an indoor clay-court stadium, and on this occasion the French lost. France, who had Guy Forget, Thierry Champion, Henri Leconte, and Arnaud Boetsch in its team, was beaten 3–2 by a Swiss team that featured Marc Rosset and Jakob Hlasek.

Seven years passed before the Davis Cup was played at the arena for a third time. Under cover, France beat the Netherlands 4–1 in the first round of the 1999 World Group, with Cedric Pioline winning all three of his rubbers against a Dutch team that included Richard Krajicek and Paul Haarhuis. On all three occasions, though, the excitement of watching tennis in such a setting must have been just as much of an attraction as the outcome of the tie. One of the appeals of the Davis Cup is that the federations don't have to stick with traditional tennis venues. ●

BROTHERS IN ARMS

Davis Cup weeks are more than just tennis. They are a unique opportunity for players to come together as a nation, to share achievements and camaraderie, and to support each other in their common goal.

Semifinals 18–20 September

Spain defeated Israel 4–1 MURCIA, SPAIN—OUTDOOR CLAY

Czech Republic defeated Croatia 4–1 POREC, CROATIA—INDOOR CLAY

Introduction

By the Saturday evening of the semifinal weekend, Spain had an unassailable 3–0 lead over Israel, and the Czech Republic had won the first three rubbers of its tie against Croatia. It would be a mistake, though, to assume that the tennis in an indoor arena by the Croatian seaside was as one-sided as the rubbers that were played at a golf complex in southern Spain. Israel never came close to beating Spain, the defending champions and serial winners. But it did not take much imagination to see that the semifinal in Porec could easily have gone the way of Croatia, the 2005 champions.

The Czech Republic's first point came through Radek Stepanek, who had been on court for almost six hours when he won a 16–14 fifth set against Ivo Karlovic, on the day the Croatian served a world-record seventy-eight aces. In the fifth set, which lasted two hours, Stepanek had staved off Karlovic's four match points. Winning the second point was not straightforward either, with Tomas Berdych a five-set winner over Marin Cilic, and by the end of the opening day there had been almost ten hours of tennis.

Spain v Israel

The *Jerusalem Post* published a provocative opinion piece on the opening day of Israel's first Davis Cup semifinal. The columnist was astonished that captain Eyal Ran and the players had agreed to compete over Rosh Hashanah, the Jewish New Year: "Just as Israeli prime ministers often eat kosher food when they travel abroad on official visits, whether they are religious or not, so too the national sports teams have a responsibility to stand up for their Jewish heritage. It was a grave mistake for captain Ran to not even attempt to get the date of the tie moved to prevent the players desecrating such an important day in such a public manner."

At least one other Israeli newspaper carried a letter from a concerned reader about the Davis Cup team playing on a holy day in the Jewish calendar.

But outside of the opinion and letter pages, few Israelis seemed to genuinely mind that the Davis Cup team would spend the Jewish New Year running around a clay court in southern Spain. The columnist

How very different to events in a temporary stadium that had been built across one of the fairways at the Polaris World La Torre Golf Resort, between the towns of Murcia and Cartagena, where the Israeli team was making its country's first appearance in the semifinals. There was less than four-and-a-half hours of play on the opening day, with David Ferrer comfortably beating Harel Levy and Juan Carlos Ferrero winning the last twelve games of his rubber against Dudi Sela, so it mattered not one bit that Spain's two top 10 players, Rafael Nadal and Fernando Verdasco, were injured.

By the next day, the Spanish and the Czechs were into the final. It would be a second successive final for Spain, and its fifth in ten years, whereas over in Porec, reaching the Davis Cup final was a new experience for the Czech Republic. Although Ivan Lendl's Czechoslovakia had won the competition in 1980, beating Italy in the final, this was the first time since the Czech Republic became a separate nation that the country's tennis players had gone so deep into the competition.

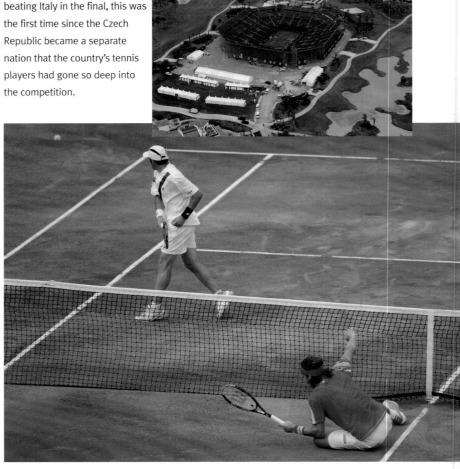

Pictured above from top:

Team Spain; Dudi Sela (ISR); Feliciano Lopez (ESP), left, and Tommy Robredo (ESP)

Pictured opposite:

David Ferrer (ESP)

for the *Jerusalem Post* even acknowledged as much, writing that he had been "shocked and confused to see little, if any, opposition to the tie being played over Rosh Hashanah." Indeed, the team embraced the fact that the tie was to be played on a holiday, as that would enable more people to follow the semifinal against the defending champions on television.

Ran and his players were perhaps the only people who believed that they had a chance of beating the winner of the 2000, 2004, and 2008 competitions. They kept telling themselves that anything was possible on clay, noting Rafael Nadal's withdrawal the week before the tie with the abdominal injury that had been bothering him at the US Open. "This is like David and Goliath," said one of the Israeli doubles players, Andy Ram. "And we all know who won that one."

The reality, though, was that Nadal's withdrawal had not significantly altered the dynamics of the tie. For one thing, Nadal still traveled to the resort, where stands had been built over one of the fairways, turning it into a seventeen-hole course for the weekend. During the matches, Nadal sat in the Spanish team box wearing a red and yellow "Espana" shirt and a white baseball cap with a bull logo on the front, while shouting "vamos" and occasionally shaking his fist. Though Spanish captain Albert Costa could not field Nadal or his other top 10 player, Fernando Verdasco,

because of a foot injury, he still had Juan Carlos Ferrero, who was having a decent year, and David Ferrer, a former top 5 player. Then there was the small matter of Spain's home record; the defending champions went into the semifinal having won their previous sixteen ties at home, and their last eighteen in the competition on clay, and for the third time that season, Spain was playing at home. For Israel, beating Russia in the quarterfinals had been an extraordinary achievement, but defeating Spain was beyond them.

Before the opening rubbers, which were played in still and sunny conditions on the Friday afternoon, a minute's silence had been held in the twelve-thousand-seat stadium to remember the victims of the flash floods that had invaded Murcia a couple of days earlier.

Costa had been supportive of Nadal's withdrawal, which had been announced midway during one of the wet-weather interruptions to the Majorcan's US Open quarterfinal victory. For the opening rubbers, Costa therefore opted to play Ferrer and Ferrero, rather than Tommy Robredo, a higher-ranked member of the team. Between them, Ferrer and Ferrero dropped just fourteen games, and neither was taken to a tiebreak or a 7–5 set, so there were barely any moments when Nadal looked worried about how the tie was playing out.

In the second set of the first rubber, Harel Levy had a 3–1 lead over Ferrer. That was the only stage of the match when Levy, who was ranked more than one hundred places below his opponent, had the better of Ferrer. Levy appeared to have concluded beforehand that his only chance of success was to play an aggressive match. While there were times when his attacking tennis was successful, he was unable to sustain a serious challenge against Ferrer, who won 6–1 6–4 6–3. "It certainly wasn't as comfortable as it might have looked," said Ferrer. "The court was very slow and it was hard to finish off the points." But Ferrer was being generous.

Looking back, Ferrero's rubber against Dudi Sela, Israel's highest-ranked player, was effectively settled in the fourth game of the second set, when the Israeli had five points to break for a 3–1 lead. Ferrero saved them all. One of the break points resulted in what must have been the rally of the tie. When Sela forced Ferrero to run wide of the court, the Spaniard came up with a drop shot that was loaded with side spin, and, when it bounced, took what appeared to be a ninety-degree turn. If Ferrero had later been given twenty attempts to re-create that shot from that position on the court, he would have made it once, or perhaps not at all. Ferrero held serve for 2–2, and Sela did not win another game in the set or indeed the match. The first set and a half of the rubber had been competitive, with the first game of the match lasting sixteen minutes, but the second half of the second set, and the entire third set, were anything but, as the Spaniard won the last eleven games of the rubber for a 6–4 6–2 6–0 victory that gave the home nation another point.

"I was really tired after the fourth game of the second set," Sela said. "He played a good game at 2–2, he broke my serve, and I think that changed everything. He played much better after that, he started moving me around, I got tired, and he took control of the match." Ferrero felt as though Sela had "started to feel the pace in the middle of the second set." It was the first time that a Davis Cup tie had been held in the region of Murcia for nine years, and by Friday evening the locals were in no doubt as to which country was going to reach the 2009 final.

Though the Israeli doubles pairing of Ram and Jonathan Erlich, the 2008 Australian Open champions, failed to beat Robredo and Feliciano Lopez, they at least managed to win their team's first set of the weekend, and also provide some entertainment. The Spanish crowd would not have minded that their players had to work hard before achieving the unassailable 3–0 lead that took them into the final. By taking the opening set in a tiebreak, Robredo and Lopez extended Spain's winning run to seven sets, but Ram and Erlich leveled the rubber at one set all with another tiebreak, despite a medical drama when play had to be suspended after a ball girl appeared to have fainted. Nadal, who was one of the first to attend to the girl, had a concerned look on his face as the medical team arrived to take her away.

That was the only live set that Israel won all weekend, as Robredo and Lopez, although predominantly singles players, used their skill and experience at doubles to win in four sets, 7–6(6) 6–7(7) 6–4 6–2. Though some of the Spanish had had the chance to play a few holes of golf between their tennis training sessions, there was never any room for complacency that weekend.

Spain was into the final for another year, with its victory dedicated to the memory of a woman who had been swept away in the floods. "There's no doubt that when the Spanish play at home, nobody can beat them," said Ram. At tennis, anyway. The only sporting contest that the Israelis had any chance of winning over the weekend was the impromptu game of football that the teams played once the tie was over. Ram and the other Israelis sounded delighted at having had the chance to play tennis against the defending champions: "This was maybe a once-in-a-lifetime experience for us but hopefully next time we can play them in Israel, with our fans behind us, and have another go."

Perhaps while Costa was sitting by the side of the court in Murcia, watching the conclusion of the doubles match and Sunday's dead singles rubbers, his thoughts were already turning to which players he would choose for December's home final. If Nadal and Verdasco were going to be fit for the final, and Ferrer, Ferrero, Lopez, and Robredo were also going to be available, who would be left out of his team? After a comfortable weekend, the new captain had plenty to think about. ●

Pictured below from top:

Juan Carlos Ferrero (ESP);

Jonathan Erlich (ISR), left, and Andy Ram (ISR)

Pictured above from top:

Standing ovation for the Czechs;

Radek Stepanek (CZE)

Croatia v Czech Republic

Equaling or breaking records for aces does not tend to be a happy or a rewarding experience for Ivo Karlovic, the tallest man in tennis, who can generate some outrageous angles with his serve. As Andy Roddick once said of the six-foot, ten-inch Croatian, "it's like he's hitting the ball out of a tree." In the first round of the 2005 Wimbledon Championships, Karlovic equaled the world record for most aces served in a match, banging fifty-one of them through a grass court, but he still lost to Italy's Daniele Bracciali. Four years later, on the Roland Garros clay, Karlovic surpassed that mark with fifty-five aces, but again lost the match to Australia's Lleyton Hewitt in five sets. And the unfortunate pattern continued for Karlovic in this Davis Cup semifinal—in a rubber that was nothing less than astonishing, he welted seventy-eight aces and yet still lost to Radek Stepanek after a 16–14 fifth set. The rubber had lasted one minute under six hours.

"I feel like I've just been in a boxing match for ten rounds," said Karlovic, who had nothing to show for his record-breaking performance. "Everything hurts."

If Stepanek had not beaten Karlovic, the weekend by the seaside in Porec could have turned out very differently indeed. As it was, the Czech Republic won the next singles rubber and the doubles match, clinching the tie in two days and reaching the final for the first time as an independent nation.

If the game of tennis simply came down to totting up the aces, Karlovic would be a multiple grand slam champion by now. Thankfully, there is more to tennis than the thud-splat-thud of unreturnable serves hitting the backstop. So what makes Karlovic's serve so tricky to return? Karlovic does not have the power of Roddick, who holds the record for the fastest serve at 155 mph, and he does not have Roger Federer's placement or variety. What makes Karlovic so dangerous is his height; the geometry of a tennis court looks totally different from up there. Standing at the other end of a tennis court from Karlovic is like being a goalkeeper in a penalty shoot-out; you are left having to guess whether to go to your left, go to your right, or stay put. Even if you make the right call, you will then have to contend with the bounce, as you are going to find yourself hitting a return from up around your ears. Facing Karlovic, you need patience.

You also need some luck. At a dinner on the Wednesday evening, a couple of days before the Czech Republic's first semifinal for thirteen years, a band had entertained the two teams. It was the same group that had played at a dinner before Croatia's first-round victory over Chile, and before its quarterfinal win over the United States, both of which had also been played in Porec. When Stepanek and the rest of the Czech team said their goodbyes for the night, reached for their coats, and moved toward the door, the band's singer called out to the visitors: "Czech team, I'm telling you that it's not a good idea to leave first. Chile and the United States were the first to leave the dinner, and they both lost." On hearing this, Stepanek immediately took off his coat and sat down again, prompting laughter around the room.

You would imagine that a match played on clay could never see one player hitting seventy-eight aces, but the match was played indoors at the Sportska Dvorana Zatika, meaning that there was no wind or glare from the sun to disrupt Karlovic's service action. "Playing Karlovic is always strange and tricky, as you

get no rhythm. You know there won't be that many rallies, and it's important to focus all the time," said Stepanek, who hit a "mere" eighteen aces. "You have only a few chances to break him, and so you have to try to take them when they come."

The opening stages of the match were no indication of how the match was going to play out, as Karlovic and Stepanek exchanged service breaks. The serve then dominated the match. The first four sets were decided on tiebreaks, and there were seventy-eight consecutive holds of serve, from the early stages of the first set until the twenty-ninth game of the fifth set, when Karlovic flunked a volley. Stepanek, who had saved four match points earlier in the fifth set, then served out the victory, to put the visitors a point up in the tie. The final set lasted more than two hours. Karlovic had hit twenty-eight aces in the fifth set alone. At the moment of victory, Stepanek dropped to his knees and rested his forehead on the frame of his racket. Later, he walked around the court with his shirt pulled over his head. It felt as though Stepanek's victory should have been worth double points.

"We weren't able to break each other. The match was going crazy," Stepanek said after his 6–7(5) 7–6(5) 7–6(6) 6–7(2) 16–14 victory. "Everyone knows about Karlovic, that he has a phenomenal serve. That is why the only thing I could do was to wait patiently for my chance. Mentally, I was very strong and calm, and that was decisive in this match. It was like a lottery, and I took my chances. I knew that patience would be important."

Previously, the record for aces in a Davis Cup rubber had been forty-seven, a mark that Karlovic had shared with Brazil's Gustavo Kuerten and Swiss Marc Rosset. In fact, that had been a rare occasion for Karlovic, when he hit a record number of aces and didn't lose, as he had served those forty-seven in beating American James Blake in July's quarterfinal. If you measured the rubber against the clock, Stepanek and Karlovic had provided the longest Davis Cup match since the 1980s, the fourth longest in history, and just twenty-three minutes short of American John McEnroe's victory over Swede Mats Wilander in the quarterfinals of the 1982 competition, which had a running time of six hours and twenty-two minutes. And that wasn't all: the eighty-two games that had been played equaled the most in Davis Cup match history.

"It was a long and exhausting match," said Stepanek. "But when you play for your country, it's worth it. It wouldn't have mattered if it had lasted for another few hours."

There was so little between the players that you wondered whether Croatia, the 2005 champions, would have won the opening tie if their fans had been a little more vocal, if they had made the most of home advantage. The traveling Czech supporters were not afraid to make themselves heard inside the hall, and there were times when it sounded as though the semifinal was being played in Prague rather than Porec. The Czech fans sometimes pushed the boundaries of sporting behavior by cheering when Karlovic missed his first serves. "The crowd was

Pictured above clockwise from top left:
Croatian fans; Marin Cilic (CRO);
Ivo Karlovic (CRO), left, and captain Goran Prpic;
The marathon opening rubber
Pictured opposite:
Czech captain Jaroslav Navratil,
left, and Radek Stepanek (CZE)

www.daviscup.com

Pictured above clockwise
from top left:

Radek Stepanek (CZE), left,
and Tomas Berdych (CZE);

Tomas Berdych (CZE);

Lovro Zovko (CRO);

Pictured below right:

Czech fans

Pictured opposite from top:

Marin Cilic (CRO);

The Czech bench

amazing, as we had a lot of fans and it was like playing at home," said Stepanek. "I was very surprised. The Croatian fans were great as well. They gave the players a lot of support. It was a great atmosphere, and it was just an honor to play tennis in front of fans like that."

It was around 8.30 p.m. in Porec when the second rubber began, with Tomas Berdych facing Marin Cilic, who only days earlier had achieved his best result at a grand slam, beating Britain's Andy Murray in straight sets in the fourth round of the US Open to reach a first slam quarterfinal. Berdych needed five sets, and three hours and forty-eight minutes, to beat Cilic, 6–3 6–3 3–6 4–6 6–3. After nine hours and forty-seven minutes of tennis on the first day of the tie, the Czech Republic was just one more victory away from the final.

Since Lukas Dlouhy had just won the US Open doubles title with Indian Leander Paes, the Czech might have expected to feature in the doubles rubber. But in the end, his weekend involved being thrown into a swimming pool by his teammates as a way of marking his success in New York, and playing in a dead singles rubber on Sunday afternoon. On Saturday, when the tie was still live, it was Stepanek and Berdych who played in the doubles rubber, and they continued their unbeaten record in the competition, winning their fifth match together. They were straight-sets winners over Cilic and Lovro Zovko, taking two and a quarter hours for their 6–1 6–3 6–4 victory, and the tie would have been decided even earlier if play had not been suspended at the start of

the third set when a bank of lights in the arena failed.

Who would have thought that Stepanek had been on court for almost six hours the day before? It was Stepanek who put the Czech Republic into the final, with an overhead winner. "When the ball went up, I thought to myself, 'don't miss it,'" said Stepanek. "But the ball went in and we were in the final."

One eyewitness likened the Czech celebrations to something you might see at a rock concert: "The cheering, chanting, and jumping up and down courtside would have been more at home at a Pearl Jam performance. An entire section of men with all body shapes removed their shirts and started to swing them in the air while singing." For Czech captain Jaroslav Navratil, the emotion was overwhelming: "This is an unbelievable success for our country," he said. Stepanek added, "I don't think it's possible to go through emotions bigger than in the Davis Cup." ●

Estadio Olimpico, Seville, Spain

Some 30,492 spectators were at the Houston Astrodome for the 1973 Battle of the Sexes to see Bobby Riggs arrive on court on a golden rickshaw carried by six blondes, a group he referred to as "Bobby's Bosom Buddies," only to then lose to Billie Jean King. But that was sexual politics dressed up as a game of tennis, and not a sanctioned match. It was at Seville's Estadio Olimpico, where Spain defeated the United States in the 2004 Davis Cup final, that the sport officially had its largest-ever live audience, with daily crowds of 27,000 at an innovative venue that was both indoors and outdoors.

Everyone who was in the Andalusian city that weekend remembers the noise, with the chants, the brass band, and the klaxons—if anyone had brought a decibel counter, this would surely have broken some record for the loudest tennis event in history. If the officials requested "silencio, por favour" once, they requested it a thousand times. By the end of the three days, even the losing team's captain, Patrick McEnroe, spoke of "the electric atmosphere."

While Spain has played in more evocative surroundings, such as bullrings, there was no doubting the ambition and innovation of contesting the final on a temporary clay court under a roof in an open-air stadium.

Some would argue that it was an American tennis player, Andy Roddick, who essentially brought the tie to Andalusia. Originally, the Royal Spanish Tennis Federation had planned that, if Spain reached a home final, the tie would be played in Madrid. However, the Spanish players knew that it would be foolish to have the tie at relative altitude— Madrid is more than six hundred meters above sea level, and tennis

balls fly quicker through the thin air—if they were going to have to deal with Andy Roddick, the man with the fastest serve in history.

Though Seville did not have a tennis arena, the federation believed they could make use of a stadium that had been built for the city's failed bid for the 2008 Summer Games—an Olympic Stadium that had never seen any Olympic sport. Though the Estadio Olimpico staged the 1999 World Athletics Championships and the final of the 2003 Uefa Cup football competition, many in Seville will have fondest memories of the weekend when Rafael Nadal won the first big prize of his career.

The clay court was built at one end of the stadium. And since no one wanted to take any chances with the December weather, a roof was needed. Remarkably, the match court, two practice courts, a roof, the structure that supported the roof, and more than a hundred executive boxes were built in six days. At first the federation had put around twenty-three thousand tickets on sale for each day's play, but it became clear that they could fit another four thousand people in the stadium, meaning the final would break the previous record for a sanctioned tennis match, the 25,578 spectators who had watched the 1954 Davis Cup final in Sydney, when Australia had defeated the United States.

After all the effort and money that had gone into the weekend—two million euros spent on the venue—the Spanish players did their bit, with two players from the Balearic island of Majorca, Nadal and Carlos Moya, winning the trophy for the home nation. Moya opened the tie with a victory over Mardy Fish, and Nadal then beat Roddick. Though the Bryan twins, Mike and Bob, won the doubles rubber against Juan Carlos Ferrero and Tommy Robredo, Moya gave Spain the Davis Cup by beating Roddick in the first of Sunday's rubbers.

The soundtrack was extraordinary. Many of the spectators were football fans watching live tennis for the first time in their lives. It took a while for the tennis players to get used to the crowd, and maybe also for the spectators to realize that sometimes a bit of quiet is needed during a tennis match.

The only contentious incident was during Roddick's match against Nadal. Just as Roddick was about to hit a volley against Nadal someone sounded a klaxon, he missed the shot, and after the American's complaint, the partisan crowd rule was invoked, so the point was replayed. McEnroe, after some misgivings on the first day about the noise from the crowd, spoke afterward of "an unforgettable experience." ●

THE DAVIS CUP EFFECT

The past and the present turned out to support their teams during the 2009 competition,
proving that once a Davis Cup player, always a Davis Cup player.

Play-offs 18–20 September

Ecuador defeated Brazil 3–2   PORTO ALEGRE, BRAZIL—INDOOR CLAY

France defeated Netherlands 4–1   MAASTRICHT, NETHERLANDS—INDOOR CLAY

India defeated South Africa 4–1   JOHANNESBURG, SOUTH AFRICA—INDOOR HARD

Serbia defeated Uzbekistan 5–0   BELGRADE, SERBIA—INDOOR HARD

Sweden defeated Romania 3–2   HELSINGBORG, SWEDEN—INDOOR HARD

Switzerland defeated Italy 3–2   GENOA, ITALY—OUTDOOR CLAY

Belgium defeated Ukraine 3–2   CHARLEROI, BELGIUM—INDOOR CLAY

Chile defeated Austria 3–2   RANCAGUA, CHILE—OUTDOOR CLAY

Introduction

A Davis Cup weekend can invigorate both young and old. Somdev Devvarman's reward, after the twenty-four-year-old took India into the World Group for the first time since 1998, was the Bollywood treatment back in New Delhi after returning from the Play-off against South Africa. Nicolas Lapentti, who is on the wrong side of thirty, propelled Ecuador into the sixteen-team elite for the first time since 2001, at an emotional tie for the player and his family in southern Brazil.

The Davis Cup can also invigorate the greatest player to have ever swung a racket, as just thirty-two hours after he lost the US Open final, Roger Federer landed in Genoa, where he kept Switzerland in the World Group, in between being photographed with Italian footballer Alessandro Del Piero and Italian fashion designer Giorgio Armani. In Belgrade, Novak Djokovic looked on from the smart seats as his Serbian colleagues defeated Uzbekistan, while in Maastricht, Frenchman Jo-Wilfried Tsonga showed the Netherlands just how to play a tiebreak.

In Sweden, Robin Soderling demonstrated against the Romanian Davis Cup team that he is a different player since his run to the final of Roland Garros. Belgium's Steve Darcis turned in such a fine performance in the live fifth rubber against Ukraine's Sergei Bubka Jr. that it proved to be an anticlimax. And it was all very different in Chile, where at 2 a.m. in Rancagua, after more than five hours on court, Nicolas Massu concluded his defeat of Austria's Stefan Koubek with a moving homage to his adoring crowd. ●

Pictured below from top:
Ecuador's captain Raul Viver;
The Brazilian bench

Brazil v Ecuador

Some would suggest that Nicolas Lapentti's most significant weekend in the Davis Cup came on Wimbledon's Court One in 2000, when Ecuador embarrassed a team that included Tim Henman and Greg Rusedski. Lapentti would disagree. Lapentti felt that the most important tie of his Davis Cup career was his thirty-seventh, when he traveled to southern Brazil for a weekend in Porto Alegre that would determine which of the South American nations would compete in the World Group in 2010.

Lapentti, a thirty-three-year-old ranked outside the world's top 100, had been thinking about retirement when he arrived in Brazil, saying that, "depending on this result, I am going to know what my future is like." Three days on an indoor clay court convinced him to carry on playing. Lapentti was on court for more than eleven hours over the weekend. By winning his two singles rubbers, and also the doubles match with his younger brother, Giovanni, he contributed the three points that took Ecuador back into the World Group for the first time since 2001.

The most memorable of the matches was Lapentti's five-set victory over Marcos Daniel, Brazil's leading singles player, which gave Ecuador the unassailable 3–1 lead. Lapentti won the first two sets only to drop the third and fourth. He had been on court for four hours and forty-two minutes when he completed his 6–4 6–4 1–6 2–6 8–6 victory. After the tennis, there were the hugs and the tears—he embraced his captain, Raul Viver; he hugged Andres Gomez, the 1990 French Open champion who had traveled to assist the team; and he wept with his parents and his brother.

Pictured above from top:

Marcos Daniel (BRA);

Nicolas Lapentti (ECU)

Pictured right:

Jo-Wilfried Tsonga (FRA)

"It is a very emotional moment for me," said Lapentti, a former top 10 player who had held a 5–2 lead in the final set and served for the match at 5–3. "I was very tired after the first two sets, and I lost the third and fourth sets, but then, when I went to the locker room after the fourth set, I told my brother that I wasn't going to lose the match. This is the beauty of Davis Cup, the energy of a team and the energy of a country."

Ecuador's winning streak was extended to six ties. Just a year and a half earlier, Ecuador had played the Netherlands Antilles in the first round of the Americas Zone Group II, a long way from the elite World Group. Ecuador beat the Netherlands Antilles, the Dominican Republic, and Paraguay to achieve promotion, and in 2009 they defeated Canada and Peru in Group I to reach the World Group Play-off round.

For Daniel, the disappointment of defeat was even greater because it occurred close to where he was born and at a venue, the Gigantinho Stadium, that is home to his football team, Internacional Porto Alegre. Daniel won the opening rubber of the tie, beating Giovanni Lapentti 7–6(3) 3–6 7–6(4) 6–2, the only live rubber that Brazil would win over the weekend before Nicolas Lapentti, twelve years older than his fellow top 100 opponent, beat Thomaz Bellucci 7–6(2) 6–4 7–5.

"I know that in the Davis Cup, experience means a lot and that the Brazilian players could feel the

pressure of the crowd a bit," said Lapentti, who, with his brother, had achieved a five-set 3–6 6–3 6–4 4–6 6–4 victory over Marcelo Melo and Andre Sa in the previous day's doubles match to set up Nicolas's decisive victory the following day. ●

Netherlands v France

Jo-Wilfried Tsonga's finest tennis came during the tiebreaks. The Frenchman played five tiebreaks over the weekend in Maastricht—two in his opening singles rubber, one in the doubles match alongside Michael Llodra, and another two in his second singles rubber—and he won them all. In fact, he won four of them fairly comfortably. The closest tiebreak was the opening set of his match against Thiemo de Bakker on the Sunday of the tie; Tsonga took that 7–5 and won the rubber in four sets to give France an unbeatable 3–1 lead.

"Jo-Wilfried was great in the tiebreaks against me, in fact he was great in all the tiebreaks over the weekend," said de Bakker, a former world junior champion. "That's when top players produce their best tennis. I have to try to copy that."

The key to playing a good tiebreak is to keep your nerve. Tsonga did just that in that fourth rubber, and de Bakker plainly did not. At 5–5 in the first-set tiebreak, the Dutchman was given a fairly routine forehand to hit, but he produced his worst stroke of the weekend, with the ball landing in the tramlines. De Bakker flung his racket across the court. Tsonga hit a big serve on the next point to take a one-set lead.

"I think I was the better player for much of the first set—just," de Bakker said. "But then I missed that forehand. And by winning the tiebreak, Jo-Wilfried also won the second set."

The Frenchman did not require a tiebreak to win that second set. But the fourth set was also decided by tennis's version of the penalty shoot-out. "I think I might have been in better shape for a fifth set than he was," de Bakker said after Tsonga's 7–6(5) 6–2 3–6 7–6(4) victory. "But again, he was excellent in the tiebreak, not giving me anything."

With Gilles Simon missing because of injury, Tsonga and Gael Monfils were France's singles nominations. On his first Davis Cup appearance, Monfils lost in four sets to de Bakker on the indoor clay. The Dutchman, who kept playing drop shots, won 6–3 5–7 6–3 6–4. For de Bakker, it was "the best win of my career, for certain." For Monfils, it was "shocking." "I wasn't the warrior I usually can be in a match, but all credit to him, he played well," said Monfils.

The French captain, Guy Forget, seemed to suggest that the occasion had gotten to Monfils. "It's difficult to prepare someone for a Davis Cup match. You can tell a guy to get in the plane and say to him, 'here's your parachute, it's no big deal, just jump, you have a parachute.' But when the guy gets there, it's different. He says, 'it's too high, I'm not jumping,' and maybe that's what happened with Gael," said Forget. "But it wasn't that bad, he shouldn't be ashamed. You

have to remember that de Bakker played a great match, worthy of a top-20 player. Against another of the Dutch players, Gael probably would have done a lot better. He didn't start very well, but that is only what can be expected when someone plays their first Davis Cup match."

Tsonga's 7–6(2) 6–2 7–6(3) victory over Jesse Huta Galung, who had come into the tie on a dreadful run of form, put the countries level after the first day. In the doubles, Tsonga and Llodra defeated de Bakker and Igor Sijsling 6–3 3–6 7–6(2) 6–4. During the doubles rubber, some of the Dutch spectators made the mistake of hissing at Tsonga during his service motion. "When they do that, it only makes me stronger," said Tsonga, who completed the French win the next day. ●

Pictured above:
Colorful fans fill the stands
Pictured below from left:
Gael Monfils (FRA);
Jesse Huta-Galung (NED)
Pictured opposite from top:
Thiemo de Bakker (NED);
Dutch fans during the doubles rubber

South Africa v India

For Somdev Devvarman, the Bollywood treatment was an insight into what life must be like on a daily basis for Sachin Tendulkar and India's other Test cricketers. When Devvarman walked out of the arrivals hall at New Delhi airport, he was bedecked with a garland of flowers, and the young tennis player found himself discussing his hair in interviews. A headline in *The Times of India* announced "the world at Som's feet," and across the country Devvarman was being spoken of as the Bright Young Thing of Indian tennis.

Devvarman had flown in from Johannesburg, where he had contributed a couple of points to give his team an unbeatable 3–1 lead in their play-off against South Africa at the Ellis Park Tennis Stadium, putting India into the World Group for the first time since 1998. This attention was all very sudden. Just a year earlier Devvarman had made his first Davis Cup appearance, losing a singles rubber against Uzbekistan in straight sets, and only a few people outside his home city of Chennai would have heard of him.

Devvarman was an American college player between 2005 and 2008, competing for the University of Virginia. In 2008, after receiving a degree in sociology, he decided to turn professional. It was in January 2009 that the wider tennis world first became aware of Devvarman's talent, when he defeated American Kevin Kim, Spaniard Carlos Moya, Croatian Ivo Karlovic, and Germany's Rainer Schuettler on the way to reaching the final of the ATP tournament in Chennai, finishing as runner-up to Croatia's Marin Cilic.

And yet the fastest way to tennis stardom in India is to achieve something special for the Davis Cup team. "I love being part of a team," said Devvarman. "My years in college were spent playing in a team. Tennis is an individual sport. But to have people to share jokes with, to share your wins with, and to pull you out of a tight spot, that's what makes it fun, and Davis Cup is the highest level of team tennis."

The Indians had reached the play-off round after Australia forfeited its Asia-Oceania tie in Chennai after citing security concerns, though the International Tennis Federation said it was safe to play. For the tie

against South Africa, they were without Leander Paes, their veteran player. Paes had only just won the US Open doubles title, with Czech Lukas Dlouhy, but he was forced to withdraw from the Davis Cup team because of shoulder and elbow injuries.

With Johannesburg some two thousand meters above sea level, visiting players often struggle with the altitude, but Devvarman seemed to be judging his shots just fine during a 7–6(5) 6–3 6–4 victory over Izak Van der Merwe. Rohan Bopanna, who was returning from a three-month break because of injury, came from a set down for a 2–6 6–4 6–2 6–4 victory over Rik De Voest, leaving India just one win away from the 2010 World Group. During the doubles rubber, India's Mahesh Bhupathi, who was partnered by Bopanna, sustained a groin strain when he was

Pictured above from top:
Somdev Devvarman (IND);
A South African fan

attempting an overhead smash, and he soon realized that he was unable to serve and volley. With the South African pairing of Wesley Moodie and Jeff Coetzee leading 6–3 3–6 4–0, the Indian team was forced to retire.

When De Voest went two sets up against Devvarman in their reverse singles rubber and broke early in the third set, it appeared as though the play-off tie would be decided in the fifth rubber. But Devvarman somehow worked his way back into the match, winning the third set, the fourth set, and then the fifth set against his friend and regular practice partner. "If the match got physical, I knew it was mine," said Devvarman after a 3–6 6–7(3) 7–6(5) 6–2 6–4 victory that took four and three-quarter hours. "When I was down two sets, I was in a place I wanted to be. I practice with Rik, and I know what his game is like. He played unbelievably well, but I knew that if I was feeling it a bit out there, Rik would be absolutely dying. It was just a matter of keeping the ball in play— then I had a chance. Obviously it was very physical. I was obviously doing a lot of work. I was running a lot, and toward the end my tactics were to get him running around the court a lot."

Devvarman had been encouraged by the support of the Indian bench. "Being calm and collected has a soothing effect on my team," said the Indian captain, Shiv Prakash Misra. "Why would I want to get unnecessarily excited?" Devvarman, who was unbeaten for the Davis Cup year after also winning both his singles matches against Chinese Taipei in March, had played some mature tennis. "That he came from two sets down shows that he has a lot of mental strength," said Paes. "Full credit to him for winning two singles matches. Somdev is the future of Indian tennis." ●

Serbia v Uzbekistan

O f the four semifinalists at the 2009 US Open, the only one who represented his country in the Davis Cup the following weekend was Roger Federer. Argentina did not play, so the new US Open champion, Juan Martin del Potro, had the weekend off in his home city of Tandil. The two defeated semifinalists, Rafael Nadal and Novak Djokovic, turned up at their respective countries' ties, but only as spectators. Djokovic, who was tired after his summer on the North American hard courts, believed—and he was not wrong with his assessment—that Serbia could beat Uzbekistan without him.

Uzbekistan had had a fine win in its previous tie, beating Japan in the Asia-Oceania zone, and had been hoping to reach the World Group for the first time. But, even without Djokovic, Serbia still had a couple of top 100 singles players in Viktor Troicki and Janko Tipsarevic, as well as a world-class doubles player in Nenad Zimonjic. The Serbian Tennis Federation offered free admission for all three days, and those who came to the Belgrade Arena watched the Balkan nation keep its place in the World Group for 2010 without losing a single rubber.

Even so, Tipsarevic and Troicki did not make life easy for themselves during their singles rubbers on the first day of the tie on the indoor hard court. Tipsarevic, a bookish type who probably would have been an academic if he was not a professional tennis player, tried to be too clever during the second set of

his four-set victory over Denis Istomin. Once Tipsarevic gathered himself and remembered that his tennis is more effective when he keeps it simple, he won the third and fourth sets. "I think I was the much better player but I tried to be too clever in the second set at times and overplayed some points when I should have just stuck with the basics," he said after his 6–2 5–7 6–1 6–4 victory. "Things fell into place after I regained my composure and I was able to play my game of being aggressive, and making my opponent move from side to side as much as possible."

Troicki, ranked in the top 40 at the time, also took the scenic route on the way to beating his opponent, Farrukh Dustov, who was outside the world's top 400. "It was my first Davis Cup match for Serbia on home soil, and I had a bit of stage fright," said Troicki, a five-set 6–4 3–6 6–3 4–6 6–2 winner. "In the end, I am glad that I came through all the trials and tribulations to give our team a 2–0 lead after the opening day. Dustov was terrific. He played way above his ATP ranking, while I took time to get into my stride and made a lot of unforced errors."

Serbia, which had lost to Rafael Nadal's Spain in the first round of the World Group, won this tie in two days, with Tipsarevic and Zimonjic dropping just seven games in beating Dustov and Istomin 6–2 6–3 6–2 in the doubles. "Janko was obviously very motivated because it was an honor for him to play with Zimonjic," said Serbia's captain, Bogdan Obradovic. "Like any other player, he can learn a lot from Nenad

about doubles, and his effervescent performance suggests that they can become a force to be reckoned with in the doubles for Serbia's Davis Cup matches."

Troicki and Illija Bozoljac, playing his first match after a ten-week injury layoff, highlighted Serbia's invincibility by winning both dead rubbers on the Sunday to a standing ovation from the crowd. "I want to thank my team for a brilliant performance, the Serbian Tennis Federation for being there for us all the time, and the fans for turning up throughout the weekend to support us," said Obradovic, whose desire for another home tie in the 2010 first round was granted when the following week, Serbia was drawn to host United States. ●

Sweden v Romania

Just one match, and one victory, can change the course of a tennis player's career, especially when that occasion is becoming the first man to defeat Rafael Nadal on the Roland Garros clay. Ever since Robin Soderling beat the Majorcan in the fourth round at Paris, and then went on to finish as runner-up to Roger Federer, he has appeared to have far greater confidence in his abilities. That extra self-belief was apparent at the Idrottens Hus in Helsinborg, where, for the first time in his Davis Cup career, Soderling won three rubbers over a weekend. In fact, Soderling did not drop a set over the three days he was on court against Romania.

"I think there are few players in the world right now who are better than Robin," Mats Wilander, Sweden's captain, said of Soderling. "He has obviously shown that in Davis Cup over the last three or four years, and now he's shown it in the grand slams. He's really at the beginning of his career and he's going to be great for the Swedish team."

In the opening rubber, Victor Hanescu had just saved Andreas Vinciguerra's three set points in the second-set tiebreak to lead 7–6(5) 7–6(10) when the Swede retired from the match because of a sprained ankle. The Swedish spectators, and perhaps even some of the Romanian fans in the crowd, felt great sympathy for Vinciguerra, who had not won a match in Davis Cup since a World Group first-round tie against Brazil in 2003. Both of Vinciguerra's singles rubbers in the 2009 World Group first-round tie against Israel had come

down to a fifth set—he lost one 11–9 and the other 8–6. It was just as well that Wilander could rely on Soderling.

Soderling needed less than an hour and a half for his 6–2 6–1 7–5 defeat of Victor Crivoi on the first day, which led the Romanian captain, Andrei Pavel, to remark that the Swede had been "hitting bombs, and everything was going in" on the indoor hard court. Soderling and his doubles partner, Robert Lindstedt, won by a score of 6–1 7–6(7) 7–6(5) against Hanescu and Horia Tecau on the Saturday, and the next day, Soderling gave Sweden a 3–1 victory with a third successive straight-sets victory, a 7–5 6–1 6–0 win over Hanescu.

Once Soderling had won the opening set, Hanescu faded away. "It feels fantastic. It was an incredibly important match for me that we just had to win," said Soderling. "Losing wasn't in the picture. My returns weren't too good in the beginning of the first set, and it took me a while to really get into the match. But once I found my tempo, he couldn't keep up. I served well and I returned well; everything was on today. I feel good after the weekend. It was three good, short matches."

As Hanescu put it: "Robin started playing some unbelievable tennis, and there wasn't much that I could do about it." ●

Pictured above from top:
Robin Soderling (SWE);
Romanian captain Andrei Pavel
Pictured left:
An injured Andreas Vinciguerra (SWE)
Pictured opposite from top:
Italian captain Corrado Barazzutti;
Roger Federer (SUI)

Italy v Switzerland

In between backstage meetings with his celebrity admirers, Roger Federer contributed two of the points that kept Switzerland in the 2010 World Group. The day before the tie at the Centro Sportivo Valletta Cambiaso in Genoa, an Italian footballer, Alessandro Del Piero, turned up to present Federer with a couple of football shirts, one with "Roger" and "No. 1" on the back, and the other an autographed Del Piero jersey. He also gave the Swiss a pair of his boots after promising that "they don't stink." Italian fashion designer Giorgio Armani was in the crowd on the Sunday of the tie, when Federer gave Switzerland an unassailable 3–1 lead and the pair was later photographed together at the stadium.

The fashion industry has been courting Federer for a while. Federer simply moves in different circles to other tennis players. A few days after the tie, he sat in the front row at Armani's show at Milan Fashion Week, next to close friend Anna Wintour, the editor of American Vogue. "I told Mr. Armani that I was planning a trip to Italy and wanted to return the favor. We didn't expect the show to be such a spectacle but I had a week off, so why not? Giorgio saw me play for my country, now I'm in his." Federer said of his Fashion Week appearance.

The world No. 1 was understandably tired when he arrived in Genoa for the tie, just thirty-two hours after he had lost the US Open final to Argentina's Juan Martin del Potro, the first time he had been beaten in New York since the 2003 tournament. Federer also indicated that he had a slight problem with his leg. If this had been a regular tour event, Federer would probably have taken the week off to recover from the disappointment and the physical exertions, but he has always tried to keep Switzerland in the World Group.

Federer had missed Switzerland's first-round tie because of a back injury, and in his absence, his countrymen had lost to the United States. There was little doubt that Federer's decision to play in Genoa, less than four days after the Monday final at the US Open, changed the outcome of the tie. "Of course I feel tired, and it's not easy because it's also a new surface and different balls, but I believe I still have a little bit

left in the tank," said Federer, who had his first practice session in the Ligurian city on Wednesday evening.

To honor the death of six Italian soldiers who had been killed by a car bomb in Afghanistan the day before the tie, the Italian players wore black armbands, the flags flew at half-mast in the stadium, and a minute's silence was observed before the opening singles rubbers.

In Stanislas Wawrinka, Switzerland has an extremely capable second player, and he dropped just seven games in winning the first rubber, with a 6–4 6–1 6–2 victory over Andreas Seppi. The Italian felt unwell on court, complaining of a headache and stomach problems, and after the second set he left the stadium to have some tests.

Such was the quality of Federer's tennis during his straight-sets victory against Simone Bolelli that it was easy to forget that it was his first appearance on a clay court for more than three months, when he had won the Coupe des Mousquetaires for the first time at Roland Garros. The Italian crowd was so impressed that they gave Federer a standing ovation after his 6–3 6–4 6–1 victory. "It wasn't easy, with the jetlag, the surface change, and then to play here in Italy. I'm very happy with the scoreline," said Federer. "Given the circumstances, I am extremely happy with my performance."

The Swiss decided to rest Federer from the doubles rubber, even though he and Wawrinka had shown in the past that they were an effective team, winning the gold medal at the Beijing Olympics. Wawrinka and Marco Chiudinelli lost 6–2 6–4 7–6(3) to Bolelli and Potito Starace, so Federer was required for the reverse singles rubbers. Starace had won his previous ten singles appearances in the Davis Cup, but it never seemed as though he stood much chance of extending his record to eleven. With a match that was interrupted by a two-hour rain delay, Federer won 6–3 6–0 6–4. It was Federer's thirteenth consecutive singles victory in Davis Cup; he had not been beaten since his defeat to Australia's Lleyton Hewitt in 2003, a match that the Swiss had led by two sets to love. "I was very happy with the quality of my game, as I definitely didn't feel at my best." Federer had dropped just fifteen games all weekend.

But even when Federer was not at his best, he was too good for Italy. You can understand why one of the Italian spectators called out over the weekend: "Roger, diventa Italiano" ("Roger, become Italian"). Starace gave his honest assessment: "We can't be expected to beat a Swiss team that includes Roger Federer." ●

Pictured above:
Simone Bolelli (ITA)
Pictured below from left:
The doubles rubber;
Roger Federer (SUI)
signs autographs

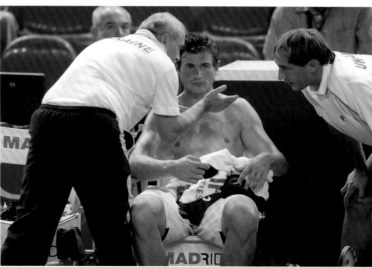

Pictured clockwise
from top left:
The Belgian team congratulates
Steve Darcis (BEL);
Sergei Bubka (UKR);
Steve Darcis (BEL)

Belgium v Ukraine

Of all the live fifth rubbers played over the course of the Davis Cup season, few can have had as little tension and drama as the one in Charleroi's Spiroudome. Very early on in the match, it was clear who was going to win, and Steve Darcis, the Belgian, dropped just three games in the first two sets against Sergei Bubka Jr., the son of the pole-vaulting great. Darcis won the third set 6–0, so the rubber was completed within an hour and a half, and Belgium had ensured it would feature in the 2010 World Group.

If the final rubber was devoid of much excitement, the doubles match provided the controversy of a disputed line-call, what the Ukrainians called their "anger burst," and Sergiy Stakhovsky's amateur photography—in the middle of the rubber, he produced his camera and took a picture of the mark on the clay. The umpire, Louise Engzell, had a busy September—she had been the official in the chair during Serena Williams's infamous US Open semifinal against Kim Clijsters, when the Californian received a point penalty at match point down after her comments directed at a female line judge.

And then Engzell had to deal with this. In the second game of the third set, Stakhovsky's partner, Bubka, struck what the Ukrainian team believed to be an ace against Xavier Malisse and Olivier Rochus. Engzell, who got down from her chair to inspect the mark on the clay, disagreed and called the serve out.

Bubka dropped his serve. The next time the Ukrainians were at that end of the court, Stakhovsky took a photograph of the mark. "If you think the ball was in you have to believe in Santa Claus and fairy tales and all that," said Stakhovsky. "I don't know what I'm going to do with the picture. Maybe I'll put it on a website. It definitely gave me an anger burst." Stakhovsky later received a fine of $750.

But the outrage appeared to propel Stakhovsky and Bubka to their four-set, 7–6(5), 3–6 6–4 7–6(4) victory that kept Ukraine in the tie in its first-ever World Group Play-off.

On the opening day, Christophe Rochus defeated Ilya Marchenko 6–3 6–4 3–6 6–2, and Darcis beat Stakhovsky 6–2 6–3 6–4. After the controversy in the doubles on Saturday afternoon, Stakhovsky came from two sets to one down in his reverse singles match on Sunday, having just lost the third set 6–0 for a 6–3 3–6 0–6 6–1 6–3 victory against Malisse that meant the play-off would be decided by a fifth rubber. "I was glad to give Junior the chance to play the last match," Stakhovsky said of presenting Bubka Jr. with the opportunity to win the tie for the Eastern Europeans. Unfortunately for Bubka, he never came close to beating Darcis, who played what he regarded as "one of the best matches of my career." "We deserve to be in the World Group," said Darcis. "We have not stolen a place in the World Group." ●

Chile v Austria

Surely the oddest episode of the Play-off weekend occurred in Rancagua, a city south of Santagio, at the Medialuna stadium, where the national rodeo championships take place every year. On this occasion, the crowds were there for tennis, rather than rodeo. Just after 2 a.m. on Monday, when the temperature had dropped to a chilly seven degrees Celsius, the spectators in the stadium suddenly started singing the national anthem. As one observer noted, it was "a simultaneously tearful and bizarre scene, made more so by the lateness of the hour and the cold," but, in truth, did anyone really expect the Chilean tennis fans to celebrate their country's return to the World Group by quietly shuffling toward the exits?

The crowd, though they were losing feeling in their fingers and toes, had stayed in their seats to watch Nicolas Massu win the fifth rubber, but it was just as well that he did not need a fifth set to beat Stefan Koubek, as completing four sets took five hours and fourteen minutes. That was because the Chilean and the Austrian both appeared to approach the outdoor clay court with pretty much the same game plan: keep the ball in play, let your opponent make the mistakes.

Inevitably, there were some very long rallies. Massu, the singles and doubles gold medalist at the 2004 Athens Olympics, had a spectacular mishap in the fourth set, when he slid across the clay and tripped over

Pictured above from top:

Chile celebrates;

Austrian captain Gilbert Schaller;

Jurgen Melzer (AUT)

Pictured opposite:

Nicolas Massu (CHI)

the line, falling heavily onto the court. Eventually, he defeated Koubek, and Austria, which had won a World Group Play-off for the previous six seasons, was relegated.

One of the first things Massu did after his 6–4 4–6 6–4 7–6(6) victory was to take a microphone and address the crowd, to thank them for staying out so late into the night. "I'd like to tell you that, without your support, I would never have won because I was so washed out," said Massu, whose nickname is "vampiro" or "vampire." "The only thing I can say is that people did not have much faith in me, in Paul [Capdeville] and in the rest of the team. They saw our victory as unlikely. I believe that nothing is impossible in life, nothing." It was after that sentence that the crowd roared their approval and began the first line of the national anthem. It seemed as though the Austrians had known all along that Massu's competitive nature would be a significant factor in the tie, with the visiting captain, Gilbert Schaller, remarking after the draw: "Massu is very well known on the circuit for his heart."

On the opening day of the tie, Massu came from a set down for a four-set, 4–6 6–4 6–4 6–3 victory against Jurgen Melzer, and Capdeville achieved a five-set, 6–4 6–4 3–6 1–6 6–4 defeat of Koubek. It was an important victory for Capdeville, Chile's first singles nomination, who had won only four games on his only previous singles appearance of the 2009 Davis Cup season, against Croatia's Marin Cilic. The week of the tie against Austria, Capdeville had suffered with a heavy cold, and from the third set of the match against Koubek he had been experiencing breathing difficulties. But having been two sets up, he won a five-setter, which lasted for three-and-a-half hours.

By the end of his singles rubber, Capdeville was tired, so it was surprising that he made himself available for the next day's doubles rubber. He and Massu lost in straight sets, 6–2 6–4 6–3, against the established pairing of Melzer and Julian Knowle, a doubles specialist. Melzer won an untidy fourth rubber in five sets, beating Capdeville 7–6(2) 4–6 6–2 5–7 6–4 in a match filled with breaks of serve. "It does not matter how well or badly I played, it just matters that I won and that the tie is still alive," said Melzer after his victory. "In a fifth match, anything can happen."

At two o'clock in the morning, Chile returned to the World Group. ●

Mullerpier, Rotterdam, Netherlands

In 2009 Jacco Eltingh, a former Davis Cup player for the Netherlands, attended a business meeting in the Mullerpier area of Rotterdam harbor. Eltingh saw for himself how the pier, which had previously been used for industrial storage and stacking, had been redeveloped into a residential area—what he called "luxury apartments," with modern conveniences and harbor views.

Eltingh's visit to the pier allowed him to spool back into Dutch Davis Cup history, as it was there, in the middle of Europe's largest port—surrounded by water, ships, cranes, and men in hard hats—that the Netherlands staged a tie in 1994, a quarterfinal against the United States that showed how the competition can come alive when you put players in the unlikeliest of locations.

"It was an amazing place to play a Davis Cup tie, as we were right there in the harbor, with the large container ships and other boats going by while we were playing tennis," recalled Eltingh, a former doubles world No. 1 who played all three days of the tie. Eltingh won all four grand slam doubles titles over the course of his career, but it sounded as though he took as much pleasure from competing on the Mullerpier as he had in Melbourne, Paris, London, and New York City.

"The top tennis players get to play in big stadiums all over the world, but when a stadium has been built for a Davis Cup tie that makes it extra special. It was incredible to be just there in the harbor with all the shipping going past, even if, since the stadium was so big, we could not see many of the ships from down on the court," said Eltingh. "The dressing rooms were between the stadium and the docks. I think the pier we were on was normally used for storage and stacking. It was probably the most unusual place that I've played Davis Cup, there was water all around, so you couldn't see into the stadium unless you had a ticket to be there. So the guys working on the docks couldn't look in to see how we were doing against the Americans."

The stadium was temporary, built just for the tie played in the middle of July, with the rubbers played on an outdoor hard court. "That was the biggest tie that we've ever had in our country," said Eltingh. "When I first started playing in the Davis Cup, we didn't get big crowds, you didn't see much of the color orange when you played at home for the Netherlands, but we had 16,000 every day for the tie against the United States. It was a great venue, and we had big opponents as well. Tennis was so alive in our country then, as there was a group of us who were high in the rankings. It was an unbelievable crowd. I think it helped that we were playing outside, as I think the atmosphere is better when you are playing in the open air rather than indoors. The atmosphere was fantastic over the weekend. It was a very fair crowd—they were cheering for us, obviously, but they didn't boo or anything at the Americans. Sometimes you get that at the Davis Cup, but they weren't a bad crowd on the pier."

Unfortunately for the Netherlands, the unusual setting and the extra crowd noise in the harbor did not help them much on the first day, when they failed to win even a set in the opening singles rubbers. Jim Courier defeated Richard Krajicek, and Pete Sampras then trounced Eltingh, dropping just four games against his Dutch opponent. But the Dutch doubles combination of Eltingh and Paul Haarhuis registered a first point for the home nation with their victory over Jared Palmer and Richey Reneberg, and Krajicek defeated Sampras in the first of the reverse singles rubbers on the Sunday, so the fifth match, Eltingh against Courier, would decide which nation reached the semifinals.

Eltingh has some strong memories of the tie. It was not just the venue that has stayed in his mind; there was also a strange noise from the crowd. "One thing I will always remember from the tie is one guy doing the loudest burp I think I've ever heard. It was so loud that everyone in the stadium heard it. It was so gross, and so loud!" said Eltingh. "The tennis was very close. It went right down to the final match. But Courier beat me in four sets in the fifth rubber. Still, I think people remember that it was a great tie." ●

EVERY KIND OF PEOPLE

It's not just the teams that turn out for Davis Cup ties. The competition spans generations, attracting everyone from fashion designers to royalty, to sporting heroes, supermodels and dignitaries.

The Final 4–6 December

Spain defeated Czech Republic 5–0 BARCELONA, SPAIN—INDOOR CLAY

The Final

Spain v Czech Republic

Only one spectator inside the Palau Sant Jordi was getting more airtime than Spain's Crown Prince Felipe. Between points, as Spain moved ever closer to retaining the Davis Cup trophy—to winning the competition for the fourth time in the Noughties—the director of the television coverage kept requesting close-up shots of Rafael Nadal. Whether he realized it or not, up in the hills above Barcelona, Nadal was Spain's cheerleader-in-chief. And who could be better for the job than Rafa? He has the most expressive face in tennis he can convey a whole range of emotions with those eyebrows alone and no one in the stadium, or watching at home on television, would have been left with any doubt as to what winning this competition meant to him.

As Fernando Verdasco and Feliciano Lopez played Radek Stepanek and Tomas Berdych, Nadal was not sitting by the side of the court. He was bouncing in his seat, calling out, shaking his fist. No wonder the television images kept flicking away from the prince to Rafa. It was plain that Nadal was getting as much pleasure from watching Verdasco and Lopez hitting winners as he would if he had been out there on the clay himself and those shots had come off his strings.

Time magazine once ran a tennis feature about "The Man Without an Ego." The subject of the story was Roger Federer, but it should have been Nadal. You can be sure that it was never Nadal's intention to take attention away from the heir to the Spanish throne. When Nadal is representing Spain in the Davis Cup, he can display his country's colors with a custom-made pair of yellow and red tennis shoes, and also share wins and defeats with his teammates. And he does not hide his emotions. "I am more of a team player than a singles player, that's my opinion," said Nadal, the world No. 2 and winner of six grand slam titles. Nadal delighted in being part of a team: "Being able to enjoy this with my teammates has been terrific."

For all his success in his solo career, for all his grand slam titles, the Davis Cup has been central to the story of Rafael "Rafa" Nadal Parera. All four of Spain's Davis Cup successes have come in the twenty-first century, and every time, Nadal has been involved,

whether directly or indirectly. Spain's first Davis Cup trophy came in the same stadium where they won their fourth. In 2000, when Spain defeated Australia in the final at the Palau Sant Jordi, the "Palace of St George," a fourteen-year-old Nadal carried his nation's flag during the on-court ceremonies. So in 2009, he would have been well aware of what "La Ensaladera," the salad bowl–shaped trophy, meant to the people of Barcelona, a city that the president of the International Tennis Federation, Francesco Ricci Bitti, described over the weekend as "the capital of tennis in Spain." The first great accomplishment of Nadal's career came in Davis Cup: before he became the French Open champion for the first time in 2005, he was a member of the Spanish team that won the trophy in 2004, contributing a point during the final at Seville's Estadio Olimpico against the United States.

Four years later, in 2008, Nadal earned his second mini replica Davis Cup trophy. Nadal had featured in Spain's quarterfinal and semifinal ties, and though a knee injury prevented him from traveling to Mar del Plata for the final against Argentina, he followed the

Pictured clockwise from top left:

Czech fans; Rafael Nadal (ESP);

David Ferrer (ESP) and captain Albert Costa

tie on television and kept in contact with the Spanish bench through text messages. As Nadal continued to have problems with his knees, he also missed Spain's quarterfinal and semifinal ties in 2009, so it was important for him to be part of the team in Catalonia. "It was disappointing not to have been at the final in 2008," said Nadal. "I have to thank the team for winning the quarterfinal and the semifinal. I wasn't there on court, but they gave me the opportunity to be here in Barcelona."

When Nadal wins a trophy, he bites it. The Davis Cup was the first piece of silverware he had bitten into since he won the clay-court tournament in Rome in May, some seven months earlier. Nadal had a successful start to the year, beating Federer at Melbourne Park in the final of the Australian Open to score his first hard-court grand slam title. At that stage, he was the undisputed world No. 1. In the middle part of the year, though, he was affected by knee injuries and his parents' divorce. He experienced his first defeat at the French Open, losing to Sweden's Robin Soderling in the fourth round, and he withdrew from Wimbledon because of the pain in both knees. Over the last two weeks of the ranking season, when he was playing on indoor hard courts, Nadal put together his longest losing run since he was seventeen, with four successive straight-sets

defeats—one in the semifinals in Paris, and then in all three of his round-robin matches at the end-of-season event in London. After all the professional and personal difficulties of 2009, what could be a better end to the tennis year than to win the Davis Cup? "That was the end to the season I needed," he said. "Winning again is a great feeling and a major achievement, particularly considering the problems I've had. You have to be sure to enjoy these moments when they happen because you don't know when the next victory will come."

Before the final began, some observers were suggesting that there could not have been a better time for Berdych, the Czech second singles nomination, to play Nadal on clay in Spain. Indeed, at the start of the week, those who didn't speak Catalan were wondering whether the "Bon Nadal" signs on display in Barcelona's streets and shop windows were an attempt by the city's mayor to encourage Rafa after his disappointing results in Paris and London. The reality was that the signs had nothing to do with tennis—in Catalan, "Bon Nadal" means "Happy Christmas." And the Czech team did not accept this idea of Nadal's vulnerability on a dusty orange-red court in Spain. Nadal had flown directly from London to Barcelona, without a stopover in Majorca, so that he had as much time as possible on the clay. As Stepanek said, it was ludicrous to suggest that Nadal would struggle playing on clay in front of the Spanish tennis public: "To take into consideration Nadal's failure in London? That doesn't work. The moment he steps on to the Barcelona clay, he will be a totally different player."

When Nadal played Berdych, it was the Majorcan's first appearance on clay since his defeat to Soderling in Paris six months earlier. Almost as soon as the smoke from the dry-ice machine had cleared from the arena, Nadal was back into his old clay-court routines. He was cleaning the baseline by scraping his yellow and red tennis shoe along the white plastic, demonstrating his rare ability to slide into shots off both his left foot and right foot, and he was hitting the whippy forehands that make him so lethal on the surface.

Berdych was only competitive in the first set. When Nadal was serving at 4–5, 0–30, the home player was two points away from losing a ninth set in succession. On the next point, Nadal went for high-risk play, hitting a heavily spun drop shot that just barely cleared the net. The ball then gripped the clay, spun backward, and Berdych arrived too late to do anything but put his response below the tape. Nadal held serve, broke in the next game, and then closed out the set. Those were the first three games of what would end up being a thirteen-game winning sequence for the Spaniard. Nadal ripped through the second and third sets. Berdych was bageled in the second set, winning

just thirteen points and no games, and Nadal also won the first four games of the third set. "There wasn't much that was working for me at that moment. It didn't happen for me. It was the worst case to be in on court," said Berdych.

No one could ever accuse Berdych of lacking ability. But this was yet another occasion when it seemed as though he was not making the most of that talent. As Andre Agassi wrote in his autobiography Open, Berdych needs to learn that he does not have to win every point by striking a winner into the corner. How about allowing your opponent to lose a few points? With Berdych playing such inconsistent tennis, and Nadal showing why he had won four French Open titles, the Czech did not get close to the Spaniard after the opening set. As one of the Spanish newspapers noted the next morning, this was Rafa remembering

Pictured clockwise from top:
Tomas Berdych (CZE); Palau Sant Jordi;
Umpire Pascal Maria with captain
Jaroslav Navratil (CZE)
Pictured opposite:
Rafael Nadal (ESP)

what it was to be Rafa. He even appeared to be picking at the pants of his shorts with greater confidence. "I played better than I did in London, but it wasn't very difficult for me to have done that," Nadal said after his 7–5 6–0 6–2 victory.

"I'm lucky to play tennis, because it's my hobby and at the same time it's my job. So for me it's not difficult to wake up every day and practice hard. Motivation is always important. It's always important to wake up with the goal to improve something. The day when I wake up and I don't feel like I have a goal, I'm going to play golf or another thing."

What of the Barcelona tennis crowd? Did they behave themselves this time? Everyone who was at the Palau Sant Jordi for the 2000 Davis Cup final will remember the hostile, spiky atmosphere. On that occasion, the Spanish fans and the Australian spectators seemed to spend most of their weekend inside the arena antagonizing each other, rather than concentrating on what was happening on the court.

This time, though, there was no such animosity at the palace from each day's capacity crowd of 16,200 spectators. Around 1,500 Czech fans had traveled to Barcelona for the final, so the Spanish and the visitors had competing bands at what had been the gymnastics venue for the 1992 Olympic Games. There were times during the changeovers when you could barely hear the music coming through the stadium's speakers. There was also occasional hissing and hooting when the Czechs asked the umpire to clamber down from his chair and check a mark on the clay. But that was to be expected. The atmosphere never got nasty. As Nadal said, "The atmosphere was unbelievable from the beginning."

Ferrer, the world No. 18, had been chosen ahead of Verdasco, even though the world No. 9 had apparently recovered from injury. "Fernando is fit and he has an important role to play in the doubles and possibly on Sunday," said Albert Costa, Spain's captain. "But David had prepared really well and he deserves to play." After the first two sets, Stepanek was 6–1 6–2 up, and it appeared as though Ferrer was two-thirds of the way to another opening day, straight-sets defeat in a Davis Cup final. A year earlier, at a time when he was struggling with his form and with personal problems, Ferrer lost heavily to Argentina's

David Nalbandian in Mar del Plata.

Stepanek, who had said that the arena was so cold during a practice session that he had walked off court with blue hands, looked extremely comfortable in a stadium warmed by the crowd, and he was playing an unorthodox, inventive, wonderfully effective brand of tennis. After winning just three games in the first two sets, Ferrer returned to the locker room to take a bathroom break and regroup. His captain went with him. The first of Ferrer's teammates to jump up from the bench and follow Ferrer and Costa into the locker room was Nadal. A day later, details emerged about what had happened in there. The Davis Cup rules state that only Costa could speak directly to Ferrer in the locker room. But according to an article in the Spanish newspaper El Pais, the players dodged the rule by encouraging Ferrer while they had their

Pictured clockwise from top:
Rafael Nadal (ESP); Radek Stepanek (CZE);
David Ferrer (ESP)
Pictured opposite:
Changeover in the second rubber

backs turned, all the while pretending to check their reflections in the mirror.

When the rubber resumed, it was a totally different match. Suddenly, Ferrer displayed a greater conviction of shot. He has always been one of the quickest players on the tour, but he was running down everything. He came back to achieve a five-set, 1–6 2–6 6–4 6–4 8–6 win over four and a quarter hours. At the moment of victory, Ferrer fell onto his back on the clay, exhausted but happy. Remarkably, it was not the first time in Ferrer's career that he had turned a two-set deficit against Stepanek into a five-set victory. Prior to the final, there had only been two occasions when Ferrer had come back from two sets down to win a match, and one of them had been against Stepanek, in the third round of the 2007 Australian Open. For Ferrer, this might just have been "the most important win of my career." How could he have felt satisfied with his contribution if, for the second year in succession, he had held up his replica trophy after winning no sets over the course of the final?

So Spain, after winning both singles rubbers on the opening day, was just one more point away from becoming the first country to win successive Davis Cup titles since Sweden retained the trophy in 1998. Czech Republic was appearing in its first final since 1980, when Ivan Lendl's Czechoslovakia had won the trophy. "Losing that match to David was tough," said Stepanek, who had done the most to take the Eastern European nation to the final. "We are playing in the Davis Cup final for the first time in twenty-nine years, so these three days mean so much to me. To lose a match like that, that's tennis. At the end David was the lucky one. But I think I should be proud of what I did today, the way I played. It's very disappointing, but my head is up. We had a great battle and I have to congratulate David for pulling it out at the end."

For Costa, Ferrer's comeback was key. "Without it," Costa said, "the final could have become complicated for us." Unfortunately for the Czechs, the only sets they won all weekend were the two that Stepanek took against Ferrer. As Lopez would say of Ferrer the next day, after Spain had retained the trophy, "this final is his."

Spain had two fresh players for the doubles rubber in Verdasco and Lopez. It is tricky to think of

another country that could have the luxury of not using a top-10 player on the first day of a Davis Cup final. Czech Republic used the same players who had competed in the singles. Who at the Palau Sant Jordi had believed that the Czech captain, Jaroslav Navratil, would stick with his original doubles nomination of Lukas Dlouhy and Jan Hajek? Stepanek and Berdych played doubles together in the first round, quarterfinal, and semifinal ties, winning all three of their rubbers. Though Stepanek had played for more than four hours late into Friday evening, moments after coming off court he suggested that he was ready

Pictured above:

Radek Stepanek (CZE) pulls up with cramp

Pictured below:

Fernando Verdasco (ESP) celebrates

with his teammates

to play in the doubles on Saturday afternoon. After all, in the semifinal against Croatia, Stepanek had been on court for six hours to beat Ivo Karlovic in the opening singles rubber, then played doubles the next day. "I think you see me walking, breathing, and talking. I think I'm physically able to play another match. I played even tougher matches before. Don't worry about me."

The doubles rubber was decided in the opening-set tiebreak. Spain's all-leftie combination led 6–3 in the tiebreak, and yet they could not convert those three set points. Then the Czechs had a set point of their own, when Berdych was serving at 7–6. Verdasco and Lopez staved off that chance and ended up taking the tiebreaker 9–7. Once they had won the opening set, the Spanish (Verdasco and Lopez on the clay, and Nadal and Crown Prince Felipe in their seats) looked increasingly assured of victory. Whatever Stepanek had said on Friday evening about his physical conditioning, it became clear that he was not in the best possible shape, with the Czech pulling up with a cramp at 1–3 down in the final set.

For the second year in succession, Verdasco was on court when Spain became the Davis Cup champion. In Mar del Plata, Verdasco won the decisive point by defeating Argentina's Jose Acasuso in the fourth singles rubber. This time, Spain's victory came a day earlier, with Verdasco and Lopez's 7–6(7) 7–5 6–2

victory giving Spain an unassailable 3–0 lead.

The final shot was a bench-clearing moment. Lopez just about had time to hold up four fingers—one finger for every Davis Cup trophy Spain has won—before he and Verdasco were lost among their teammates, captain Costa, and the other coaches and members of the backroom staff. When that group hug broke up, they celebrated with their families, and then with Crown Prince Felipe, who had walked down to the side of the court. This was yet another victory that Nadal could share with the prince. When Nadal won the 2008 Wimbledon title, he went for a precarious walk along the roofs of the television commentary boxes in Centre Court to reach the Royal Box, where he celebrated with Prince Felipe and his wife, Princess Letizia.

The players gave the bumps to their captain and to Juan Carlos Ferrero. In 2000 Ferrero had won the winning point for Spain with his defeat of Australian Lleyton Hewitt. Nine years later, the former world No. 1 and 2003 French Open champion did not make the team. But Ferrero had played an important role in Spain's Davis Cup success, winning a decisive fifth rubber in the quarterfinal against Germany. Ferrero was touched by how the crowd chanted his name and the players threw him high into the air.

There was no repeat of the animosity between Spain and the beaten finalists that had arisen in 2000. The Czech players and captain were quick to congratulate the Spanish on their victory, on winning the Davis Cup final in two days. "We are very happy with this season because we were in the final for the first time since 1980," said Navratil. "But, you know, our opponent, Team Spain, was very strong, very tough. I just have to congratulate the Spanish team for winning the Davis Cup for the second year in succession." In return, the Spanish congratulated the Czechs on their year, for having reached their first final in almost thirty years.

Spain's various winning streaks continued. With the victory in Catalonia, Spain had won its last eight ties, a Spanish record. The team also extended Spain's winning run at home to eighteen ties, and its unbeaten run on clay to twenty ties. Its last defeat on clay, and also its last defeat at home, was the loss to Brazil in the first round of the 1999 World Group.

The statistics kept coming on top of the Montjuic Hill—Costa also achieved the player-captain double. Nine years earlier in Barcelona, Costa won the Davis Cup as a player, and now he had won the competition in his first year as captain. "I think the most important thing for me is the players," said Costa. "Without the players there is no chance for the captain. So that's the most important thing. It's a special moment for me. To have the chance to win the Davis Cup as a player and now as a captain, I think I'm a very lucky man."

There was enough to keep the ticket holders entertained on a "dead" Sunday. Nadal demonstrated his selflessness by playing in a best-of-three-sets singles rubber. Some players of his standing would not have agreed to that request the day after winning the Davis Cup. Nadal took his match seriously, beating Hajek in straight sets, and Ferrer then defeated Dlouhy in straight sets as well. Spain was the first country since Sweden in 1997 to win all five rubbers at a Davis Cup final. It was only then that Spain's players and captain, some of whom were showing the effects of Saturday evening's celebrations, were presented with their miniature replica trophies to hold above their heads on the dais. Cheers of "campeones, campeones" and "España, España" bounced around the Palau Sant Jordi.

Over the weekend, Nadal looked as happy as he had been all year. At the official dinner on Sunday evening, which was held at Barcelona's old stock exchange, Nadal was photographed enjoying the speeches. One shot stood out. It was of Nadal throwing his head back and laughing. ●

Pictured above:
Fernando Verdasco (ESP), Rafael Nadal (ESP) and Feliciano Lopez (ESP)
Pictured below:
Crown Prince Felipe congratulates Fernando Verdasco (ESP)
Pictured opposite from top:
Feliciano Lopez (ESP) and Fernando Verdasco (ESP) deliver Spain its fourth title;
The 2009 champions and finalists

Player of the Year: Radek Stepanek

Born November 27 1978 in Karvina, Czech Republic
Turned professional 1996

There have been times during his career when Radek Stepanek hasn't been to everyone's taste, as his cartoonish on-court ways don't always endear him to his opponents or their supporters. Yet over a weekend in Barcelona, there was no mistaking the respect and admiration that Spain's Davis Cup players had for Stepanek. And during the prize ceremony at the Palau Sant Jordi, he was the Czech player who was given the loudest applause. At the age of thirty-one, in the autumn of his tennis life, Stepanek has been making friends and influencing people.

Given that Spain was the 2009 Davis Cup champion, you would be forgiven for thinking that the Player of the Year should be a Rafa, a David, a Feliciano, a Fernando, a Tommy, or a Juan Carlos. But given that there was not one Spanish player who dominated the Davis Cup year—five different Spaniards played in live singles rubbers over the four ties—this yearbook has opted for the alternative choice of one of the defeated finalists, someone who lost a singles rubber and a doubles rubber in Barcelona.

If this was anyone's year it was Stepanek's. Czech Republic would not have gone very far in the World Group without its veteran from Karvina, a coal-mining town in the northeastern corner of the country. The 2009 Davis Cup year brought the best out of Stepanek, but he did not just contribute with his racket. He also provided leadership, especially with his words of encouragement and his tactical advice for Tomas Berdych, his young teammate and doubles partner at all four ties. For Stepanek, this was still a team effort. "Davis Cup means so much to me. I gave everything, all my heart, to the Davis Cup," said Stepanek. "It is a special event. When you play a tournament, the only person you have is you, yourself. When you lose, you can talk to yourself. But in the Davis Cup, you have responsibility. You have the whole nation behind your back; you have all the people supporting you. It's a completely different feeling."

Stepanek has never been one of the gray men of tennis. One of the reasons the Spanish spectators showed their appreciation for Stepanek was because of his style of play. In an era when most players are happy to stand on the baseline all day, biffing and bashing topspin forehands, Stepanek takes a different approach, playing a brand of unorthodox, inventive, colorful tennis. It includes attacking the net whenever possible, occasionally when it looks impossible to do so, plus making use of various spins, angles, and deception. It was clear in 2009 just how awkward an opponent Stepanek could be, as he gave his country the winning point at their first round, quarterfinal, and semifinal ties.

At the first-round tie against France in Ostrava, Stepanek's victory over Gilles Simon took the Czechs through. When they played Argentina in the quarterfinals, also in Ostrava, Stepanek won the decisive fifth rubber against Juan Monaco, and at the semifinal in the Croatian seaside town of Porec, Stepanek and Berdych achieved an insurmountable 3–0 lead by beating Marin Cilic and Lovro Zovko in the doubles rubber.

But if there is one match that stands out from Stepanek's year, it is the singles rubber he played against Ivo Karlovic in Porec. Though the Croat served a world-record seventy-eight aces that day, Stepanek gave an unbelievably resilient performance for a five-set, six-hour victory. The first four sets were all decided in tiebreaks, and then Stepanek took the fifth set 16–14. Even after all that tennis, Stepanek still made himself available to play in the doubles rubber the next day.

Such was the quality of Stepanek's tennis in the opening two sets of his singles rubber against Spain's David Ferrer on the first day of the final that he dropped just three games. Ferrer was a very distant second. However, after regrouping during a bathroom break, Ferrer came back to win in five sets. The next day, Stepanek and Berdych suffered their first doubles defeat of the Davis Cup year. Stepanek was clearly suffering physically after his long four-and-a-quarter-hour singles match against Ferrer the night before, and the Czechs lost in straight sets.

So, once again, Spain had won the Davis Cup. But Stepanek, who may never get another opportunity to play in a Davis Cup final, said he was proud of his efforts. Who had a greater effect on his country's fortunes in 2009 than Stepanek did on Czech Republic's adventures in the World Group? ●

THE FINAL TOUCHES
There was plenty happening on and offcourt to add some flavor to the 2009 Davis Cup by BNP Paribas Final.

WORLD GROUP

First Round 6-8 March

Argentina defeated Netherlands 5-0, Buenos Aires, ARG, Clay (O): Juan Ignacio Chela (ARG) d. Jesse Huta Galung (NED) 62 26 62 67(4) 62; Juan Monaco (ARG) d. Thiemo de Bakker (NED) 61 62 76(1); Lucas Arnold Ker/Martin Vassallo Arguello (ARG) d. Jesse Huta Galung/Rogier Wassen (NED) 64 75 63; Martin Vassallo Arguello (ARG) d. Matwe Middelkoop (NED) 62 64; Juan Ignacio Chela (ARG) d. Thiemo de Bakker (NED) 75 62.

Czech Republic defeated France 3-2, Ostrava, CZE, Carpet (I): Tomas Berdych (CZE) d. Gilles Simon (FRA) 76(3) 46 76(2) 63; Jo-Wilfried Tsonga (FRA) d. Radek Stepanek (CZE) 75 62 76(1); Tomas Berdych/Radek Stepanek (CZE) d. Richard Gasquet/Michael Llodra (FRA) 63 16 64 62; Radek Stepanek (CZE) d. Gilles Simon (FRA) 76(2) 63 76(0); Jo-Wilfried Tsonga (FRA) d. Jan Hernych (CZE) 62 67(5) 76(0).

USA defeated Switzerland 4-1, Birmingham, AL, USA, Hard (I): Stanislas Wawrinka (SUI) d. James Blake (USA) 36 64 63 76(3); Andy Roddick (USA) d. Marco Chiudinelli (SUI) 61 63 76(5); Bob Bryan/Mike Bryan (USA) d. Yves Allegro/Stanislas Wawrinka (SUI) 63 64 36 76(2); Andy Roddick (USA) d. Stanislas Wawrinka (SUI) 64 64 62; James Blake (USA) d. Marco Chiudinelli (SUI) 64 76(6).

Croatia defeated Chile 5-0, Porec, CRO, Hard (I): Mario Ancic (CRO) d. Nicolas Massu (CHI) 63 63 76(4); Marin Cilic (CRO) d. Paul Capdeville (CHI) 61 62 61; Mario Ancic/Marin Cilic (CRO) d. Paul Capdeville/Nicolas Massu (CHI) 63 63 36 64; Roko Karanusic (CRO) d. Guillermo Hormazabal (CHI) 75 63; Ivo Karlovic (CRO) d. Hans Podlipnik-Castillo (CHI) 63 76(4).

Israel defeated Sweden 3-2, Malmo, SWE, Carpet (I): Thomas Johansson (SWE) d. Harel Levy (ISR) 67(3) 64 75 46 86; Dudi Sela (ISR) d. Andreas Vinciguerra (SWE) 46 63 36 63 119; Simon Aspelin/Robert Lindstedt (SWE) d. Amir Hadad/Andy Ram (ISR) 64 16 76(4) 64; Dudi Sela (ISR) d. Thomas Johansson (SWE) 36 61 46 64 62; Harel Levy (ISR) d. Andreas Vinciguerra (SWE) 64 46 64 36 86.

Russia defeated Romania 4-1, Sibiu, ROU, Carpet (I): Marat Safin (RUS) d. Victor Crivoi (ROU) 76(5) 64 64; Mikhail Youzhny (RUS) d. Victor Hanescu (ROU) 64 62 64; Marius Copil/Horia Tecau (ROU) d. Marat Safin/Dmitry Tursunov (RUS) 46 67(2) 76(4) 76(5) 64; Dmitry Tursunov (RUS) d. Victor Hanescu (ROU) 46 57 63 64 62; Teimuraz Gabashvili (RUS) d. Victor Crivoi (ROU) 64 62.

Germany defeated Austria 3-2, Garmisch-Partenkirchen, GER, Hard (I): Stefan Koubek (AUT) d. Rainer Schuettler (GER) 64 75 57 62; Philipp Kohlschreiber (GER) d. Jurgen Melzer (AUT) 67(4) 46 64 63 63; Nicolas Kiefer/Philipp Kohlschreiber (GER) d. Julian Knowle/Alexander Peya (AUT) 63 76(6) 36 64; Nicolas Kiefer (GER) d. Jurgen Melzer (AUT) 76(3) 64 64; Stefan Koubek (AUT) d. Christopher Kas (GER) 62 63.

Spain defeated Serbia 4-1, Benidorm, ESP, Clay (O): David Ferrer (ESP) d. Novak Djokovic (SRB) 63 63 76(4); Rafael Nadal (ESP) d. Janko Tipsarevic (SRB) 61 60 62; Viktor Troicki/Nenad Zimonjic (SRB) d. Feliciano Lopez/Tommy Robredo (ESP) 76(5) 64 76(7); Rafael Nadal (ESP) d. Novak Djokovic (SRB) 64 64 61; David Ferrer (ESP) d. Viktor Troicki (SRB) 60 63.

Quarterfinals 10-12 July

Czech Republic defeated Argentina 3-2, Ostrava, CZE, Carpet (I): Tomas Berdych (CZE) d. Juan Monaco (ARG) 64 26 26 63 62; Juan Martin del Potro (ARG) d. Ivo Minar (CZE) 61 63 63; Tomas Berdych/Radek Stepanek (CZE) d. Jose Acasuso/Leonardo Mayer (ARG) 61 64 63; Juan Martin del Potro (ARG) d. Tomas Berdych (CZE) 64 64 64; Radek Stepanek (CZE) d. Juan Monaco (ARG) 76(5) 63 62.

Croatia defeated USA 3-2, Porec, CRO, Clay (I): Ivo Karlovic (CRO) d. James Blake (USA) 67(5) 46 63 76(3) 75; Marin Cilic (CRO) d. Mardy Fish (USA) 46 63 67(3) 61 86; Bob Bryan/Mike Bryan (USA) d. Roko Karanusic/Lovro Zovko (CRO) 63 61 63; Marin Cilic (CRO) d. James Blake (USA) 63 63 46 62; Bob Bryan (USA) d. Roko Karanusic (CRO) 57 63 76(4).

Israel defeated Russia 4-1, Tel Aviv, ISR, Hard (I): Harel Levy (ISR) d. Igor Andreev (RUS) 64 62 46 62; Dudi Sela (ISR) d. Mikhail Youzhny (RUS) 36 61 60 75; Jonathan Erlich/Andy Ram (ISR) d. Igor Kunitsyn/Marat Safin (RUS) 63 64 67(3) 46 64; Igor Andreev (RUS) d. Dudi Sela (ISR) 4-3 ret.; Harel Levy (ISR) d. Igor Kunitsyn (RUS) 64 46 76(2).

Spain defeated Germany 3-2, Marbella, ESP, Clay (O): Fernando Verdasco (ESP) d. Andreas Beck (GER) 60 36 67(4) 62 61; Philipp Kohlschreiber (GER) d. Tommy Robredo (ESP) 63 64 64; Feliciano Lopez/Fernando Verdasco (ESP) d. Nicolas Kiefer/Mischa Zverev (GER) 63 76(1) 67(6) 63; Philipp Kohlschreiber (GER) d. Fernando Verdasco (ESP) 64 62 16 26 86; Juan Carlos Ferrero (ESP) d. Andreas Beck (GER) 64 64 64.

Semifinals 18-20 September

Czech Republic defeated Croatia 4-1, Porec, CRO, Clay (I): Radek Stepanek (CZE) d. Ivo Karlovic (CRO) 67(5) 76(5) 76(6) 67(2) 1614; Tomas Berdych (CZE) d. Marin Cilic (CRO) 63 63 36 46 63; Tomas Berdych/Radek Stepanek (CZE) d. Marin Cilic/Lovro Zovko (CRO) 61 63 64; Jan Hajek (CZE) d. Roko Karanusic (CRO) 76(4) 64; Lovro Zovko (CRO) d. Lukas Dlouhy (CZE) 63 64.

Spain defeated Israel 4-1, Murcia, ESP, Clay (O): David Ferrer (ESP) d. Harel Levy (ISR) 61 64 63; Juan Carlos Ferrero (ESP) d. Dudi Sela (ISR) 64 62 60; Feliciano Lopez/Tommy Robredo (ESP) d. Jonathan Erlich/Andy Ram (ISR) 76(6) 67(7) 64 62; David Ferrer (ESP) d. Andy Ram (ISR) 63 61; Harel Levy (ISR) d. Feliciano Lopez (ESP) 75 62.

Final 4-6 December

Spain defeated Czech Republic, Barcelona, ESP, Clay (I): Rafael Nadal (ESP) d. Tomas Berdych (CZE) 75 60 62; David Ferrer (ESP) d. Radek Stepanek (CZE) 16 26 64 64 86; Feliciano Lopez/Fernando Verdasco (ESP) d. Tomas Berdych/Radek Stepanek (CZE) 76(7) 75 62; Rafael Nadal (ESP) d. Jan Hajek (CZE) 63 64; David Ferrer (ESP) d. Lukas Dlouhy (CZE) 64 62.

World Group Play-offs 18-20 September

Chile defeated Austria 3-2, Rancagua, CHI, Clay (O): Nicolas Massu (CHI) d. Jurgen Melzer (AUT) 46 64 64 63; Paul Capdeville (CHI) d. Stefan Koubek (AUT) 64 64 36 16 64; Julian Knowle/Jurgen Melzer (AUT) d. Paul Capdeville/Nicolas Massu (CHI) 62 64 63; Jurgen Melzer (AUT) d. Paul Capdeville (CHI) 76(2) 46 62 57 64; Nicolas Massu (CHI) d. Stefan Koubek (AUT) 64 46 64 76(6).

Belgium defeated Ukraine 3-2, Charleroi, BEL, Clay (I): Christophe Rochus (BEL) d. Illya Marchenko (UKR) 63 64 36 62; Steve Darcis (BEL) d. Sergiy Stakhovsky (UKR) 62 63 64; Sergei Bubka/Sergiy Stakhovsky (UKR) d. Xavier Malisse/Olivier Rochus (BEL) 76(5) 36 64 76(4); Sergiy Stakhovsky (UKR) d. Xavier Malisse (BEL) 63 36 06 61 63; Steve Darcis (BEL) d. Sergei Bubka (UKR) 62 61 60.

Ecuador defeated Brazil 3-2, Porto Alegre, BRA, Clay (I): Marcos Daniel (BRA) d. Giovanni Lapentti (ECU) 76(3) 36 76(4) 62; Nicolas Lapentti (ECU) d. Thomaz Bellucci (BRA) 76(2) 64 75; Giovanni Lapentti/Nicolas Lapentti (ECU) d. Marcelo Melo/Andre Sa (BRA) 36 63 64 46 64; Nicolas Lapentti (ECU) d. Marcos Daniel (BRA) 64 64 16 26 86; Thomaz Bellucci (BRA) d. Julio-Cesar Campozano (ECU) 62 64.

France defeated Netherlands 4-1, Maastricht, NED, Clay (I): Thiemo de Bakker (NED) d. Gael Monfils (FRA) 63 57 63 64; Jo-Wilfried Tsonga (FRA) d. Jesse Huta Galung (NED) 76(2) 62 76(3); Michael Llodra/Jo-Wilfried Tsonga (FRA) d. Thiemo de Bakker/Igor Sijsling (NED) 63 36 76(2) 64; Jo-Wilfried Tsonga (FRA) d. Thiemo de Bakker (NED) 76(5) 62 36 76(4); Jeremy Chardy (FRA) d. Jesse Huta Galung (NED) 63 62.

India defeated South Africa 4-1, Johannesburg, RSA, Hard (I): Somdev Devvarman (IND) d. Izak van der Merwe (RSA) 76(5) 63 64; Rohan Bopanna (IND) d. Rik de Voest (RSA) 26 64 62 64; Jeff Coetzee/Wesley Moodie (RSA) d. Mahesh Bhupathi/Rohan Bopanna (IND) 63 36 4-0 ret.; Somdev Devvarman (IND) d. Rik de Voest (RSA) 36 67(3) 76(5) 62 64; Yuki Bhambri (IND) d. Izak van der Merwe (RSA) 36 63 64.

Serbia defeated Uzbekistan 5-0, Belgrade, SRB, Hard (I): Janko Tipsarevic (SRB) d. Denis Istomin (UZB) 62 57 61 64; Viktor Troicki (SRB) d. Farrukh Dustov (UZB) 64 36 63 46 62; Janko Tipsarevic/Nenad Zimonjic (SRB) d. Farrukh Dustov/Denis Istomin (UZB) 62 63 62; Viktor Troicki (SRB) d. Murad Inoyatov (UZB) 46 64 63; Ilia Bozoljac (SRB) d. Vaja Uzakov (UZB) 61 64.

Sweden defeated Romania 3-2, Helsingborg, SWE, Hard (I): Victor Hanescu (ROU) d. Andreas Vinciguerra (SWE) 76(5) 76(10) ret.; Robin Soderling (SWE) d. Victor Crivoi (ROU) 62 61 75; Robert Lindstedt/Robin Soderling (SWE) d. Victor Hanescu/Horia Tecau (ROU) 61 76(7) 76(5); Robin Soderling (SWE) d. Victor Hanescu (ROU) 75 61 60; Marius Copil (ROU) d. Andreas Vinciguerra (SWE) 46 ret.

Switzerland defeated Italy 3-2, Genoa, ITA, Clay (O): Stanislas Wawrinka (SUI) d. Andreas Seppi (ITA) 64 61 62; Roger Federer (SUI) d. Simone Bolelli (ITA) 63 64 61; Simone Bolelli/Potito Starace (ITA) d. Marco Chiudinelli/Stanislas Wawrinka (SUI) 62 64 76(3); Roger Federer (SUI) d. Potito Starace (ITA) 63 60 64; Fabio Fognini (ITA) d. Michael Lammer (SUI) 75 76(4).

GROUP I

Americas Zone
First Round 6-8 March
Colombia defeated Uruguay 5-0, Bogota, COL, Clay (O): Alejandro Falla (COL) d. Marcel Felder (URU) 64 60 67(4) 63; Santiago Giraldo (COL) d. Federico Sansonetti (URU) 64 75 61; Juan-Sebastian Cabal/Alejandro Falla (COL) d. Ariel Behar/Marcel Felder (URU) 63 57 76(6) 64; Carlos Salamanca (COL) d. Dario Acosta (URU) 60 63; Juan-Sebastian Cabal (COL) d. Federico Sansonetti (URU) 62 63.

Ecuador defeated Canada 3-2, Toronto, CAN, Hard (I): Nicolas Lapentti (ECU) d. Frederic Niemeyer (CAN) 63 76(4) 76(4); Frank Dancevic (CAN) d. Giovanni Lapentti (ECU) 64 64 75; Daniel Nestor/Frederic Niemeyer (CAN) d. Giovanni Lapentti/Nicolas Lapentti (ECU) 64 63 63; Nicolas Lapentti (ECU) d. Frank Dancevic (CAN) 63 57 46 76(6) 61; Giovanni Lapentti (ECU) d. Frederic Niemeyer (CAN) 26 76(5) 63 63.

Second Round 8-10 May
Brazil defeated Colombia 4-1, Tunja, COL, Clay (O): Thomaz Bellucci (BRA) d. Alejandro Falla (COL) 76(5) 36 76(6) 62; Franco Ferreiro (BRA) d. Santiago Giraldo (COL) 63 64 67(3) 76(1); Marcelo Melo/Andre Sa (BRA) d. Juan-Sebastian Cabal/Alejandro Falla (COL) 63 76(4) 46 46 63; Thomaz Bellucci (BRA) d. Carlos Salamanca (COL) 67(5) 61 75; Juan-Sebastian Cabal (COL) d. Franco Ferreiro (BRA) 62 63.

Ecuador defeated Peru 4-1, Quito, ECU, Clay (O): Giovanni Lapentti (ECU) d. Ivan Miranda (PER) 62 63 75; Nicolas Lapentti (ECU) d. Mauricio Echazu (PER) 62 75 63; Giovanni Lapentti/Nicolas Lapentti (ECU) d. Sergio Galdos/Ivan Miranda (PER) 75 63 63; Carlos Avellan (ECU) d. Ivan Miranda (PER) 64 64; Sergio Galdos (PER) d. Julio-Cesar Campozano (ECU) 64 67(2) 62.

Brazil and Ecuador advanced to World Group Play-offs on 18-20 September 2009.

First Round Relegation Play-off 10-12 July
Canada defeated Peru 3-2, Lima, PER, Clay (O): Peter Polansky (CAN) d. Ivan Miranda (PER) 76(4) 64 64; Luis Horna (PER) d. Bruno Agostinelli (CAN) 62 76(2) 46 75; Daniel Nestor/Frederic Niemeyer (CAN) d. Luis Horna/Ivan Miranda (PER) 67(3) 75 76(4) 46 63; Luis Horna (PER) d. Frederic Niemeyer (CAN) 76(4) 46 64 75; Bruno Agostinelli (CAN) d. Ivan Miranda (PER) 76(5) 16 63 64.

Second Round Relegation Play-off 18-20 September
Uruguay defeated Peru 4-1, Lima, PER, Clay (O): Marcel Felder (URU) d. Luis Horna (PER) 62 63 61; Pablo Cuevas (URU) d. Mauricio Echazu (PER) 64 63 62; Pablo Cuevas/Marcel Felder (URU) d. Luis Horna/Ivan Miranda (PER) 76(2) 36 63 62; Federico Sansonetti (URU) d. Ivan Miranda (PER) 75 76(2); Mauricio Echazu (PER) d. Ariel Behar (URU) 62 63.

Peru relegated to Americas Zone Group II in 2010.

Asia/Oceania Zone
First Round 6-8 February
Chinese Taipei defeated Kazakhstan 4-1, Hsinchuang, TPE, Carpet (I): Mikhail Kukushkin (KAZ) d. Ti Chen (TPE) 67(9) 57 61 75 64; Yeu-Tzuoo Wang (TPE) d. Andrey Golubev (KAZ) 76(4) 63 62; Tsung-Hua Yang/Chu-Huan Yi (TPE) d. Alexey Kedryuk/Yuriy Schukin (KAZ) 67(5) 76(6) 76(4) 64; Ti Chen (TPE) d. Yuriy Schukin (KAZ) 46 63 26 76(3) 61; Yeu-Tzuoo Wang (TPE) d. Mikhail Kukushkin (KAZ) 26 63 63.

Second Round 6-8 March
Australia defeated Thailand 3-2, Nonthaburi, THA, Hard (O): Lleyton Hewitt (AUS) d. Kittiphong Wachiramanowong (THA) 63 62 61; Danai Udomchoke (THA) d. Brydan Klein (AUS) 62 62 75; Carsten Ball/Chris Guccione (AUS) d. Sanchai Ratiwatana/Sonchat Ratiwatana (THA) 76(3) 64 64; Danai Udomchoke (THA) d. Lleyton Hewitt (AUS) 26 46 76(2) 64 61; Chris Guccione (AUS) d. Kittiphong Wachiramanowong (THA) 63 75 76(3).

India defeated Chinese Taipei 3-2, Kaohsiung, TPE, Hard (O): Somdev Devvarman (IND) d. Ti Chen (TPE) 75 64 64; Yen-Hsun Lu (TPE) d. Rohan Bopanna (IND) 76(2) 62 62; Mahesh Bhupathi/Leander Paes (IND) d. Tsung-Hua Yang/Chu-Huan Yi (TPE) 64 76(0) 67(2) 62; Somdev Devvarman (IND) d. Yen-Hsun Lu (TPE) 61 62 63; Tsung-Hua Yang (TPE) d. Rohan Bopanna (IND) 63 67(6) 76(5).

Japan defeated China, P.R. 5-0, Osaka, JPN, Carpet (I): Go Soeda (JPN) d. Shao-Xuan Zeng (CHN) 62 76(4) 63; Kei Nishikori (JPN) d. Ze Zhang (CHN) 64 75 62; Satoshi Iwabuchi/Takao Suzuki (JPN) d. Shao-Xuan Zeng/Ze Zhang (CHN) 62 63 62; Takao Suzuki (JPN) d. Di Wu (CHN) 62 63; Go Soeda (JPN) d. Ze Zhang (CHN) 46 63 62.

Uzbekistan defeated Korea, Rep. 4-1, Namangan, UZB, Clay (I): Hyung-Taik Lee (KOR) d. Farrukh Dustov (UZB) 75 76(8) 64; Denis Istomin (UZB) d. Kyu-Tae Im (KOR) 63 62 64; Farrukh Dustov/Denis Istomin (UZB) d. Kyu-Tae Im/Hyung-Taik Lee (KOR) 26 62 36 63 64; Denis Istomin (UZB) d. Hyung-Taik Lee (KOR) 63 16 63 36 63; Murad Inoyatov (UZB) d. Yong-Kyu Lim (KOR) 36 61 63.

Third Round 8-10 May
India defeated Australia w/o, Chennai, IND, Hard (O).

Uzbekistan defeated Japan 3-2, Namangan, UZB, Clay (I): Denis Istomin (UZB) d. Yuichi Sugita (JPN) 63 62 62; Farrukh Dustov (UZB) d. Tatsuma Ito (JPN) 64 63 36 63; Farrukh Dustov/Denis Istomin (UZB) d. Satoshi Iwabuchi/Takao Suzuki (JPN) 67(7) 63 76(3) 46 63; Tatsuma Ito (JPN) d. Murad Inoyatov (UZB) 76(5) 64; Takao Suzuki (JPN) d. Vaja Uzakov (UZB) 46 63 63.

India and Uzbekistan advanced to World Group Play-offs on 18-20 September 2009.

Second Round Relegation Play-offs 10-12 July
Kazakhstan defeated Thailand 5-0, Nonthaburi, THA, Hard (O): Andrey Golubev (KAZ) d. Perakiat Siriluethaiwattana (THA) 62 63 62; Mikhail Kukushkin (KAZ) d. Kittiphong Wachiramanowong (THA) 62 64 62; Alexey Kedryuk/Yuriy Schukin (KAZ) d. Sanchai Ratiwatana/Kittiphong Wachiramanowong (THA) 46 64 46 64 61; Andrey Golubev (KAZ) d. Kittiphong Wachiramanowong (THA) 61 64; Alexey Kedryuk (KAZ) d. Perakiat Siriluethaiwattana (THA) 76(6) 76(6).

Korea, Rep. defeated China, P.R. 3-2, Chuncheon City, KOR, Hard (O): Kyu-Tae Im (KOR) d. Mao-Xin Gong (CHN) 63 60 62; Hyung-Taik Lee (KOR) d. Shao-Xuan Zeng (CHN) 63 64 62; Shao-Xuan Zeng/Ze Zhang (CHN) d. Kyu-Tae Im/Hyung-Taik Lee (KOR) 75 36 76(5) 64; Ze Zhang (CHN) d. Yong-Kyu Lim (KOR) 26 67(0) 64 76(7) 2-0 ret.; Kyu-Tae Im (KOR) d. Shao-Xuan Zeng (CHN) 60 62 63.

Third Round Relegation Play-off 18-20 September
China, P.R. defeated Thailand 4-1, Jiaxing, CHN, Hard (I): Shao-Xuan Zeng (CHN) d. Kittiphong Wachiramanowong (THA) 57 61 62 64; Danai Udomchoke (THA) d. Ze Zhang (CHN) 63 63 62; Shao-Xuan Zeng/Ze Zhang (CHN) d. Sanchai Ratiwatana/Sonchat Ratiwatana (THA) 26 46 64 75 62; Shao-Xuan Zeng (CHN) d. Danai Udomchoke (THA) 26 64 36 61 64; Mao-Xin Gong (CHN) d. Kittiphong Wachiramanowong (THA) 75 36 63.

Thailand relegated to Asia/Oceania Zone Group II in 2010.

Europe/Africa Zone
First Round 6-8 March
South Africa defeated FYR Macedonia 5-0, Johannesburg, RSA, Hard (O): Izak van der Merwe (RSA) d. Predrag Rusevski (MKD) 26 62 62 64; Rik de Voest (RSA) d. Lazar Magdincev (MKD) 63 62 61; Jeff Coetzee/Rik de Voest (RSA) d. Lazar Magdincev/Predrag Rusevski (MKD) 61 76(1) 62; Raven Klaasen (RSA) d. Ilija Martinoski (MKD) 62 62; Izak van der Merwe (RSA) d. Dimitar Grabuloski (MKD) 64 60.

Second Round 6-8 March
Italy defeated Slovak Republic 4-1, Cagliari, ITA, Clay (O): Potito Starace (ITA) d. Dominik Hrbaty (SVK) 61 62 64; Fabio Fognini (ITA) d. Lukas Lacko (SVK) 16 63 62 16 61; Michal Mertinak/Filip Polasek (SVK) d. Flavio Cipolla/Potito Starace (ITA) 75 46 60 26 97; Fabio Fognini (ITA) d. Dominik Hrbaty (SVK) 76(1) 61 63; Flavio Cipolla (ITA) d. Lukas Lacko (SVK) 62 75.

Ukraine defeated Great Britain 4-1, Glasgow, GBR, Hard (I): Illya Marchenko (UKR) d. Josh Goodall (GBR) 76(2) 76(5) 76(5); Sergiy Stakhovsky (UKR) d. Chris Eaton (GBR) 63 36 63 64; Sergei Bubka/Sergiy Stakhovsky (UKR) d. Colin Fleming/Ross Hutchins (GBR) 64 36 63 57 64; Ivan Sergeyev (UKR) d. Josh Goodall (GBR) 76(3) 63; Chris Eaton (GBR) d. Illya Marchenko (UKR) 63 46 76(5).

Belgium defeated Poland 4-1, Liege, BEL, Clay (I): Kristof Vliegen (BEL) d. Michal Przysiezny (POL) 16 63 64 16 63; Xavier Malisse (BEL) d. Jerzy Janowicz (POL) 76(2) 63 63; Steve Darcis/Olivier Rochus (BEL) d. Marcin Matkowski/Grzegorz Panfil (POL) 63 76(1) 63; Jerzy Janowicz (POL) d. Kristof Vliegen (BEL) 62 64; Olivier Rochus (BEL) d. Grzegorz Panfil (POL) 63 62.

8-10 May South Africa defeated Belarus 5-0, Johannesburg, RSA, Hard (O): Izak van der Merwe (RSA) d. Uladzimir Ignatik (BLR) 64 4-3 ret.; Rik de Voest (RSA) d. Andrei Karatchenia (BLR) 61 64 61; Jeff Coetzee/Rik de Voest (RSA) d. Max Mirnyi/Siarhei Betau (BLR) 63 64 76(5); Raven Klaasen (RSA) d. Siarhei Betau (BLR) 61 64; Izak van der Merwe (RSA) d. Andrei Karatchenia (BLR) 61 63.

Belgium, Italy, South Africa and Ukraine advanced to World Group Play-offs on 18-20 September.

First Round Relegation Play-off 10-12 July
Belarus defeated FYR Macedonia 4-1, Minsk, BLR, Hard (O): Dimitar Grabuloski (MKD) d. Andrei Vasilevski (BLR) 57 67(2) 63 76(5) 63; Uladzimir Ignatik (BLR) d. Lazar Magdincev (MKD) 62 75 63; Alexander Bury/Max Mirnyi (BLR) d. Dimitar Grabuloski/Lazar Magdincev (MKD) 61 76(2) 61; Uladzimir Ignatik (BLR) d. Dimitar Grabuloski (MKD) 63 61 64; Andrei Vasilevski (BLR) d. Ilija Martinoski (MKD) 64 62.

Second Round Relegation Play-offs 18-20 September
Slovak Republic defeated FYR Macedonia 5-0, Bratislava, SVK, Hard (I): Dominik Hrbaty (SVK) d. Dimitar Grabuloski (MKD) 62 64 64; Lukas Lacko (SVK) d. Lazar Magdincev (MKD) 61 61 63; Martin Klizan/Filip Polasek (SVK) d. Dimitar Grabuloski/Lazar Magdincev (MKD) 63 63 63; Lukas Lacko (SVK) d. Shendrit Deari (MKD) 63 60; Dominik Hrbaty (SVK) d. Tomislav Jotovski (MKD) 60 60.

Poland defeated Great Britain 3-2, Liverpool, GBR, Hard (I): Andy Murray (GBR) d. Michal Przysiezny (POL) 64 62 64; Jerzy Janowicz (POL) d. Daniel Evans (GBR) 63 63 76(5); Mariusz Fyrstenberg/Marcin Matkowski (POL) d. Ross Hutchins/Andy Murray (GBR) 75 36 63 62; Andy Murray (GBR) d. Jerzy Janowicz (POL) 63 64 63; Michal Przysiezny (POL) d. Daniel Evans (GBR) 62 61 75.

Great Britain and FYR Macedonia relegated to Europe/Africa Zone Group II in 2010.

GROUP II

Americas Zone
First Round 6-8 March
Mexico defeated Jamaica 5-0, Mexico City, MEX, Clay (O): Bruno Echagaray (MEX) d. Damar Johnson (JAM) 62 61 62; Santiago Gonzalez (MEX) d. Damion Johnson (JAM) 64 62 60; Luis-Manuel Flores/Santiago Gonzalez (MEX) d. Damar Johnson/Damion Johnson (JAM) 63 61 61; Miguel Gallardo-Valles (MEX) d. Christopher Lawson (JAM) 60 63; Bruno Echagaray (MEX) d. Brandon Burke (JAM) 62 60.

Venezuela defeated Netherlands Antilles 4-1, Barquisimeto, VEN, Hard (O): Piero Luisi (VEN) d. Martijn van Haasteren (AHO) 75 62 64; Jose de Armas (VEN) d. Romano Tatuhey (AHO) 36 63 62 64; Jose de Armas/Yohny Romero (VEN) d. Romano Tatuhey/Martijn van Haasteren (AHO) 63 63 76(7); Martijn van Haasteren (AHO) d. Luis David Martinez (VEN) 63 63; Piero Luisi (VEN) d. Nick van Rosberg (AHO) 63 61.

Dominican Republic defeated Guatemala 5-0, Santo Domingo, DOM, Clay (O): Jhonson Garcia (DOM) d. Christopher Diaz-Figueroa (GUA) 64 62 60; Victor Estrella (DOM) d. Julen Uriguen (GUA) 36 62 4-3 ret.; Victor Estrella/Jhonson Garcia (DOM) d. Christopher Diaz-Figueroa/Cristian Paiz (GUA) 61 75 64; Jose Hernandez (DOM) d. Christopher Diaz-Figueroa (GUA) 36 60 63; Jesus Francisco Felix (DOM) d. Christian Saravia (GUA) 61 64.

Paraguay defeated Bahamas 4-1, Lambare, PAR, Clay (O): Ramon Delgado (PAR) d. Timothy Neilly (BAH) 61 64 62; Devin Mullings (BAH) d. Diego Galeano (PAR) 46 75 4-1 ret.; Ramon Delgado/Diego Galeano (PAR) d. Bjorn Munroe/Marvin Rolle (BAH) 61 60 62; Ramon Delgado (PAR) d. Devin Mullings (BAH) 61 76(3) 61; Diego Galeano (PAR) d. Timothy Neilly (BAH) 64 61.

Second Round 10-12 July
Venezuela defeated Mexico 3-2, Maracaibo, VEN, Hard (O): Daniel Vallverdu (VEN) d. Cesar Ramirez (MEX) 63 62 62; Jose De Armas (VEN) d. Miguel Gallardo-Valles (MEX) 63 62 62; Jose De Armas/Piero Luisi (VEN) d. Luis-Manuel Flores/Santiago Gonzalez (MEX) 67(8) 63 64 75; Cesar Ramirez (MEX) d. Jhonnatan Medina-Alvarez (VEN) 61 1-0 ret.; Luis-Manuel Flores (MEX) d. Piero Luisi (VEN) 46 63 63.

Dominican Republic defeated Paraguay 3-2, Provincia Duarte, DOM, Clay (O): Jose Hernandez (DOM) d. Diego Galeano (PAR) 60 61 62; Victor Estrella (DOM) d. Nicolas Salama (PAR) 61 60 2-0 ret.; Victor Estrella/Jose Hernandez (DOM) d. Jose Benitez/Diego Galeano (PAR) 62 62 62; Diego Galeano (PAR) d. Jesus Francisco Felix (DOM) 36 61 61; Jose Benitez (PAR) d. Amaury Gomez (DOM) 64 76(7).

Final 18-20 September
Dominican Republic defeated Venezuela 3-2; Santo Domingo, DOM, Clay (O): Victor Estrella (DOM) d. Daniel Vallverdu (VEN) 64 63 46 75; Jose De Armas (VEN) d. Jose Hernandez (DOM) 63 61 36 61; Jose De Armas/Daniel Vallverdu (VEN) d. Victor Estrella/Jhonson Garcia (DOM) 64 76(6) 61; Victor Estrella (DOM) d. Jose De Armas (VEN) 63 26 76(6) 36 61; Jhonson Garcia (DOM) d. Daniel Vallverdu (VEN) 63 63 75.

Dominican Republic promoted to Americas Zone Group I in 2010.

Relegation Play-offs 10-12 July
Netherlands Antilles defeated Jamaica 5-0, Curacao, AHO, Hard (O): Alexander Blom (AHO) d. Christopher Lawson (JAM) 46 62 4-2 ret.; Romano Tatuhey (AHO) d. Dominic Pagon (JAM) 61 63 64; Romano Tatuhey/Martijn van Haasteren (AHO) d. Tyler Chin/Dominic Pagon (JAM) 61 61 64; Alexander Blom (AHO) d. Tyler Chin (JAM) 62 61; Martijn van Haasteren (AHO) d. Christopher Lawson (JAM) 64 62.

Guatemala defeated Bahamas 3-2, Nassau, BAH, Hard (O): Devin Mullings (BAH) d. Julen Uriguen (GUA) 63 64 62; Christopher Diaz-Figueroa (GUA) d. Timothy Neilly (BAH) 75 61 62; Christopher Diaz-Figueroa/Sebastien Vidal (GUA) d. Devin Mullings/Marvin Rolle (BAH) 76(5) 75 46 36 86; Devin Mullings (BAH) d. Cristian Paiz (GUA) 75 36 61 61; Julen Uriguen (GUA) d. Marvin Rolle (BAH) 67(5) 64 46 62 86.

Bahamas and Jamaica relegated to Americas Zone Group III in 2010.

Asia/Oceania Zone
First Round 6-8 March
Philippines defeated Hong Kong, China 4-1, Victoria Park, HKG, Hard (O): Martin Sayer (HKG) d. Treat Huey (PHI) 64 76(0) 62; Cecil Mamiit (PHI) d. Hiu-Tung Yu (HKG) 76(2) 61 61; Treat Huey/Cecil Mamiit (PHI) d. Brian Hung/Martin Sayer (HKG) 75 63 76(4); Cecil Mamiit (PHI) d. Martin Sayer (HKG) 64 46 36 76(4) 97; Francis Casey Alcantara (PHI) d. Michael Lai (HKG) 64 64.

Pakistan defeated Oman 4-1, Muscat, OMA, Hard (O): Aisam Qureshi (PAK) d. Khalid Al Nabhani (OMA) 62 63 62; Aqeel Khan (PAK) d. Mohammed Al Nabhani (OMA) 46 67(5) 64 63 61; Aqeel Khan/Aisam Qureshi (PAK) d. Khalid Al Nabhani/Mohammed Al Nabhani (OMA) 64 62 57 62; Mohammed Al Nabhani (OMA) d. Yasir Khan (PAK) 62 64; Jalil Khan (PAK) d. Khalid Al Nabhani (OMA) 64 76(2).

Indonesia defeated Kuwait 3-2, Solo, INA, Hard (O): Christopher Rungkat (INA) d. Ahmad Rabeea Muhammad (KUW) 62 63 62; Mohammad Ghareeb (KUW) d. Sunu-Wahyu Trijati (INA) 61 64 76(2); Ketut-Nesa Arta/Christopher Rungkat (INA) d. Mohammad Ghareeb/Mohammad-Khaliq Siddiq (KUW) 36 61 63 60; Mohammad Ghareeb (KUW) d. Christopher Rungkat (INA) 75 61 26 67(6) 63; Prima Simpatiaji (INA) d. Mohammad-Khaliq Siddiq (KUW) 64 60 62.

New Zealand defeated Malaysia 5-0, Auckland, NZL, Hard (I): Jose Statham (NZL) d. Razlan Rawi (MAS) 61 61 60; Daniel King-Turner (NZL) d. Yew-Ming Si (MAS) 64 61 64; G.D. Jones/Daniel King-Turner (NZL) d. Adam Jaya/Yew-Ming Si (MAS) 61 64 62; G.D. Jones (NZL) d. Adam Jaya (MAS) 63 63; Adam Thompson (NZL) d. Abd-Hazli Bin Zainuddin (MAS) 60 62.

Second Round 10-12 July
Philippines defeated Pakistan 3-2, Manila, PHI, Clay (I): Treat Huey (PHI) d. Aqeel Khan (PAK) 64 75 62; Cecil Mamiit (PHI) d. Jalil Khan (PAK) 61 62 61; Treat Huey/Cecil Mamiit (PHI) d. Aqeel Khan/Jibran Mohammadi (PAK) 62 64 60; Aqeel Khan (PAK) d. Patrick-John Tierro (PHI) 61 76(7); Jalil Khan (PAK) d. Francis Casey Alcantara (PHI) 16 76(8) 63.

New Zealand defeated Indonesia 5-0, Hamilton, NZL, Hard (I): Daniel King-Turner (NZL) d. Sunu-Wahyu Trijati (INA) 64 61 64; G.D. Jones (NZL) d. Christopher Rungkat (INA) 75 46 63 62; G.D. Jones/Daniel King-Turner (NZL) d. Ketut-Nesa Arta/Christopher Rungkat (INA) 46 75 76(4) 64; Daniel King-Turner (NZL) d. Ayrton Wibowo (INA) 64 61; Mikal Statham (NZL) d. Sunu-Wahyu Trijati (INA) 61 60.

Third Round 18-20 September
Philippines defeated New Zealand 4-1, Manila, PHI, Clay (I): Treat Huey (PHI) d. Daniel King-Turner (NZL) 64 67(5) 60 ret.; Cecil Mamiit (PHI) d. Jose Statham (NZL) 64 75 62; Treat Huey/Cecil Mamiit (PHI) d. G.D. Jones/Mikal Statham (NZL) 76(4) 63 75; Johnny Arcilla (PHI) d. Mikal Statham (NZL) 63 26 64; Jose Statham (NZL) d. Vicente Elberto Anasta (PHI) 61 75.

Philippines promoted to Asia Oceania Zone Group I in 2010.

Relegation Play-offs 10-12 July
Hong Kong, China defeated Oman 5-0, Chinese Recreation Club, HKG, Hard (O): Hiu-Tung Yu (HKG) d. Khalid Al Nabhani (OMA) 63 60 61; Martin Sayer (HKG) d. Mohammed Al Nabhani (OMA) 61 75 63; Cheuk-Wai Hui/Brian Hung (HKG) d. Khalid Al Nabhani/Mohammed Al Nabhani (OMA) 62 63 63; Cheuk-Wai Hui (HKG) d. Mohammed Al Nabhani (OMA) 60 64; Brian Hung (HKG) d. Sulaiman Al Rawahi (OMA) 61 61.

Malaysia defeated Kuwait 4-1, Kuala Lumpur, MAS, Hard (I): Yew-Ming Si (MAS) d. Ahmad Rabeea Muhammad (KUW) 61 64 63; Mohammad Ghareeb (KUW) d. Razlan Rawi (MAS) 61 26 64 64; Yew-Ming Si/Selvam Veerasingam (MAS) d. Musaad Al Jazzaf/Ahmad Rabeea Muhammad (KUW) 76(2) 26 63 62; Yew-Ming Si (MAS) d. Hassan Al Mousa (KUW) 62 61 61; Razlan Rawi (MAS) d. Ahmad Rabeea Muhammad (KUW) w/o.

Kuwait and Oman relegated to Asia/Oceania Zone Group III in 2010.

Europe/Africa Zone
First Round 6-8 March

Lithuania defeated Georgia 3-2, Vilnius, LTU, Hard (I): Ricardas Berankis (LTU) d. George Khrikadze (GEO) 61 63 61; Lado Chikhladze (GEO) d. Gvidas Sabeckis (LTU) 64 61 62; Lado Chikhladze/Irakli Labadze (GEO) d. Daniel Lencina-Ribes/Gvidas Sabeckis (LTU) 76(3) 61 62; Ricardas Berankis (LTU) d. Lado Chikhladze (GEO) 63 64 61; Dovydas Sakinis (LTU) d. Irakli Labadze (GEO) 61 62 64.

Slovenia defeated Egypt 5-0, Otocec, SLO, Carpet (I): Grega Zemlja (SLO) d. Sherif Sabry (EGY) 75 76(6) 62; Blaz Kavcic (SLO) d. Karim Maamoun (EGY) 60 62 62; Andrej Kracman/Grega Zemlja (SLO) d. Karim Maamoun/Sherif Sabry (EGY) 62 63 63; Andrej Kracman (SLO) d. Mohamed Safwat (EGY) 76(4) 63; Blaz Kavcic (SLO) d. Mahmoud Ezz (EGY) 36 76(5) 64.

Latvia defeated Moldova 5-0, Jurmala, LAT, Carpet (I): Andis Juska (LAT) d. Andrei Gorban (MDA) 64 76(4) 61; Deniss Pavlovs (LAT) d. Andrei Ciumac (MDA) 76(8) 61 64; Andis Juska/Deniss Pavlovs (LAT) d. Radu Albot/Andrei Ciumac (MDA) 62 62 62; Karlis Lejnieks (LAT) d. Radu Albot (MDA) 76(6) 63; Adrians Zguns (LAT) d. Maxim Dubarenco (MDA) 62 36 62.

Bulgaria defeated Hungary 3-2, Gyor, HUN, Carpet (I): Todor Enev (BUL) d. Attila Balazs (HUN) 62 46 64 64; Grigor Dimitrov (BUL) d. Adam Kellner (HUN) 76(5) 64 67(5) 76(5); Kornel Bardoczky/Robert Varga (HUN) d. Grigor Dimitrov/Todor Enev (BUL) 16 62 36 62 62; Grigor Dimitrov (BUL) d. Attila Balazs (HUN) 76(2) 36 63 36 60; Adam Kellner (HUN) d. Tihomir Grozdanov (BUL) 46 62 76(3).

Finland defeated Denmark 3-2, Kolding, DEN, Hard (I): Jarkko Nieminen (FIN) d. Martin Pedersen (DEN) 63 61 63; Frederik Nielsen (DEN) d. Timo Nieminen (FIN) 26 64 62 63; Henri Kontinen/Jarkko Nieminen (FIN) d. Frederik Nielsen/Rasmus Norby (DEN) 64 64 75; Jarkko Nieminen (FIN) d. Frederik Nielsen (DEN) 61 63 36 57 61; Martin Pedersen (DEN) d. Henri Kontinen (FIN) 64 64.

Monaco defeated Montenegro 5-0, Roquebrune Cap Martin, MON, Clay (O): Jean-Rene Lisnard (MON) d. Goran Tosic (MNE) 75 75 46 63; Benjamin Balleret (MON) d. Daniel Danilovic (MNE) 63 63 63; Guillaume Couillard/Jean-Rene Lisnard (MON) d. Daniel Danilovic/Goran Tosic (MNE) 61 67(3) 63 76(5); Guillaume Couillard (MON) d. Nemanja Kontic (MNE) 62 61; Benjamin Balleret (MON) d. Goran Tosic (MNE) 75 64.

Ireland defeated Algeria 4-1, Algiers, ALG, Clay (O): Eddy Chala (ALG) d. James McGee (IRL) 76(4) 57 64 64; Conor Niland (IRL) d. Slimane Saoudi (ALG) 63 63; James McGee/Colin O'Brien (IRL) d. Abdelhak Hameurlaine/Slimane Saoudi (ALG) 75 36 67(3) 62 64; Conor Niland (IRL) d. Eddy Chala (ALG) 76(11) 62 61; Colin O'Brien (IRL) d. Ouassel Hared (ALG) 64 64.

Cyprus defeated Portugal 3-2, Nicosia, CYP, Hard (O): Frederico Gil (POR) d. Photos Kallias (CYP) 60 62 61; Marcos Baghdatis (CYP) d. Rui Machado (POR) 63 75 64; Marcos Baghdatis/Photos Kallias (CYP) d. Frederico Gil/Leonardo Tavares (POR) 64 36 46 63 61; Marcos Baghdatis (CYP) d. Frederico Gil (POR) 62 75 62; Joao Sousa (POR) d. Philippos Tsangaridis (CYP) 63 61.

Second Round 10-12 July

Slovenia defeated Lithuania 5-0, Otocec, SLO, Clay (O): Grega Zemlja (SLO) d. Ricardas Berankis (LTU) 61 64 63; Blaz Kavcic (SLO) d. Gvidas Sabeckis (LTU) 62 63 61; Andrej Kracman/Grega Zemlja (SLO) d. Ricardas Berankis/Vadim Pinko (LTU) 76(2) 63 63; Janez Semrajc (SLO) d. Ricardas Berankis (LTU) 63 75; Grega Zemlja (SLO) d. Dovydas Sakinis (LTU) 64 26 61.

Latvia defeated Bulgaria 4-1, Plovdiv, BUL, Clay (O): Andis Juska (LAT) d. Tihomir Grozdanov (BUL) 67(5) 62 63 64; Ernests Gulbis (LAT) d. Todor Enev (BUL) 75 62 62; Ernests Gulbis/Deniss Pavlovs (LAT) d. Todor Enev/Ivaylo Traykov (BUL) 64 64 64; Tihomir Grozdanov (BUL) d. Adrians Zguns (LAT) 64 63; Andis Juska (LAT) d. Valentin Dimov (BUL) 64 64.

Finland defeated Monaco 3-2, Naantali, FIN, Clay (O): Benjamin Balleret (MON) d. Timo Nieminen (FIN) 16 46 61 64 64; Henri Kontinen (FIN) d. Guillaume Couillard (MON) 46 46 76(4) 76(5) 62; Benjamin Balleret/Guillaume Couillard (MON) d. Harri Heliovaara/Henri Kontinen (FIN) 63 76(7) 63; Henri Laaksonen (FIN) d. Clement Morel (MON) 75 62 67(4) 26 63; Henri Kontinen (FIN) d. Benjamin Balleret (MON) 63 64 61.

Cyprus defeated Ireland 3-2, Nicosia, CYP, Hard (O): Marcos Baghdatis (CYP) d. Louk Sorensen (IRL) 67(5) 64 36 75 64; Conor Niland (IRL) d. Photos Kallias (CYP) 57 63 5-0 ret.; Marcos Baghdatis/Photos Kallias (CYP) d. James McGee/Colin O'Brien (IRL) 62 57 62 62; Marcos Baghdatis (CYP) d. Conor Niland (IRL) 46 63 61 63; Colin O'Brien (IRL) d. Demetrios Leontis (CYP) 76(2) 63.

Third Round 18-20 September

Latvia defeated Slovenia 3-2, Jurmala, LAT, Carpet (I): Grega Zemlja (SLO) d. Andis Juska (LAT) 61 61 64; Ernests Gulbis (LAT) d. Luka Gregorc (SLO) 46 67(3) 64 64 86; Luka Gregorc/Grega Zemlja (SLO) d. Ernests Gulbis/Deniss Pavlovs (LAT) 67(5) 64 62 26 64; Ernests Gulbis (LAT) d. Grega Zemlja (SLO) 62 36 63 75; Andis Juska (LAT) d. Blaz Kavcic (SLO) 63 64 62.

Finland defeated Cyprus 3-2, Salo, FIN, Hard (I): Jarkko Nieminen (FIN) d. Photos Kallias (CYP) 62 61 60; Marcos Baghdatis (CYP) d. Henri Kontinen (FIN) 63 63 62; Henri Kontinen/Jarkko Nieminen (FIN) d. Marcos Baghdatis/Photos Kallias (CYP) 67(4) 16 62 63 75; Marcos Baghdatis (CYP) d. Jarkko Nieminen (FIN) 75 63 36 64; Henri Kontinen (FIN) d. Photos Kallias (CYP) 60 75 60.

Finland and Latvia promoted to Europe/Africa Zone Group I in 2010.

Relegation Play-offs 10-12 July
Egypt defeated Georgia 5-0, Cairo, EGY, Clay (O): Karim Maamoun (EGY) d. George Khrikadze (GEO) 60 5-0 ret.; Sherif Sabry (EGY) d. Nodar Itonishvili (GEO) 62 64 60; Karim Maamoun/Sherif Sabry (EGY) d. Nodar Itonishvili/George Khrikadze (GEO) 60 62 61; Mohamed Mamoun (EGY) d. Nodar Itonishvili (GEO) 61 63; Omar Hedayet (EGY) d. Alexander Tavkhelidze (GEO) 16 62 62.

Hungary defeated Moldova 3-2, Godollo, HUN, Clay (O): Attila Balazs (HUN) d. Radu Albot (MDA) 61 64 46 64; Andrei Gorban (MDA) d. Denes Lukacs (HUN) 64 26 75 61; Attila Balazs/Robert Varga (HUN) d. Radu Albot/Andrei Ciumac (MDA) 63 46 46 75 64; Attila Balazs (HUN) d. Andrei Gorban (MDA) 64 60 64; Radu Albot (MDA) d. Denes Lukacs (HUN) 63 62.

Denmark defeated Montenegro 3-2, Lyngby, DEN, Clay (O): Goran Tosic (MNE) d. Frederik Nielsen (DEN) 57 64 76(5) 64; Martin Pedersen (DEN) d. Daniel Danilovic (MNE) 76(5) 64 61; Daniel Danilovic/Goran Tosic (MNE) d. Frederik Nielsen/Martin Pedersen (DEN) 62 63 63; Frederik Nielsen (DEN) d. Daniel Danilovic (MNE) 36 61 62 64; Martin Pedersen (DEN) d. Goran Tosic (MNE) 64 63 62.

Portugal defeated Algeria 5-0, Oran, ALG, Clay (O): Rui Machado (POR) d. Valentin Rahmine (ALG) 60 60 60; Frederico Gil (POR) d. Abdelhak Hameurlaine (ALG) 61 62 64; Frederico Gil/Leonardo Tavares (POR) d. Abdelhak Hameurlaine/Valentin Rahmine (ALG) 61 62 63; Leonardo Tavares (POR) d. Valentin Rahmine (ALG) 61 60; Joao Sousa (POR) d. Sid-Ali Akkal (ALG) 63 60.

Algeria, Georgia, Moldova and Montenegro relegated to Europe/Africa Zone Group III in 2010.

GROUP III

Americas Zone
Date: 22-26 April **Venue:** La Libertad, El Salvador **Surface:** Clay (O)
Group A: Barbados, Bolivia, El Salvador
Group B: Costa Rica, Cuba, Honduras, Puerto Rico

Group A
22 April El Salvador defeated Bolivia 3-0: Marcelo Arevalo (ESA) d. Mauricio Estivariz (BOL) 64 64; Rafael Arevalo (ESA) d. Mauricio Doria-Medina (BOL) 61 61; Marcelo Arevalo/Rafael Arevalo (ESA) d. Mauricio Doria-Medina/Mauricio Estivariz (BOL) 57 64 63.

23 April Bolivia defeated Barbados 2-1: Mauricio Estivariz (BOL) d. Darian King (BAR) 60 60; Haydn Lewis (BAR) d. Mauricio Doria-Medina (BOL) 64 75; Mauricio Estivariz/Jose-Roberto Velasco (BOL) d. Haydn Lewis/Russell Moseley (BAR) 61 46 61.

24 April El Salvador defeated Barbados 2-1: Darian King (BAR) d. Rodrigo Rappaccioli (ESA) 36 75 63; Rafael Arevalo (ESA) d. Haydn Lewis (BAR) 63 61; Marcelo Arevalo/Rafael Arevalo (ESA) d. Haydn Lewis/Russell Moseley (BAR) 46 63 64.

Final Positions: 1. El Salvador, 2. Bolivia, 3. Barbados.

Group B
22 April Cuba defeated Costa Rica 3-0: William Dorantes Sanchez (CUB) d. Ignaci Roca (CRC) 61 75; Edgar Hernandez-Perez (CUB) d. Federico Chavarria (CRC) 75 64; Favel-Antonio Freyre-Perdomo/Sandor Martinez-Breijo (CUB) d. Federico Chavarria/Fernando Martinez-Manrique (CRC) 76(1) 76(3).

Puerto Rico defeated Honduras 2-1: Keny Turcios (HON) d. Gilberto Alvarez (PUR) 26 75 76(5); Jose Emilio Sierra-Short (PUR) d. Alejandro Obando (HON) 63 36 62; Gilberto Alvarez/Ricardo Gonzalez-Diaz (PUR) d. Alejandro Obando/Keny Turcios (HON) 63 61.

23 April Costa Rica defeated Honduras 3-0: Federico Chavarria (CRC) d. Keny Turcios (HON) 64 75; Fernando Martinez-Manrique (CRC) d. Alejandro Obando (HON) 61 64; Fernando Martinez-Manrique/Ignaci Roca (CRC) d. Alejandro Obando/Ricardo Pineda (HON) 60 61.

Cuba defeated Puerto Rico 3-0: William Dorantes Sanchez (CUB) d. Jose Emilio Sierra-Short (PUR) 62 60; Edgar Hernandez-Perez (CUB) d. Ricardo Gonzalez-Diaz (PUR) 64 46 63; Favel-Antonio Freyre-Perdomo/Sandor Martinez-Breijo (CUB) d. Gilberto Alvarez/Gabriel Flores Ruiz (PUR) 63 64.

24 April Puerto Rico defeated Costa Rica 2-1: Gilberto Alvarez (PUR) d. Ignaci Roca (CRC) 76(3) 63; Ricardo Gonzalez-Diaz (PUR) d. Federico Chavarria (CRC) 64 67(6) 76(1); Pablo Nunez/Ignaci Roca (CRC) d. Gabriel Flores Ruiz/Jose Emilio Sierra-Short (PUR) 67(5) 64 76(4).

Cuba defeated Honduras 3-0: William Dorantes Sanchez (CUB) d. Keny Turcios (HON) 61 61; Edgar Hernandez-Perez (CUB) d. Alejandro Obando (HON) 60 62; Favel-Antonio Freyre-Perdomo/Sandor Martinez-Breijo (CUB) d. Alejandro Obando/Ricardo Pineda (HON) 62 64.

Final Positions: 1. Cuba, 2. Puerto Rico, 3. Costa Rica, 4. Honduras.

Play-offs for 1st-4th Positions:
Results carried forward: El Salvador defeated Bolivia 3-0; Cuba defeated Puerto Rico 3-0.

25 April El Salvador defeated Cuba 3-0: Marcelo Arevalo (ESA) d. William Dorantes Sanchez (CUB) 63 75; Rafael Arevalo (ESA) d. Edgar Hernandez-Perez (CUB) 60 63; Marcelo Arevalo/Rodrigo Rappaccioli (ESA) d. Favel-Antonio Freyre-Perdomo/Sandor Martinez-Breijo (CUB) 76(1) 64.

Bolivia defeated Puerto Rico 2-1: Mauricio Estivariz (BOL) d. Gilberto Alvarez (PUR) 76(5) 62; Ricardo Gonzalez-Diaz (PUR) d. Mauricio Doria-Medina (BOL) 67(1) 75 75; Mauricio Estivariz/Jose-Roberto Velasco (BOL) d. Gilberto Alvarez/Ricardo Gonzalez-Diaz (PUR) 62 62.

26 April El Salvador defeated Puerto Rico 3-0: Marcelo Arevalo (ESA) d. Gabriel Flores Ruiz (PUR) 62 60; Rafael Arevalo (ESA) d. Jose Emilio Sierra-Short (PUR) 60 60; Marcelo Arevalo/Rodrigo Rappaccioli (ESA) d. Gabriel Flores Ruiz/Jose Emilio Sierra-Short (PUR) 67(4) 61 63.

Bolivia defeated Cuba 2-1: Mauricio Estivariz (BOL) d. William Dorantes Sanchez (CUB) 64 60; Mauricio Doria-Medina (BOL) d. Edgar Hernandez-Perez (CUB) 63 60; Favel-Antonio Freyre-Perdomo/Sandor Martinez-Breijo (CUB) d. Marco-Antonio Rojas/Jose-Roberto Velasco (BOL) 64 76(3).

Play-offs for 5th-7th Positions:
Result carried forward: Costa Rica defeated Honduras 3-0.

25 April Barbados defeated Honduras 3-0: Russell Moseley (BAR) d. Keny Turcios (HON) 57 61 61; Haydn Lewis (BAR) d. Alejandro Obando (HON) 62 60; Darian King/Seanon Williams (BAR) d. Marco Ricardo Osorio/Ricardo Pineda (HON) 76(3) 46 60.

26 April Costa Rica defeated Barbados 2-1: Federico Chavarria (CRC) d. Darian King (BAR) 62 63; Haydn Lewis (BAR) d. Fernando Martinez-Manrique (CRC) 63 63; Federico Chavarria/Fernando Martinez-Manrique (CRC) d. Haydn Lewis/Russell Moseley (BAR) 36 76(3) 62.

Final Positions: 1. El Salvador, 2. Bolivia, 3. Cuba, 4. Puerto Rico, 5. Costa Rica, 6. Barbados, 7. Honduras.

Bolivia and El Salvador promoted to Americas Zone Group II in 2010. Barbados and Honduras relegated to Americas Zone Group IV in 2010.

Asia/Oceania Zone
Date: 15-18 April **Venue:** Aleppo, Syria **Surface:** Hard (O)
Group A: Lebanon, Pacific Oceania, Singapore, Tajikistan
Group B: Iran, Saudi Arabia, Sri Lanka, Syria

Group A
15 April Pacific Oceania defeated Tajikistan 3-0: Juan Sebastien Langton (POC) d. Bakhtiyor Sadulloev (TJK) 64 62; Michael Leong (POC) d. Sergey Makashin (TJK) 62 62; Brett Baudinet/Cyril Jacobe (POC) d. Bakhtiyor Sadulloev/Mirkhusein Yakhyaev (TJK) 61 62.

Lebanon defeated Singapore 2-1: Stanley Armando (SIN) d. Brahim Saffiedine (LIB) 64 26 62; Karim Alayly (LIB) d. Abdul-Hakim Jamaludin (SIN) 61 61; Karim Alayly/Jicham Zaatini (LIB) d. Stanley Armando/Daniel Heryanta Dewandaka (SIN) 61 60.

16 April Pacific Oceania defeated Singapore 3-0: Juan Sebastien Langton (POC) d. Stanley Armando (SIN) 36 62 75; Michael Leong (POC) d. Abdul-Hakim Jamaludin (SIN) 60 63; Brett Baudinet/Cyril Jacobe (POC) d. Abdul-Hakim Jamaludin/Marcus Dexian Tay (SIN) 76(3) 63.

Lebanon defeated Tajikistan 2-1: Mirkhusein Yakhyaev (TJK) d. Brahim Saffiedine (LIB) 60 63; Karim Alayly (LIB) d. Bakhtiyor Sadulloev (TJK) 63 61; Karim Alayly/Jicham Zaatini (LIB) d. Sergey Makashin/Mirkhusein Yakhyaev (TJK) 75 64.

17 April Pacific Oceania defeated Lebanon 2-1: Juan Sebastien Langton (POC) d. Jicham Zaatini (LIB) 64 36 64; Karim Alayly (LIB) d. Brett Baudinet (POC) 46 1-3 ret.; Brett Baudinet/Cyril Jacobe (POC) d. Karim Alayly/Jicham Zaatini (LIB) 57 63 64.

Tajikistan defeated Singapore 3-0: Mirkhusein Yakhyaev (TJK) d. Marcus Dexian Tay (SIN) 63 64; Sergey Makashin (TJK) d. Stanley Armando (SIN) 75 60; Sergey Makashin/Mirkhusein Yakhyaev (TJK) d. Stanley Armando/Daniel Heryanta Dewandaka (SIN) 62 75.

Final Positions: 1. Pacific Oceania, 2. Lebanon, 3. Singapore, 4. Tajikistan.

Group B
15 April Sri Lanka defeated Iran 2-1: Anoosha Shahgholi (IRI) d. Rajeev Rajapakse (SRI) 76(1) 57 60; Harshana Godamanna (SRI) d. Rouzbeh Kamran (IRI) 63 62; Harshana Godamanna/Rajeev Rajapakse (SRI) d. Anoosha Shahgholi/Ashkan Shokoofi (IRI) 60 62.

Syria defeated Saudi Arabia 3-0: Romain Radwan (SYR) d. Fahad Al Saad (KSA) 76(2) 63; Issam Tawil (SYR) d. Saleh Alrajeh (KSA) 63 75; Hayan Marouf/Roy Radwan (SYR) d. Fahad Al Saad/Bader Mohammed Almuqail (KSA) 63 64.

16 April Sri Lanka defeated Saudi Arabia 3-0: Rajeev Rajapakse (SRI) d. Fahad Al Saad (KSA) 61 57 64; Harshana Godamanna (SRI) d. Saleh Alrajeh (KSA) 64 60; Harshana Godamanna/Rajeev Rajapakse (SRI) d. Omar Al Thagib/Bader Mohammed Almuqail (KSA) 62 63.

Syria defeated Iran 3-0: Roy Radwan (SYR) d. Ashkan Shokoofi (IRI) 46 62 64; Romain Radwan (SYR) d. Anoosha Shahgholi (IRI) 75 6-6 ret.; Hayan Marouf/Issam Tawil (SYR) d. Rouzbeh Kamran/Omid Souri (IRI) 62 64.

17 April Sri Lanka defeated Syria 3-0: Rajeev Rajapakse (SRI) d. Romain Radwan (SYR) 46 75 61; Harshana Godamanna (SRI) d. Issam Tawil (SYR) 57 62 62; Harshana Godamanna/Rajeev Rajapakse (SRI) d. Hayan Marouf/Issam Tawil (SYR) 62 62.

Saudi Arabia defeated Iran 2-1: Omid Souri (IRI) d. Omar Al Thagib (KSA) 64 63; Fahad Al Saad (KSA) d. Anoosha Shahgholi (IRI) 64 3-1 ret.; Fahad Al Saad/Bader Mohammed Almuqail (KSA) d. Anoosha Shahgholi/Ashkan Shokoofi (IRI) 57 63 64.

Final Positions: 1. Sri Lanka, 2. Syria, 3. Iran, 4. Saudi Arabia.

Play-offs for 1st-4th Positions:
Results carried forward: Sri Lanka defeated Syria 3-0; Pacific Oceania defeated Lebanon 2-1.

18 April Sri Lanka defeated Lebanon 3-0: Rajeev Rajapakse (SRI) d. Brahim Saffiedine (LIB) 64 62; Harshana Godamanna (SRI) d. Karim Alayly (LIB) 64 63; Sankha Atukorale/Harshana Godamanna (SRI) d. Rami Osman/Brahim Saffiedine (LIB) 60 61.

Pacific Oceania defeated Syria 2-1: Hayan Marouf (SYR) d. Juan Sebastien Langton (POC) 60 64; Michael Leong (POC) d. Issam Tawil (SYR) 61 63; Brett Baudinet/Cyril Jacobe (POC) d. Hayan Marouf/Roy Radwan (SYR) 60 64.

19 April Pacific Oceania defeated Sri Lanka 3-0: Juan Sebastien Langton (POC) d. Rajeev Rajapakse (SRI) 76(4) 64; Michael Leong (POC) d. Harshana Godamanna (SRI) 75 61; Brett Baudinet/Cyril Jacobe (POC) d. Sankha Atukorale/Harshana Godamanna (SRI) 46 62 64.

Syria defeated Lebanon 3-0: Hayan Marouf (SYR) d. Rami Osman (LIB) 61 63; Issam Tawil (SYR) d. Brahim Saffiedine (LIB) 63 62; Romain Radwan/Roy Radwan (SYR) d. Rami Osman/Brahim Saffiedine (LIB) 5-0 ret.

Play-offs for 5th-8th Positions:
Results carried forward: Tajikistan defeated Singapore 3-0; Saudi Arabia defeated Iran 2-1.

18 April Iran defeated Tajikistan 2-1: Anoosha Shahgholi (IRI) d. Mirkhusein Yakhyaev (TJK) 64 46 62; Sergey Makashin (TJK) d. Rouzbeh Kamran (IRI) 62 75; Anoosha Shahgholi/Ashkan Shokoofi (IRI) d. Sergey Makashin/Mirkhusein Yakhyaev (TJK) 63 61.

Saudi Arabia defeated Singapore 3-0: Fahad Al Saad (KSA) d. Marcus Dexian Tay (SIN) 61 61; Saleh Alrajeh (KSA) d. Abdul-Hakim Jamaludin (SIN) 61 61; Omar Al Thagib/Bader Mohammed Almuqail (KSA) d. Abdul-Hakim Jamaludin/Marcus Dexian Tay (SIN) 62 64.

19 April Saudi Arabia defeated Tajikistan 3-0: Fahad Al Saad (KSA) d. Sergey Makashin (TJK) 36 75 75; Saleh Alrajeh (KSA) d. Bakhtiyor Sadulloev (TJK) 76(2) 62; Omar Al Thagib/Bader Mohammed Almuqail (KSA) d. Bakhtiyor Sadulloev/Mirkhusein Yakhyaev (TJK) 5-3 ret.

Iran defeated Singapore 3-0: Anoosha Shahgholi (IRI) d. Marcus Dexian Tay (SIN) 61 60; Rouzbeh Kamran (IRI) d. Abdul-Hakim Jamaludin (SIN) 60 76(2); Anoosha Shahgholi/Ashkan Shokoofi (IRI) d. Abdul-Hakim Jamaludin/Marcus Dexian Tay (SIN) 63 62.

Final Positions: 1. Pacific Oceania, 2. Sri Lanka, 3. Syria, 4. Lebanon, 5. Saudi Arabia, 6. Iran, 7. Tajikistan, 8. Singapore.

Pacific Oceania and Sri Lanka promoted to Asia/Oceania Zone Group II in 2010. Singapore and Tajikistan relegated to Asia/Oceania Zone Group IV in 2010.

Europe/Africa Zone - Venue I
Date: 29 April-3 May **Venue:** Istanbul, Turkey **Surface:** Hard (O)
Group A: Botswana, Estonia, Iceland, Luxembourg
Group B: Greece, Madagascar, Rwanda, Turkey

Group A
29 April Luxembourg defeated Iceland 3-0: Gilles Kremer (LUX) d. Arnar Sigurdsson (ISL) 26 76(5) 63; Mike Scheidweiler (LUX) d. Birkir Gunnarsson (ISL) 60 60; Gilles Kremer/Mike Scheidweiler (LUX) d. Magnus Gunnarsson/Teitur Marshall (ISL) 61 61.

Estonia defeated Botswana 3-0: Jaak Poldma (EST) d. Matshidiso Malope (BOT) 60 60; Jurgen Zopp (EST) d. Thabiso Mabaka (BOT) 60 60; Mait Kunnap/Jurgen Zopp (EST) d. Shingirai Muzondiwa/Lefa Ashley Sibanda (BOT) 61 61.

30 April Luxembourg defeated Botswana 3-0: Laurent Bram (LUX) d. Lefa Ashley Sibanda (BOT) 60 61; Mike Scheidweiler (LUX) d. Thabiso Mabaka (BOT) 60 61; Laurent Bram/Philippe Grandjean (LUX) d. Matshidiso Malope/Shingirai Muzondiwa (BOT) 62 61.

Estonia defeated Iceland 3-0: Jaak Poldma (EST) d. Magnus Gunnarsson (ISL) 60 60; Jurgen Zopp (EST) d. Teitur Marshall (ISL) 62 61; Vladimir Ivanov/Mait Kunnap (EST) d. Magnus Gunnarsson/Arnar Sigurdsson (ISL) 61 64.

1 May Estonia defeated Luxembourg 3-0: Jaak Poldma (EST) d. Gilles Kremer (LUX) 76(6) 62; Jurgen Zopp (EST) d. Mike Scheidweiler (LUX) 46 63 76(2); Mait Kunnap/Jaak Poldma (EST) d. Laurent Bram/Philippe Grandjean (LUX) 64 63.

Iceland defeated Botswana 2-1: Arnar Sigurdsson (ISL) d. Matshidiso Malope (BOT) 60 60; Thabiso Mabaka (BOT) d. Teitur Marshall (ISL) 62 61; Magnus Gunnarsson/Arnar Sigurdsson (ISL) d. Thabiso Mabaka/Matshidiso Malope (BOT) 64 63.

Final Positions: 1. Luxembourg, 2. Estonia, 3. Iceland, 4. Botswana.

Group B
29 April Turkey defeated Greece 2-1: Haluk Akkoyun (TUR) d. Konstantinos Economidis (GRE) 76(4) 60; Marsel Ilhan (TUR) d. Alexandros Jakupovic (GRE) 64 62; Alexandros Jakupovic/Dimitris Kleftakos (GRE) d. Baris Erguden/Ergun Zorlu (TUR) 63 36 63.

Madagascar defeated Rwanda w/o.

30 April Greece defeated Madagascar 3-0: Konstantinos Economidis (GRE) d. Jacob Rasolondrazana (MAD) 63 63; Alexandros Jakupovic (GRE) d. Tony Rajaobelina (MAD) 62 63; Alexandros Jakupovic/Dimitris Kleftakos (GRE) d. Erick Counil/Thierry Rajaobelina (MAD) 63 46 63.

Turkey defeated Rwanda 3-0: Haluk Akkoyun (TUR) d. Dieu-Donne Habiyambere (RWA) 60 61; Marsel Ilhan (TUR) d. Olivier Nkunda (RWA) 61 60; Baris Erguden/Ergun Zorlu (TUR) d. Dieu-Donne Habiyambere/Olivier Nkunda (RWA) 60 61.

1 May Greece defeated Rwanda 3-0: Dimitris Kleftakos (GRE) d. Dieu-Donne Habiyambere (RWA) 61 61; Alexandros Jakupovic (GRE) d. Olivier Nkunda (RWA) 61 61; Konstantinos Economidis/Dimitris Kleftakos (GRE) d. Dieu-Donne Habiyambere/Olivier Nkunda (RWA) 60 60.

Turkey defeated Madagascar 2-1: Erick Counil (MAD) d. Haluk Akkoyun (TUR) 63 62; Marsel Ilhan (TUR) d. Jacob Rasolondrazana (MAD) 76(1) 63; Marsel Ilhan/Ergun Zorlu (TUR) d. Thierry Rajaobelina/Jacob Rasolondrazana (MAD) 62 64.

Final Positions: 1. Greece, 2. Turkey, 3. Madagascar, 4. Rwanda.

Play-offs for 1st-4th Positions:
Results carried forward: Turkey defeated Greece 2-1; Estonia defeated Luxembourg 3-0.

2 May Estonia defeated Turkey 2-1: Jaak Poldma (EST) d. Haluk Akkoyun (TUR) 61 76(4); Marsel Ilhan (TUR) d. Jurgen Zopp (EST) 64 64; Mait Kunnap/Jurgen Zopp (EST) d. Marsel Ilhan/Ergun Zorlu (TUR) 61 62.

Luxembourg defeated Greece 2-1: Dimitris Kleftakos (GRE) d. Gilles Kremer (LUX) 64 16 61; Mike Scheidweiler (LUX) d. Alexandros Jakupovic (GRE) 57 63 76(4); Gilles Kremer/Mike Scheidweiler (LUX) d. Alexandros Jakupovic/Dimitris Kleftakos (GRE) 46 62 63.

3 May Turkey defeated Luxembourg 2-0: Haluk Akkoyun (TUR) d. Gilles Kremer (LUX) 76(2) 61; Marsel Ilhan (TUR) d. Mike Scheidweiler (LUX) 67(6) 64 64.

Estonia defeated Greece 3-0: Jaak Poldma (EST) d. Dimitris Kleftakos (GRE) 3-0 ret.; Jurgen Zopp (EST) d. Alexandros Jakupovic (GRE) 5-0 ret.; Mait Kunnap/Jurgen Zopp (EST) d. Alexandros Jakupovic/Dimitris Kleftakos (GRE) w/o.

Play-offs for 5th-8th Positions:
Results carried forward: Madagascar defeated Rwanda w/o; Iceland defeated Botswana 2-1.

2 May Madagascar defeated Iceland 2-1: Arnar Sigurdsson (ISL) d. Thierry Rajaobelina (MAD) 61 63; Jacob Rasolondrazana (MAD) d. Birkir Gunnarsson (ISL) 61 61; Erick Counil/Jacob Rasolondrazana (MAD) d. Magnus Gunnarsson/Arnar Sigurdsson (ISL) 64 63.

Rwanda defeated Botswana 2-1: Dieu-Donne Habiyambere (RWA) d. Lefa Ashley Sibanda (BOT) 61 36 75; Thabiso Mabaka (BOT) d. Olivier Nkunda (RWA) 75 62; Dieu-Donne Habiyambere/Olivier Nkunda (RWA) d. Matshidiso Malope/Shingirai Muzondiwa (BOT) 63 57 63.

3 May Madagascar defeated Botswana 3-0: Thierry Rajaobelina (MAD) d. Lefa Ashley Sibanda (BOT) 62 61; Jacob Rasolondrazana (MAD) d. Thabiso Mabaka (BOT) 61 64; Erick Counil/Jacob Rasolondrazana (MAD) d. Matshidiso Malope/Shingirai Muzondiwa (BOT) 60 61.

Iceland defeated Rwanda 2-1: Arnar Sigurdsson (ISL) d. Dieu-Donne Habiyambere (RWA) 60 60; Olivier Nkunda (RWA) d. Birkir Gunnarsson (ISL) 62 16 75; Magnus Gunnarsson/Arnar Sigurdsson (ISL) d. Dieu-Donne Habiyambere/Mathieu Uwizeyimana (RWA) 61 61.

Final Positions: 1. Estonia, 2. Turkey, 3. Luxembourg, 4. Greece, 5. Madagascar, 6. Iceland, 7. Rwanda, 8. Botswana.

Estonia, Greece, Luxembourg and Turkey promoted to Europe/Africa Zone Group II in 2010.

Europe/Africa Zone – Venue II
Date: 1-5 April **Venue:** La Marsa, Tunisia **Surface:** Clay (O)
Group A: Morocco, Nigeria, San Marino, Tunisia
Group B: Andorra, Bosnia/Herzegovina, Namibia, Norway

Group A
1 April Morocco defeated San Marino 3-0: Reda El Amrani (MAR) d. Alberto Brighi (SMR) 61 61; Rabie Chaki (MAR) d. Giacomo Zonzini (SMR) 64 62; Talal Ouahabi/Mehdi Ziadi (MAR) d. Domenico Vicini/Giacomo Zonzini (SMR) 63 62.

Tunisia defeated Nigeria 3-0: Haithem Abid (TUN) d. Lawal Shehu (NGR) 61 61; Malek Jaziri (TUN) d. Abdul-Mumin Babalola (NGR) 62 60; Haithem Abid/Malek Jaziri (TUN) d. Abdul-Mumin Babalola/Lawal Shehu (NGR) 64 61.

2 April Morocco defeated Nigeria 3-0: Rabie Chaki (MAR) d. Candy Idoko (NGR) 61 62; Talal Ouahabi (MAR) d. Sunday Emmanuel (NGR) 62 63; Reda El Amrani/Mehdi Ziadi (MAR) d. Abdul-Mumin Babalola/Lawal Shehu (NGR) 63 62.

Tunisia defeated San Marino 3-0: Haithem Abid (TUN) d. Giacomo Zonzini (SMR) 60 60; Malek Jaziri (TUN) d. Diego Zonzini (SMR) 62 61; Haithem Abid/Malek Jaziri (TUN) d. Domenico Vicini/Diego Zonzini (SMR) 61 62.

3 April Morocco defeated Tunisia 2-1: Haithem Abid (TUN) d. Reda El Amrani (MAR) 63 63; Rabie Chaki (MAR) d. Malek Jaziri (TUN) 63 75; Rabie Chaki/Mehdi Ziadi (MAR) d. Anis Ghorbel/Malek Jaziri (TUN) 61 61.

Nigeria defeated San Marino 3-0: Abdul-Mumin Babalola (NGR) d. Domenico Vicini (SMR) 61 64; Sunday Emmanuel (NGR) d. Diego Zonzini (SMR) 57 62 60; Candy Idoko/Lawal Shehu (NGR) d. Domenico Vicini/Diego Zonzini (SMR) 76(0) 76(5).

Final Positions: 1. Morocco, 2. Tunisia, 3. Nigeria, 4. San Marino.

Group B

1 April Norway defeated Andorra 3-0: Erling Tveit (NOR) d. Hector Hormigo-Herrera (AND) 61 61; Stian Boretti (NOR) d. Jean-Baptiste Poux-Gautier (AND) 62 63; Stian Boretti/Erling Tveit (NOR) d. Pau Gerbaud-Farras/Jordi Vila-Vila (AND) 62 62.

Bosnia/Herzegovina defeated Namibia 3-0: Ismar Gorcic (BIH) d. Jean Erasmus (NAM) 61 61; Aldin Setkic (BIH) d. Jurgens Strydom (NAM) 60 62; Mirza Basic/Tomislav Brkic (BIH) d. Jean Erasmus/Jurgens Strydom (NAM) 62 63.

2 April Norway defeated Namibia 3-0: Erling Tveit (NOR) d. Jean Erasmus (NAM) 62 60; Stian Boretti (NOR) d. Jurgens Strydom (NAM) 60 67(4) 63; Stian Boretti/Erling Tveit (NOR) d. Jean Erasmus/Warren Frewer (NAM) 61 61.

Bosnia/Herzegovina defeated Andorra 3-0: Ismar Gorcic (BIH) d. Hector Hormigo-Herrera (AND) 62 61; Aldin Setkic (BIH) d. Pau Gerbaud-Farras (AND) 61 60; Mirza Basic/Tomislav Brkic (BIH) d. Hector Hormigo-Herrera/Jordi Vila-Vila (AND) 63 63.

3 April Bosnia/Herzegovina defeated Norway 2-1: Ismar Gorcic (BIH) d. Erling Tveit (NOR) 62 46 75; Aldin Setkic (BIH) d. Stian Boretti (NOR) 63 75; Stian Boretti/Erling Tveit (NOR) d. Mirza Basic/Tomislav Brkic (BIH) 64 63.

Andorra defeated Namibia 2-1: Jordi Vila-Vila (AND) d. Jean Erasmus (NAM) 61 46 76(5); Jean-Baptiste Poux-Gautier (AND) d. Jurgens Strydom (NAM) 46 63 61; Jean Erasmus/Jurgens Strydom (NAM) d. Pau Gerbaud-Farras/Hector Hormigo-Herrera (AND) 63 63.

Final Positions: 1. Norway, 2. Bosnia/Herzegovina, 3. Namibia, 4. Andorra.

Play-offs for 1st-4th Positions:

Results carried forward: Morocco defeated Tunisia 2-1; Bosnia/Herzegovina defeated Norway 2-1.

4 April Morocco defeated Bosnia/Herzegovina 2-1: Rabie Chaki (MAR) d. Ismar Gorcic (BIH) 75 64; Talal Ouahabi (MAR) d. Aldin Setkic (BIH) 75 75; Ismar Gorcic/Aldin Setkic (BIH) d. Rabie Chaki/Mehdi Ziadi (MAR) 62 62.

Norway defeated Tunisia 2-1: Erling Tveit (NOR) d. Ouassim Derbal (TUN) 62 61; Malek Jaziri (TUN) d. Stian Boretti (NOR) 76(1) 62; Stian Boretti/Erling Tveit (NOR) d. Ouassim Derbal/Malek Jaziri (TUN) 75 75.

5 April Norway defeated Morocco 2-1: Erling Tveit (NOR) d. Rabie Chaki (MAR) 61 26 61; Stian Boretti (NOR) d. Talal Ouahabi (MAR) 61 60; Rabie Chaki/Mehdi Ziadi (MAR) d. Stian Boretti/Erling Tveit (NOR) 67(4) 62 76(3).

Bosnia/Herzegovina defeated Tunisia 2-1: Ismar Gorcic (BIH) d. Ouassim Derbal (TUN) 61 76(4); Malek Jaziri (TUN) d. Aldin Setkic (BIH) 46 62 75; Ismar Gorcic/Aldin Setkic (BIH) d. Ouassim Derbal/Malek Jaziri (TUN) 76(4) 61.

Play-offs for 5th-8th Positions:

Results carried forward: Nigeria defeated San Marino 3-0; Andorra defeated Namibia 2-1.

4 April Andorra defeated Nigeria 3-0: Pau Gerbaud-Farras (AND) d. Abdul-Mumin Babalola (NGR) 63 63; Jean-Baptiste Poux-Gautier (AND) d. Sunday Emmanuel (NGR) 63 64; Jean-Baptiste Poux-Gautier/Jordi Vila-Vila (AND) d. Candy Idoko/Lawal Shehu (NGR) 61 63.

Namibia defeated San Marino 2-1: Domenico Vicini (SMR) d. Jean Erasmus (NAM) 62 64; Jurgens Strydom (NAM) d. Giacomo Zonzini (SMR) 64 64; Jean Erasmus/Jurgens Strydom (NAM) d. Domenico Vicini/Giacomo Zonzini (SMR) 67(2) 60 63

5 April Nigeria defeated Namibia 2-1: Lawal Shehu (NGR) d. Jean Erasmus (NAM) 62 63; Jurgens Strydom (NAM) d. Sunday Emmanuel (NGR) 63 64; Candy Idoko/Lawal Shehu (NGR) d. Jean Erasmus/Jurgens Strydom (NAM) 61 63.

Andorra defeated San Marino 2-1: Giacomo Zonzini (SMR) d. Hector Hormigo-Herrera (AND) 64 36 62; Jean-Baptiste Poux-Gautier (AND) d. Diego Zonzini (SMR) 60 62; Pau Gerbaud-Farras/Jean-Baptiste Poux-Gautier (AND) d. Alberto Brighi/Domenico Vicini (SMR) 57 63 61.

Final Positions: 1. Norway, 2. Bosnia/Herzegovina, 3. Morocco, 4. Tunisia, 5. Andorra, 6. Nigeria, 7. Namibia, 8. San Marino.

Norway and Bosnia/Herzegovina promoted to Europe/Africa Zone Group II in 2010.

GROUP IV

Americas Zone
Date: 1-5 April **Venue:** Dhaka, Bangladesh **Surface:** Hard (O)

22 April Aruba defeated Bermuda 2-1: Gavin Manders (BER) d. Mitchell De Jong (ARU) 63 61; Gian Hodgson (ARU) d. Jenson Bascome (BER) 63 76(6); Gian Hodgson/Harry van Reek (ARU) d. Jenson Bascome/Gavin Manders (BER) 46 64 76(4).

US Virgin Islands defeated Panama 2-1: Giuseppe Guarnieri (PAN) d. Brian Karlsson Oldfield (ISV) 60 62; Kristepher Elien (ISV) d. Luis Fernando Garcia (PAN) 46 61 62; Kristepher Elien/Brian Karlsson Oldfield (ISV) d. Walner Espinoza/Jose Gilbert Gomez (PAN) 76(8) 62.

23 April Aruba defeated US Virgin Islands 2-1: Mitchell De Jong (ARU) d. Terrance Eugene Highfield (ISV) 63 64; Kristepher Elien (ISV) d. Gian Hodgson (ARU) 62 16 76(4); Gian Hodgson/Harry van Reek (ARU) d. Kristepher Elien/Terrance Eugene Highfield (ISV) 16 76(6) 64.

Bermuda defeated Trinidad & Tobago 2-1: Gavin Manders (BER) d. Vaughn Wilson (TRI) 62 62; Richard Chung (TRI) d. Jenson Bascome (BER) 76(7) 76(5); Jenson Bascome/Gavin Manders (BER) d. Richard Chung/Jerome Ward (TRI) 62 61.

24 April Trinidad & Tobago defeated Panama 2-1: Giuseppe Guarnieri (PAN) d. Jerome Ward (TRI) 63 67(3) 64; Richard Chung (TRI) d. Luis Fernando Garcia (PAN) 62 76(8); Richard Chung/Vaughn Wilson (TRI) d. Walner Espinoza/Luis Fernando Garcia (PAN) 64 62.

Bermuda defeated US Virgin Islands 2-1: Gavin Manders (BER) d. Terrance Eugene Highfield (ISV) 63 36 76(3); Kristepher Elien (ISV) d. Jenson Bascome (BER) 64 62; Jenson Bascome/Gavin Manders (BER) d. Kristepher Elien/Terrance Eugene Highfield (ISV) 64 46 63.

25 April Aruba defeated Panama 2-1: Giuseppe Guarnieri (PAN) d. Mitchell De Jong (ARU) 75 62; Gian Hodgson (ARU) d. Walner Espinoza (PAN) 61 60; Gian Hodgson/Harry van Reek (ARU) d. Walner Espinoza/Jose Gilbert Gomez (PAN) 63 63.

US Virgin Islands defeated Trinidad & Tobago 2-1: Brian Karlsson Oldfield (ISV) d. Jerome Ward (TRI) 46 61 62; Kristepher Elien (ISV) d. Richard Chung (TRI) 63 62; Richard Chung/Vaughn Wilson (TRI) d. Kemit-Amon Francis Lewis/Brian Karlsson Oldfield (ISV) 63 61.

26 April Aruba defeated Trinidad & Tobago 2-1: Jerome Ward (TRI) d. Harry van Reek (ARU) 64 67(7) 63; Gian Hodgson (ARU) d. Richard Chung (TRI) 46 62 75; Mitchell de Jong/Harry van Reek (ARU) d. Richard Chung/Vaughn Wilson (TRI) 61 64.

Bermuda defeated Panama 3-0: Gavin Manders (BER) d. Jose Gilbert Gomez (PAN) 62 64; Jenson Bascome (BER) d. Giuseppe Guarnieri (PAN) 26 63 6-6 ret.; Nicholas Thuell/Jacob Trott (BER) d. Walner Espinoza/Jose Gilbert Gomez (PAN) 76(5) 63.

Final Positions: 1. Aruba, 2. Bermuda, 3. US Virgin Islands, 4. Trinidad & Tobago, 5. Panama.

Aruba and Bermuda promoted to Americas Zone Group III in 2010.

Asia/Oceania Zone
Date: 1-5 April **Venue:** Dhaka, Bangladesh **Surface:** Hard (O)

Group A

1 April Vietnam defeated Bahrain 3-0: Quang-Huy Ngo (VIE) d. Khaled Al Thawadi (BRN) 62 62; Bui-Tri Nguyen (VIE) d. Abdulla Mohamed Ahmed Mohamed (BRN) 62 60; Quoc-Khanh Le/Thanh-Hoang Tran (VIE) d. Khaled Al Thawadi/Abdulla Mohamed Ahmed Mohamed (BRN) 62 61.

United Arab Emirates defeated Yemen 3-0: Mahmoud-Nader Al Baloushi (UAE) d. Ahmed Saif (YEM) 61 61; Hamad Abbas Janahi (UAE) d. Momen Hasan (YEM) 62 61; Rashed Al Falasi/Faisal Bastaki (UAE) d. Mohammed Saif/Fahd Thabit (YEM) 60 60.

2 April Vietnam defeated Iraq w/o. United Arab Emirates defeated Bahrain 2-1: Khaled Al Thawadi (BRN) d. Faisal Bastaki (UAE) 61 60; Hamad Abbas Janahi (UAE) d. Abdulla Mohamed Ahmed Mohamed (BRN) 61 64; Mahmoud-Nader Al Baloushi/Hamad Abbas Janahi (UAE) d. Esam Abdulaal/Khaled Al Thawadi (BRN) 16 62 64;

3 April United Arab Emirates defeated Iraq w/o. Bahrain defeated Yemen 2-1: Khaled Al Thawadi (BRN) d. Momen Hasan (YEM) 62 61; Ahmed Saif (YEM) d. Abdulla Mohamed Ahmed Mohamed (BRN) 16 64 4-0 ret.; Esam Abdulaal/Khaled Al Thawadi (BRN) d. Ahmed Saif/Fahd Thabit (YEM) 60 60.

4 April Bahrain defeated Iraq w/o.

Vietnam defeated Yemen 3-0: Quang-Huy Ngo (VIE) d. Momen Hasan (YEM) 60 61; Bui-Tri Nguyen (VIE) d. Mohammed Saif (YEM) 62 60; Quoc-Khanh Le/Thanh-Hoang Tran (VIE) d. Mohammed Saif/Fahd Thabit (YEM) 61 61.

5 April Yemen defeated Iraq w/o.

Vietnam defeated United Arab Emirates 2-1: Quang-Huy Ngo (VIE) d. Mahmoud-Nader Al Baloushi (UAE) 64 76(4); Hamad Abbas Janahi (UAE) d. Bui-Tri Nguyen (VIE) 64 62; Quoc-Khanh Le/Thanh-Hoang Tran (VIE) d. Mahmoud-Nader Al Baloushi/Hamad Abbas Janahi (UAE) 60 76(1).

Group A Final Positions: 1. Vietnam, 2. United Arab Emirates, 3. Bahrain, 4. Yemen, 5. Iraq.

Group B

1 April Bangladesh defeated Jordan 2-1: Shibu Lal (BAN) d. Khaled Naffa (JOR) 64 76(2); Sree-Amol Roy (BAN) d. Ahmed Al Hadid (JOR) 76(0) 61; Fabio Badra/Tareq Talal Shkakwa (JOR) d. Ranjan Ram/Omar-Faruk Sunny (BAN) 26 63 76(8).

Qatar defeated Myanmar 2-1: Abdulla Al Haji (QAT) d. Min Min (MYA) 62 62; Sultan Khalfan Al Alawi (QAT) d. Maung Nge Hnaung (MYA) 76(5) 61; Min Min/Maung Nge Hnaung (MYA) d. Jabor Al Mutawa/Mousa Zayed (QAT) 61 63.

2 April Bangladesh defeated Turkmenistan 3-0: Shibu Lal (BAN) d. Jamshid Ilmuradov (TKM) 61 61; Sree-Amol Roy (BAN) d. Eziz Davletov (TKM) 62 64; Shibu Lal/Ranjan Ram (BAN) d. Bahtiyar Atabaev/Eziz Davletov (TKM) 61 63.

Jordan defeated Myanmar 2-1: Maung Nge Hnaung (MYA) d. Fabio Badra (JOR) 76(5) 64; Ahmed Al Hadid (JOR) d. Aung Kyaw Naing (MYA) 61 61; Ahmed Al Hadid/Khaled Naffa (JOR) d. Min Min/Maung Nge Hnaung (MYA) 67(3) 61 63.

3 April Myanmar defeated Turkmenistan 3-0: Maung Nge Hnaung (MYA) d. Jamshid Ilmuradov (TKM) 60 63; Aung Kyaw Naing (MYA) d. Eziz Davletov (TKM) 64 63; Min Min/Maung Nge Hnaung (MYA) d. Ibragim Byashimov/Jamshid Ilmuradov (TKM) 62 64.

Jordan defeated Qatar 3-0: Fabio Badra (JOR) d. Abdulla Al Haji (QAT) 76(5) 64; Ahmed Al Hadid (JOR) d. Sultan Khalfan Al Alawi (QAT) 26 62 63; Khaled Naffa/Tareq Talal Shkakwa (JOR) d. Jabor Al Mutawa/Mousa Zayed (QAT) 63 60.

4 April Bangladesh defeated Qatar 3-0: Shibu Lal (BAN) d. Jabor Al Mutawa (QAT) 60 60; Sree-Amol Roy (BAN) d. Abdulla Al Haji (QAT) 62 75; Shibu Lal/Ranjan Ram (BAN) d. Jabor Al Mutawa/Mousa Zayed (QAT) 60 61.

Jordan defeated Turkmenistan 3-0: Fabio Badra (JOR) d. Bahtiyar Atabaev (TKM) 62 16 64; Ahmed Al Hadid (JOR) d. Ibragim Byashimov (TKM) 60 62; Khaled Naffa/Tareq Talal Shkakwa (JOR) d. Eziz Davletov/Jamshid Ilmuradov (TKM) 62 62.

5 April Bangladesh defeated Myanmar 2-1: Maung Nge Hnaung (MYA) d. Shibu Lal (BAN) 64 64; Sree-Amol Roy (BAN) d. Aung Kyaw Naing (MYA) 61 63; Ranjan Ram/Sree-Amol Roy (BAN) d. Min Min/Maung Nge Hnaung (MYA) 61 46 64.

Qatar defeated Turkmenistan 3-0: Sultan Khalfan Al Alawi (QAT) d. Bahtiyar Atabaev (TKM) 60 60; Mousa Zayed (QAT) d. Eziz Davletov (TKM) 64 62; Jabor Al Mutawa/Mousa Zayed (QAT) d. Bahtiyar Atabaev/Eziz Davletov (TKM) 36 61 62.

Group B Final Positions: 1. Bangladesh, 2. Jordan, 3. Qatar, 4. Myanmar, 5. Turkmenistan.

Bangladesh and Vietnam promoted to Asia/Oceania Zone Group III in 2010.

Europe/Africa Zone Group IV
Date: 29 April–3 May **Venue:** Abidjan, Cote d'Ivoire **Surface:** Hard (O)

29 April Ghana defeated Armenia 3-0: Emmanuel Mensah (GHA) d. Ashot Gevorgyan (ARM) 64 75; Mohammed Salifu (GHA) d. Harutyun Sofyan (ARM) 62 61; Emmanuel Mensah/Mohammed Salifu (GHA) d. Ashot Gevorgyan/Henrik Nikoghosyan (ARM) 61 61.

Cote d'Ivoire defeated Cameroon 2-1: Celestin Nkoueleue (CMR) d. Lavry Sylvain N'Yaba (CIV) 64 61; Valentin Sanon (CIV) d. Germain Ayinda (CMR) 62 61; Lavry Sylvain N'Yaba/Valentin Sanon (CIV) d. Pierre Damien Ayissi Djomo/Celestin Nkoueleue (CMR) 63 63.

30 April Cote d'Ivoire defeated Armenia 2-1: Lavry Sylvain N'Yaba (CIV) d. Ashot Gevorgyan (ARM) 64 63; Valentin Sanon (CIV) d. Harutyun Sofyan (ARM) 62 63; Ashot Gevorgyan/Henrik Nikoghosyan (ARM) d. Yeboua Koffi Etienne Bini/Akre Francis Koffi (CIV) 75 57 64.

Ghana defeated Zimbabwe 3-0: Emmanuel Mensah (GHA) d. Andrew Mawire (ZIM) 63 62; Mohammed Salifu (GHA) d. Takanyi Garanganga (ZIM) 36 76(7) 4-1 ret.; Emmanuel Mensah/Mohammed Salifu (GHA) d. Andrew Mawire/Mbonisi Ndimande (ZIM) 63 63.

1 May Zimbabwe defeated Armenia 2-1: Mbonisi Ndimande (ZIM) d. Ashot Gevorgyan (ARM) 67(1) 64 61; Harutyun Sofyan (ARM) d. Takanyi Garanganga (ZIM) 61 63; Andrew Mawire/Mbonisi Ndimande (ZIM) d. Ashot Gevorgyan/Harutyun Sofyan (ARM) 64 62.

Ghana defeated Cameroon 3-0: Emmanuel Mensah (GHA) d. Celestin Nkoueleue (CMR) 61 63; Mohammed Salifu (GHA) d. Germain Ayinda (CMR) 61 61; Robert Mensah Kpodo/Menford Owusu (GHA) d. Pierre Damien Ayissi Djomo/Augustin Ntouba (CMR) 64 46 75.

2 May Armenia defeated Cameroon 3-0: Ashot Gevorgyan (ARM) d. Pierre Damien Ayissi Djomo (CMR) 62 63; Harutyun Sofyan (ARM) d. Celestin Nkoueleue (CMR) 63 64; Henrik Nikoghosyan/Harutyun Sofyan (ARM) d. Pierre Damien Ayissi Djomo/Augustin Ntouba (CMR) 62 63.

Zimbabwe defeated Cote d'Ivoire 2-1: Mbonisi Ndimande (ZIM) d. Lavry Sylvain N'Yaba (CIV) 36 75 61; Valentin Sanon (CIV) d. Andrew Mawire (ZIM) 61 61; Andrew Mawire/Mbonisi Ndimande (ZIM) d. Lavry Sylvain N'Yaba/Valentin Sanon (CIV) 62 76(5).

3 May Zimbabwe defeated Cameroon 3-0: Mbonisi Ndimande (ZIM) d. Augustin Ntouba (CMR) 63 60; Andrew Mawire (ZIM) d. Celestin Nkoueleue (CMR) 62 76(3); Andrew Mawire/Mbonisi Ndimande (ZIM) d. Germain Ayinda/Augustin Ntouba (CMR) 63 61.

Ghana defeated Cote d'Ivoire 3-0: Emmanuel Mensah (GHA) d. Lavry Sylvain N'Yaba (CIV) 61 64; Mohammed Salifu (GHA) d. Valentin Sanon (CIV) 76(3) 64; Robert Mensah Kpodo/Menford Owusu (GHA) d. Yeboua Koffi Etienne Bini/Akre Francis Koffi (CIV) 62 62.

Final Positions: 1. Ghana, 2. Zimbabwe, 3. Cote d'Ivoire, 4. Armenia, 5. Cameroon.

Acknowledgements

The first Davis Cup final I saw live was in 2004, at Seville's Estadio Olimpico. At the time, much was made of the fact that Spain's tie against the United States drew a record crowd of more than 27,000 spectators a day. But, looking back at that final, the most significant aspect was not the number of people in seats, but that this was the weekend when Rafael Nadal parked his tank on the world stage. When he appeared at the 2004 final, Nadal had yet to win a grand slam. At that stage in his career, the eighteen-year-old hadn't even played a match on the clay of Roland Garros.

Five years later, and I was in Barcelona for another Spanish home final, for a reminder of what the Davis Cup final means to Spain, and to Nadal. After all he has achieved, Nadal doesn't do blasé and he doesn't do self-enchanted. After a frustrating middle and end to the 2009 season on the singles tour, it was clear how much he craved more success in the Davis Cup. Nadal, a winner of six grand slam titles, needed Spain to win the Davis Cup if he was to go into the close season thinking happy thoughts.

My favorite story of the 2009 Davis Cup year, however, was the day when Ivo Karlovic hit seventy-eight aces but still lost. That is almost twenty games' worth of aces. Nothing personal against Karlovic, but there was something reassuring about how Stepanek, after watching all those serves fizz past him, could still go on to win the match.

Thank you to everyone who has helped me with this book. In alphabetical order, they are: Chris Archer, Nicola Arzani, Chris Bowers, Jo Burnham, Chris Clarey, Barry Cowan, Rhian Evans, the editor Emily Forder-White, Craig Gabriel, Simon Higson, Nick Imison, Mitzi Ingram-Evans, Barry Millns, Neil Robinson, Danielle Rossingh, Radek Stepanek, and Barbara Travers. And special thanks to Amy, Sarah, George, Rob, Katie, and James.

Mark Hodgkinson

Photography Credits

- **Oren Aharoni, YNET** 67 (bottom middle)
- **Ron Angle** 23 (top and bottom), 24, 25, 45, 102 (top right)
- **Mihai Barbu** 30, 31, 32, 33, 103 (top left)
- **Virginie Bouyer** 47 (bottom middle), 87 (bottom right), 88, 89, 103 (bottom left)
- **Reg Caldecott** 66 (bottom left), 90, 91
- **Sergio Carmona** 11 (bottom), 14-15, 16, 17, 18, 19, 60, 61, 62, 63, 66 (top left), 70, 71, 72, 73, 74, 82 (top left), 83 (top right), 103 (bottom middle), 107 (except top left), 108 (bottom left), 109, 118 (middle right)
- **Antonio Costantini** 103 (bottom right)
- **Antoine Couvercelle** 20, 21, 22, 23 (middle), 67 (top right)
- **Arne Forsell** 38, 39, 40, 66 (middle right), 94
- **Jean-Loup Gautreau/AFP** 65
- **GEPA** 34, 35, 36, 37, 47 (top left)
- **Manuel Gonzalez** 46 (top left), 47 (top right), 98, 99
- **Nir Keidar** 47 (bottom right), 50, 51, 52, 67 (bottom right)
- **Henk Koster** 100, 101
- **Sergio Llamera** 41, 42, 43, 46 (bottom right), 47 (bottom left), 82 (top right)
- **Maurer/Zimmer** 56, 57, 58, 59, 116
- **Andy Mueller/EQ Images** 96 (bottom right), 102 (top left)
- **Pascal Parrot/Corbis** 64
- **Photonews** 46 (top right), 67 (top left), 97
- **Marcelo Ruschel** 46 (middle right), 66 (top right), 83 (except bottom right), 86, 87 (top left and middle left)
- **Srdjan Stevanovic** 67 (middle top), 82 (bottom right), 92, 93, 103 (top right)
- **Tonelli** 84-85, 95, 96 (top and bottom left)
- **Paul Zimmer** endpapers (front and back), 5, 6, 8, 11 (top), 12, 26, 27, 28, 29, 46 (bottom left), 48-49, 53, 54, 55, 66 (bottom right), 67 (bottom left), 68-69, 75, 76, 77, 78, 79, 80, 81, 82 (bottom left), 83 (bottom left), 102 (bottom left and right), 104-105, 106, 107 (top left), 108 (except bottom left), 110, 111, 112, 113, 114, 115, 118 (except middle right), 119